HOW TO AIRBNB®

Maximize Your Rental Income by Short-Term Renting... the Right Way

(Revised & Expanded 2021 Edition)

by Jeffrey S. Malfatti, Esq.

Copyright © 2020 Jeffrey S. Malfatti, Esq.

All rights reserved. Reproduction, adaptation, or translation of this material is prohibited without prior written permission of the author. This book has been registered with the U.S. Copyright Office.

Airbnb® and the Bélo are registered trademarks of Airbnb, Inc. This book is not published by, associated with, or endorsed by Airbnb, Inc.

HomeAway®, Vrbo®, Booking.com®, Houfy®, Sonder®, Lyric®, Waanderjaunt®, The Guild®, Lodgify®, Guesty®, Wimdu®, TripAdvisor®, MisterBNB®, Fresh Step® and other brands or brand names mentioned in this book are trademarks and/or registered trademarks of their respective owners in the U.S. and other countries, and the author does not claim any ownership of or association with them.

Cover image (starburst) designed by Starline / Freepik (freepik.com/starline).

iStock images © 2020 iStock, used under Standard Licenses.

Illustrations of the Bywater Bungalow and the Duplex are copyright © 2020 the author.

Important Disclaimers

The author of this book is not a financial adviser, and nothing in this book should be interpreted as financial advice, either specifically directed to the reader or in general. The author draws upon his knowledge of the short-term rental industry, financial markets, historical incidents, personal and anecdotal knowledge, and other information solely to provide illustrations of general concepts and to, at times, speculate on general trends. The author *does not and would not* advise any reader on how to invest his or her money or property.

Similarly, though the author may occasionally refer to tax consequences of potental investments or circumstances in this book, **the author does not purport to give any tax advice to the reader whatsoever.** Tax advice should be sought from a Certified Public

Accountant, Certified Financial Planner, or licensed tax attorney when making any decisions in regard to the reader's personal tax situation.

Finally, though the author is an attorney licensed to practice law in the State of Louisiana, **the author *is not your attorney* and *does not represent you in any legal matter whatsoever*.** Legal information provided in this book should be regarded as general legal information related to the general business of short-term renting. Examples offered in this book should be viewed as for illustration purposes only. No matter how similar the reader's circumstances may seem to those in the book, **only an attorney licensed in the reader's own jurisdiction is qualified to provide legal advice on the reader's personal legal issues or circumstances.**

About the Author

Jeffrey S. Malfatti, Esq. is a licensed attorney who assists clients on matters related to short-term rentals as well as hosting two short-term rentals himself, in New Orleans, Louisiana. He was educated at Tulane Law School, Tulane School of Public Health and Tropical Medicine, and UCLA, where he studied English. He was born in San Francisco and raised in Northern California.

Visit AmericanBNB.Com to read the author's blog, Q&A from readers, and for other useful information. **Be sure to visit the author's YouTube channel, AmericanBNB, for more content about short-term renting.**

Contents

HOW TO AIRBNB® 1
Maximize Your Rental Income by Short-Term Renting... the Right Way 1
   Important Disclaimers 2
   About the Author 3
Everything Has Changed. Now What? 4
Who Is This Book For? 10
   What's a New Host to Do? 11
Addressing the Covid-19 Crisis 13
   Reasons for Optimism 14
How Do the STR Platforms Work? 17
   High-Touch vs. High-Profit 19
   What Can Be an STR? 20
How Much Can You Make? 22
Real-Life Examples 23
   The Bywater Bungalow 23
   Duplex 28
Expenses 34
   STR vs. LTR Expenses 35
Who Can Start a Short-Term Rental Business? 41
   Are you in an area where out-of-town visitors would like to stay? .41
   Are you near somewhere tourists regularly visit or business travelers frequent? ..42
   Are you near public transportation? 42
   Is it legal? 43
   But Who Would Even Know? 44
   Europe 45
   Jail 45
   Can Renters Operate STRs? 46
Can STRs Be a Full-Time Job? 47

Property Owners	47
Rental Property	52
Rental Arbitrage	53

How to Survive Covid-19 57
Is Short-Term Renting for You? 60

Study the STRs in Your Immediate Area	61
Read the Reviews of Comparable STRs in Your Area	61
Do the comps have features you don't?	64
Set your prices a bit lower at first	64

Legal 65
Neighbors 67
Some Types of Short-Term Rentals 70

Room Rental, Urban Setting	70
Room Rental, Suburban or Rural	71
Whole-House Rental, Tourist Destination	72
If You Normally Live There, But Vacate When You Rent	73
Separate Towels, Linens, Etc.	74
Do Not Leave Your Pets!	75
Whole-Apartment Rental	75
Apartment in a Building	76
Non-Traditional Space	76

Does Operating an STR Fit Your Lifestyle? 78

Guests Have to Arrive	78
Early Check-in	79
Set Firm Rules and Stick by Them	81
Make Your Life Way, Way Easier.	82
You need to be reachable—or it may cost you	82
Cleaning	84
A Positive Note	88
The Secret to a Clean	88
Hiring a Cleaner	88
Check-Out	89
Bathtubs	91

Analyzing Your Market 93

    Measure Twice, Cut Once 93

    Vacancy Costs Money 94

    Legalities 94

    Enforcement 96

Marketing Your Property 98

    What about Vrbo? 100

    What Did That Have to Do with Marketing? 101

        Booking.Com 101

        Other Sites 103

        Direct Booking 105

    Getting Started with Direct Booking 107

        Advertising Your Property 108

    Getting Customers During Slow Seasons 111

        Toys 111

        Festivals 112

The New Airbnb Guest 113

    Are Hosts to Blame for Newer Guests' Behavior? 114

    Do Guests Game the System? 115

        Under-Promise and Over-Deliver 117

Guests with No Reviews 120

What Kind of Town Are You? 126

    Seasonal 127

    Times When Short-Term Renting is Not the Right Choice 129

    Make Your Property "Findable" 130

    Gaming Calendaring 131

    Your Town Type 133

        Big City 133

        Historical Destination 134

        Event Destination 134

        Family Destination 136

        College Town 137

        Nothing Town 137

STR Saturation 138

    Know Your Competition 139

- Know Yourself 140
- Know Other Hosts 140

Evaluate Your Property 143
- Curb Appeal 144
- Walk-Through 144
- Dining Room 150
- Kitchen 150
- Bathrooms 152
- Bedrooms 152
- Themed Rooms 153

Your Target Market 154
- The Bargain Traveler 154
- "The Middle" 156
  - Front Yard 157
  - Foyer 157
  - Living Room 158
  - Dining Room 159
  - Kitchen 159
  - Bedrooms 160
  - Specific Products 163
- The Upscale Traveler 163
- The Luxury Traveler 165
  - Where to List 166

Outdoor Space 168

Income Potential 171
- First: Calculate Your Expected Revenues 172
- If you can find comps that are 50% booked for the upcoming 30 days… 173
- If you cannot find comps that are 50% booked for the upcoming 30 days 174
- Second: Calculate Your Expenses 175
- Where to Find Information about Rates Online 177
- InsideAirbnb.Com 177
- BeyondPricing.Com 178
- Airbnb's Price Tips 180
- Mark Up to Mark Down 180

Getting Your First Bookings 182
Cash Flow vs. "Cash Flow" 182

Upselling & Add-Ons 185
Upselling 185
Add-On Sales 185
Upsells and Add-Ons for Your STR Business 186

Legal (Again) 189
City and County-Level Regulations 189
State-Level Regulations 191
Do You Need a Lawyer? 191

Homeowner's Insurance 193
Insurance from the STR Platforms 195
Airbnb's "Host Guarantee" 195
HomeAway's Primary Liability Coverage 197

Rental Agreements 199
Airbnb 199
HomeAway 201
Sample Short-Term Rental Agreement 202

Waivers, Releases of Liability, and Other Contracts 203

Taxes 204

Now Accepting Reservations! 205
Sync Your Calendars 205
What Platform Charges the Most? 205
Vrbo Example 206
Airbnb Example 208

Creating Your Listing 210

Your Listing: The Specifics 213
Headline 214
Photos 216
Who Takes the Photos? 217
To Watermark or Not to Watermark? 217
"About this listing" (Summary) 219
"The Space" (Description) 220
House Rules 223

House Rules on Airbnb 224

  House Rules for Vrbo 226

  (Dis)Allowing Children & Infants 228

  Pets 230

  Pot Smoking 231

Service Animals, Emotional Support Animals, Therapy Animals 233

  ADA 233

  FHA and Section 104 236

    A Word of Warning 239

  Miniature Horses 241

  It May Get Worse Before It Gets Worse 241

  Local Rules and Regulations about Animals 242

Accepting Reservations & Screening Guests 245

  The Booking Process 245

  Instant Book 246

  Other Ways to Screen Guests 248

    Should I Accept A Guest with No Reviews? 249

    Should I Accept Local Guests? 249

  Read the Guest's Profile 250

  Talk to Your Guests 251

    What brings you to town? 251

    How many people will be staying at the rental? 252

Speaking of Number of Guests 253

  Recommendation 255

    Should I Charge More for More Guests? 256

Cancelling 259

  Your Policy 259

  Airbnb Policies 259

    Flexible 260

    Flexible or Non-refundable 260

    Moderate 260

    Moderate or Non-refundable 260

    Strict 260

    Strict or Non-refundable 261

- Long-Term ... 261
  - Super Strict 30 Days and Super Strict 60 Days ... 261
- Vrbo Policies ... 261
  - Relaxed ... 261
  - Moderate ("recommended") ... 261
  - Firm ... 262
  - Strict ... 262
  - No Refund ... 262
- What You Need to Consider ... 262
- Everybody Has an Excuse ... 263
  - Extenuating Circumstances ... 264
  - Super-Predators ... 265
  - Trip/Travelers Insurance ... 266

Cancellation by the Host ... 267
Search Rankings ... 269
- Airbnb ... 269
- HomeAway ... 271
- A Couple More Tips ... 272

When Guests Arrive ... 273
- Greeting Your Guests ... 276
- Be Ready on Time ... 276
- The Hazards of Self-Check-In ... 277
  - You don't get a chance to tell them about the little quirks ... 277
  - You don't get a chance to create a personal bond ... 277
  - You don't get to size them up ... 278
  - You miss out on a chance to fix major errors ... 278
- Gift Baskets ... 279

Your Welcome Binder ... 280
When Guests Check Out ... 281
Safety & Security ... 283
- Pre-Arrival ... 283
- Your Appetite for Risk ... 284
- Point of Clarification ... 284
- How Identity Thieves Make Their Living ... 285

Scams 287
    Check-Refund Scam 287
    Stolen-Listing Scam 289
    Phishing Scam 289
Physical Security 290
    Security Cameras 290
    Alarm System 292
    Motion-Sensitive Floodlights 292
    Personal Safety 293
    Lights on Timers 293

Minimum Standards 294
"Hosting on Airbnb" 294
    Professional Hospitality Businesses 296
HomeAway Marketplace Standards 298
My Two Cents 299

Hiring a Property Manager 300

Consider Reviews at Every Stage 303
Creating your Listing 303
Taking Reservations and Booking Guests 306
Guest Arrival and Check-in 307
During the Guest's Stay 307
Guest Departure & Asking for Reviews 308
Post-Departure 309
    Overall Rating 310
    Game Theory and Reviewing 311
Airbnb 314
Vrbo 317
Responding to Reviews 318
    Take a Deep Breath...and a Few Days 319
    Keep it Brief 319
    Keep It Positive 320

Final Thoughts 321
Notes 331

Everything Has Changed. Now What?

I have no doubt that for the rest of our lives, all of us who were alive and conscious when Covid-19 hit will remember it as *the* defining time of our professional, and probably personal, lives.

Did anyone's job or business go on as normal? I am having trouble thinking of a single type of job that could go on exactly the same as before. Maybe "eccentric hermit artist"?

And, unfortunately for us, travel was affected the worst.

At various points in March and April of 2020, *well over half of the world's population* was under a lockdown, stay-at-home, shelter-in-place, or similar order.[1] Countries closed their borders. The virus hit different countries and parts of the world at different times, so the closures were always shifting.

Needless to say, few people wanted to leave their homes, let alone travel for leisure. Ride on a stuffy airplane, or stay in a hotel or short-term rental ("STR") where you couldn't be sure who stayed there before you, or whether everything had been cleaned well enough to remove all possible traces of the Virus? No thanks, the world said. That is, the half of the world who wasn't locked down. And most of the developed world, as well as the "second world," was.

I don't have to tell anyone already in the STR business that the result was devastation. Our bookings all canceled. *All*. I saw my calendar for New Orleans' busiest months—March through May, roughly—in 2020 go from jammed to completely devoid of reservations.

In fact, as of this writing, in June 2020, I have *no* bookings on my calendar for the rest of the year, and have not had anyone keep a reservation since the week preceding March 15. The only plus I can see in all this is that I was able to switch off the power to my rental and save a few months of electrical bills. And it didn't matter if I ran out of any supplies. The whole toilet paper shortage (was that real?) didn't affect me, since I already had a supply on hand for the rentals.

But now we are in the Recovery. It's sort of like when you're at the start of a rollercoaster and finally reach the top where you spend a moment going slowly around the track before the first giant plunge comes.

Nerve-wracking, I mean. Not that bookings are plunging—maybe this is not the best metaphor—but that we do not know what's coming, and that's scary. Maybe bookings will stay at or new zero for months. Some are even asking if it is the end of Airbnb, or of short-term rentals in general.

I don't think that will come to pass. But what will?

Early signs, as I write this in June 2020, are slightly encouraging, compared to the years-long catastrophe that many Cassandras were fearing. (OK, I was fearing it. Sheltering in place can do that to you.)

The message boards and websites I frequent have seen hosts going from begging in vain for ideas on how to get bookings, to cheerfully announcing that they are getting inquiries and bookings for upcoming months.

Some hosts, anyway. Mostly the ones by the beach. We still have a long way to go.

For this Second Edition, I added several sections (and reviewed the others, bringing them up to date), including the very pertinent:

How to Attract Guests During Slow Times

I did not write about this in the First Edition, which was a significant omission, because, as more STR markets have become saturated, it is clearly a more pervasive question than I realized. I suppose I assumed that STR hosts in areas that were very seasonal knew they were going to make all their money in the busy season and virtually none in the off-season. That's how it's always been with vacation rentals, long before Airbnb and "short-term rentals" were a thing.

But I have since realized it is not hopeless, and there is a lot you can do. And since the question now applies to both the Covid-19 recovery and slow times of year in general, I've gathered a lot of ideas and put them in this edition for your money-making pleasure.

Rental Arbitrage: Leveraging Yourself Rich

I also added quite a bit of information and analysis of rental arbitrage, which in the past couple of years has exploded as a topic in the STR industry.

The general method of being an STR host used to be that the host owned, or sometimes was the renter of a property, and wanted to either STR the entire place or just a room. If they were successful, they might decide to buy another property, then maybe another one when they could save up the 20% minimum down payment that banks usually required for investment property. Or maybe they just used their profits to fix up their primary rental and do all the repairs and upgrades they've wanted to do for a long time but could never afford to do.

So, the default mode of operating STRs kept most people operating either a room or one whole property, or maybe two, but rarely more than a few, if you were really ambitious. Personally, I thought very few landlords would be open to the idea of allowing someone to rent their place then use it as an STR, allowing a constant stream of strangers to come and go. Sure, you could probably find one if you were willing to face a lot of rejection. But it sounded like a lot of work and trouble.

But then some people found this was not the case, and built mini-empires of rentals they were permitted to use as STRs by their landlords. I have learned a tremendous amount about rental arbitrage since then, and I go into a lot more detail about how to do that in this edition.

Marketing

A new section on Marketing of STRs has been added. Though the last edition was peppered with lots of ideas and commentary on how to attract guests, this edition has dedicated an entire section specifically to Marketing. And not coincidentally, because marketing is going to be a huge part of surviving the Covid-19 recovery, unless you are one of the lucky owners of a beach house.

We will discuss how to go about obtaining **direct bookings**, which has become probably the #1 topic of interest among Airbnb hosts who feel they were badly burned by Airbnb, in particular, refunding all their bookings during the height of the Covid-19 crisis.

I'll discuss other platforms beyond Airbnb and Vrbo that you may consider, including revisiting Booking.com (which in the previous edition I recommended avoiding), some non-traditional ones, and other ideas for marketing your property, including how to create a website for your propert(ies) and, more importantly, how to get them ranked reasonably highly in Google searches.

Current technologies have made it simple to create a beautiful website with just a few clicks, and if nothing else, you should create a "billboard" type website for your propert(ies). We will go over what that means and why you should do it, even if you do no further online marketing.

Today's STR Guest

As the STR industry has evolved over time, so have STR guests.

STRs have obtained visibility far beyond just the Airbnb and Vrbo websites. Prospective guests used to have to seek out STRs to rent by typing in specific URLs. And a prerequisite to that was knowing that STRs even *existed*.

But today, STRs are put before travelers in everything from Expedia and Hotels.com searches to Google searches, as part of the just-launched Google Travel, which intends to be another big player right alongside every vacation property purveyor.

This new accessibility to STRs brings with it a new kind of customer. In short, a customer who does not really know what an STR is, does not know (or really care about) the unwritten, and sometimes written, rules that those of us who have been hosting and staying at STRs for years know and mostly follow.

This is a natural evolution and should not be resisted. Sure, you will still have your "old school" guests. They are not going to stop staying at STRs. But you also have a new breed and you need to adapt to them—not vice versa.

As with pretty much everything, the person paying is the one who has to be catered to. Being in denial about that is pointless. It means you are behind the curve. I bring this up because a common reaction by hosts is to get angry about these "bad guests" and wonder what they need to do to keep them from booking. But that isn't possible if you want to survive—there's too much competition, and too much Covid-19 (at least right now)—so adapt. Let your competitors be the ones behind the curve.

Speaking of which, the new breed doesn't give 5-star reviews across the board. They just don't. We'll talk about that, too.

Covid-19 Specific Information

The Covid-19 crisis has led to change after change by the STR platforms and their policies, often from week to week. Airbnb infamously decided to refund guests for all the bookings they made for stays between March 15 and June 30. Or actually, no, they didn't: they just decided that the hosts would definitely not get the money they were entitled to based on their cancellation policies. Airbnb figured out a way to keep much of it.

More on that drama later.

Cleaning. Cleaning your properties between guests has become a critical matter for safety and to comply with both Airbnb's and Vrbo's rules. We go through the polices and exactly what you need to do to follow them.

In the case of Airbnb, this is very important, because if you do not opt-in to their "enhanced cleaning protocols," they will automatically make you keep your rental vacant for 72 hours between reservations. If you opt-in, you only need to keep it vacant for 24 hours. Since the things on the enhanced cleaning list are things you should be doing anyway, you need to make sure to opt-in and commit to following the protocols. This includes passing a quiz, which we will discuss.

Airbnb also has a safety checklist which you need to make sure to update within your listing.

Vrbo also emphasizes their new Cleaning Guidelines[2], and has added a Health and Safety tab to your property's description. It's critical that you update this. We will talk more about cleaning, safety, and Vrbo.

Housing Covid-19 First Responders. We will discuss how each company is addressing providing housing for first responders. I will not spend a lot of time on that because it was primarily an issue at the beginning of the crisis, and is not so much now, as our medical facilities have adapted. But if Covid-19 follows the surge/retreat/surge/retreat pattern that some think it will, it could become relevant again during the surges, particularly if they are unpredictable.

And So Much More

Of course. I'm writing this section after the fact. I can't remember every single new thing I put into the Second Edition. But I assure you, I went over every word and updated everything that has changed. And *everything* has changed, metaphorically speaking.

Jeffrey S. ("Josh") Malfatti, Esq.

New Orleans, LA

June 7, 2020

Who Is This Book For?

This book explains, in simple terms, everything you need to know to start and run aa short-term rental (which I will refer to as "STR" from now on). You may have heard STRs referred to as "Airbnbs," but we are well beyond one company having a lock on the STR market. It's possible Airbnb won't even be around in a couple of years, since the Covid-19 crisis has put the company's survival in question.[3] But STRs are not going away.

In this book, we will primarily focus on the two most popular platforms, Airbnb and Vrbo, though we will also discuss many other options for obtaining customers, including direct bookings (where the guest books directly through you, avoiding fees—on both sides).

This book will take you through exactly what you need to do to start your own STR, and do it right, avoiding mistakes that can cost you money and time.

In short, this book is for the beginner.

But it is also valuable for the more experienced STR host. Every topic I discuss starts with an explanation of the basics, but then offers much more, in the form of advice from experienced hosts including myself.

By reading this book while preparing to launch your STR business, you will be advised on how to do something experienced hosts did not have the opportunity to do: avoid costly mistakes when you first get started.

I have owned and operated multiple short-term rentals for several years in New Orleans, Louisiana, hosting hundreds (thousands?) of guests and groups.

I am quite sure that this book will educate you about not only the basics, but topics that have never even crossed your mind, that can improve your STR business, helping you make more money faster and leave your guests happier having met their expectations. This leads to better reviews and more money for you. Which, ultimately, is the reason we are all doing this.

Money.

Though many hosts enjoy (or claim to enjoy) the constant interaction with new and interesting people from around the country and around the globe, most STR hosts will tell you that, at the end of the day, the fact that they can make double or triple from their rental property by renting it as an STR instead of as a long-term rental ("LTR") is the reason they do it. Period.

What's a New Host to Do?

In the ultra-competitive STR environment of today, many areas are seeing floods of people becoming STR hosts, and those of us with experience watch them flail about without the slightest clue of what to do. We wonder why they do things that are sure to have dire effects on their businesses for years to come.

The reason is that they didn't have a book like this to walk them through the things they needed to know, and decided to try to learn "on the fly" or "by trial and error." Maybe they felt they had no choice.

But this is not a good business. The financial stakes are too high, and mistakes you make at the beginning can haunt you and negatively affect you for years to come. Reviews you get in your first month—when you are making mistakes left and right, and causing guests to dock you on reviews—do not go away in a year. Or two years. They sit there, dragging down your average rating.

And if you get even one horrible review (which, in the Airbnb system, is three stars) for doing something wrong you did not even know was wrong, you will need *19* five-star reviews in order to bring your average to 4.9, which is considered excellent. If you are willing to settle for a 4.8 average, still quite good, you only need 9 five-star reviews to get there. Of course, your average will be lower than that until you actually get the 9 five-star reviews. And believe it or not, if your review average ever falls below 4.7, you will get a warning from Airbnb saying if you do not improve, you risk having your listing removed.

They may give you more slack if your low review comes right when you start, taking into account you are still learning. I would hope, anyway. They may not.

In short, you need to know what you're doing right out of the gate.

If you are just starting out, you really do need a book like this. Though you may not realize it now, you can use every piece of advice you can get.

In short, keep reading. You and your bank account will thank me.

This book will take you through exactly what you need to do to start your own STR, and do it right, avoiding mistakes that can cost you money and time.

In short, this book is for the absolute beginner, though it contains advice and information that hosts of all levels can use.

Addressing the Covid-19 Crisis

Nothing has ever thrown the short-term rental ("STR") industry into as big a crisis as Covid-19.

Bookings, and travel generally, were down about 90% for the first few months of the crisis in the US, international borders were closed, and stay-at-home orders were in effect. When recovery first began, it really only benefited certain properties, mostly those by at the beach or out in the wilderness, places where people could escape to to be outdoors and socially distance.

On top of that, while many STR hosts had already reduced their rates by up to 50%, many guests were ruthless about seeking further discounts. They knew it was a buyer's market and guests clearly had the upper hand. Some hosts chose to stay vacant, others chose to make what little money they could, despite the strenuous extra cleaning required. Still others went a different route, like exiting the STR business altogether, either selling their properties to avoid foreclosure, or finding long-term tenants.

The Covid-19 crisis showed us the worst that could happen in many ways. Not only were people avoiding travel, first by governmental order, then out of concern for their personal safety, but when they did begin traveling, they refused to pay enough to allow hosts to realistically continue operating.

Additionally, through no fault of guests or anyone else, cleaning rentals between guests became hugely more intensive. Airbnb currently offers hosts two options—either do normal cleaning between guests and leave the property vacant for 72 hours between bookings, or do "enhanced cleaning," and allow 24 hours between bookings. Both cost money, either in terms of lost days' rentals, increased cleaning costs, or both. Vrbo followed up with their own version of enhanced cleaning policies. We will discuss these policies in detail in later chapters.

In short, STR hosts got hit from every angle during the Covid-19 crisis, and the slow recovery afterwards. It was simply a terrible industry to be in. And as of this writing, the STR industry has not really emerged. Not nearly.

Reasons for Optimism

It's common knowledge that the bubonic plague outbreak of 1347-1351 was good for the poor, economically speaking.[4] (Not a happy subject, I know, but hear me out.)

After 30% of Europeans died, in that one outbreak, there were fewer serfs to work the land.

But the *demand* for their work did not change, because there was as much land to farm as ever (farming was the big thing back then). So, inevitably, wages went up.

Suddenly the poor were able to buy better food, or even acquire land of their own. Wealthy landowners at first tried to avoid paying serfs more, and laws were handed down requiring that they work for the same low wages they were getting before the plague.

It didn't work. Workers were needed in order for landowners to make money, and with the supply drastically reduced, landowners found ways around the new laws. They provided serfs with what we now call fringe benefits, like extra food and money under the table, and sometimes gave them their own plots of land, so they were no longer solely working for The Man.

Surprisingly, the Dark Ages, if you managed to dodge the plague, were not a terrible time be a serf.

I view STR hosts, at least the ones who are still standing when the pandemic is over, as the serfs of Covid-19.

It may not be until mid-2021, or later, that things return to normalcy. In the meantime, I predict about half of hosts will have exited the market. The recovery will not be sudden and fast, it will be incremental and slow. But hosts who outlast the exodus will, eventually, benefit.

Recovery will come in an unpredictable, scattershot fashion, with some properties and cities recovering faster and others recovering much more slowly. Currently, the media are debating debate whether STRs safer or less-safe than hotels, from a Covid-19 perspective.

Personally, I vote for STRs, but maybe I'm biased. STRs are much better at enabling social distancing, but hotels are better able to enforce cleaning standards, if they choose to.

Ultimately, what employers decide, whether logical or not, will have a huge impact. If I had to guess, I'd say they would lean toward hotels, the more traditional option. But you never know. They could remain ambivalent, or even conclude STRs are safer. They will also, almost certainly, find that STRs can be a lot cheaper than hotels, which in a recovering market may make the difference.

STR hosts who have left the industry, meanwhile, will be enjoying the comparatively minimal amount of work involved in being LTR hosts, if they still own their properties at all. The absence of stress from worrying about turnovers, cleanings, and reviews will be welcomed. They will likely no longer be closely following what is happening in the STR industry, except those who are determined to get back in as soon as they can.

Because LTR-ing is easier, and evicting a tenant is a process, I predict that a significant majority of former STR hosts will drag their feet before converting back to STRs, or never go back to STR-ing at all.

Even when they do realize it may be viable again to operate an STR, there will hurdles. As I said, I believe the recovery will be scattershot, and income will be hard to predict. Uncertainty is something that people who left the market when Covid-19 hit do not like, cannot afford, or both. If they could live with uncertainty and could afford a period of downtime, they might have just waited it out.

Switching your property from an LTR to an STR requires more than just kicking out a tenant and reactivating a listing. You will have to fix up/freshen up the rental again (painting, repairs, furnishing or re-furnishing, depending on your circumstances). Even if you rented your property out as an LTR furnished, so you did not have to move everything out, your LTR tenants will certainly have taken the shine off many of your things. Repairing, replacing, or just thoroughly cleaning the property will take time and money, for an uncertain return.

Because, what if it all happens again? It could. Covid-19 itself will probably enter a pattern of surging and receding several times until we have a cure or vaccine. It's uncharted territory in the modern world. First-world problems, indeed!

In the modern world, infectious disease seems to come up more often as the population becomes denser and more bugs seem to emerge. SARS 1 arrived in 2003, H1N1 in 2009, MERS in 2012. Covid-19 is essentially SARS 2,[5] though far more contagious and less deadly.

None of those, lucky for us, became catastrophic like Covid-19 did. But risk-averse people will think carefully and fret about the "next one."

This is to say nothing of the rental arbitrage companies that have taken out dozens, hundreds, or even, in a couple cases, *thousands* of long-term leases on properties for the sole purpose of using them as STRs. They have done that, and furnished them with everything you need for an STR. Most of these units aim for the higher-end market, so their initial costs were undoubtedly significant.

Will they survive the difficult part of the crisis?

Or will it be just us serfs?

How Do the STR Platforms Work?

Now to get back to the basics, for the person who is just starting out, and for whom this book was originally written.

Airbnb is a platform for people to advertise properties (houses, apartments, single rooms, or even shared, hostel-like rooms) for rent on a short-term basis. That can mean anything from one night on up.

Someone looking for a short-term rental goes on a website like Airbnb.com, Vrbo.com, Booking.com, or many others, and browses the listings. The person can input selection criteria like number of bedrooms, number of actual beds, location, whether the property is a "whole home" or shared, number of bathrooms, pool, or any number of features.

They can also search by certain other qualities, some peculiar to this industry, like whether the owner is a "Superhost" (on Airbnb) or "Premier Partner" (on Vrbo) and how many reviews the owner has.

The vast majority of short-term rentals function as privately-owned and operated alternatives to hotels or hostels.

So, what do STRs have that hotels and hostels do not?

To be frank, they offer more for less. More space for less money. They offer a place that, usually, is embedded in a real neighborhood, not on a tourist strip where every person the traveler will bump into is likely to be another tourist.

Often, an STR offers a *host*, who can explain things to the traveler about the city they are visiting, and make suggestions on places to eat and things that locals enjoy so that the guest can avoid tourist traps. A traveler probably won't get this from the typically brusque front desk clerk at the Marriott, or even from the mysterious concierge at any major hotel, whose desk so often seems to be vacant.

But mostly, STRs offer a lot of space for a lower price than you would get at a hotel. I keep coming back to that because, as many times as you will hear people say that Airbnb is really about the experience of meeting new people, for most travelers, it honestly comes down to dollars and cents. Hotels have gotten very expensive (partly because they have to pay numerous taxes and follow a labyrinth of regulations), and most Airbnb owners are willing to charge a lot less. Many are just operating an STR as a side business for some extra cash, and often don't pay those taxes or follow all the rules, even if they should be.

On the flip side, there are many things that short-term rentals *do not* offer that hotels do. Like room service, valet parking (or, often, any parking), maid service, the ability of the traveler to check their bags before check-in or leave them long after check-out, and lots of extra available rooms in case there's a problem or a guest is dissatisfied with the one they are assigned.

When a guest rents an STR, they are renting one specific property—as you would if you were renting a ski cabin or beach house. If you rent a ski cabin and you don't like it, you can't just call the owner and ask him to put you in another ski cabin. He's not a hotel, and probably doesn't have another ski cabin. It doesn't work like that.

In contrast to hotels, STRs often have private outdoor spaces like landscaped patios, back yards to grill in, or even hot tubs and pools that only the guest and their group can use. You aren't going to get these things in most hotels, unless you are willing to pay a few thousand dollars a night for a luxury suite. But you can often find an STR with these kinds of amenities for just a few hundred dollars per night, depending on the city.

The downside, for the guest, is that the rental agreement for an STR is for one specific property, and if something goes seriously wrong with the property, the owner may very well have nothing else to offer.

The STR platforms do not own properties themselves (though some have made investments in resort-like developments, but let's ignore that for now) and are simply online marketplaces on which private owners offer private properties to rent.

This means that STRs are not standardized *at all*. This is actually one of the things that makes them appealing to many. But the lack of homogeneity can lead to confusion and dissatisfaction if it's not clear to a guest, especially a "newbie" guest, what they are getting.

As new guests who have never rented an STR before book an STR for the first time, confusion about what they are getting can create problems. They may think they have rented "an Airbnb" and "an Airbnb" is a specific thing with specific rules and perhaps is even owned by Airbnb, Inc. It isn't.

Not only that, but every property owner (in STR parlance, "host") is unique as well.

Many hosts are "high-touch"—they spend a lot of time talking with their guests, even going out on the town with them and showing them around. This is not required by any means (I certainly don't do it), but is just some hosts' style. Particularly for hosts who are renting out just a room in their apartment or house, it can be both fun and financially advantageous (more bookings, happier guests) to spend a lot of time with their guests, if they want that.

Most people renting out whole apartments and whole houses have less opportunity to provide a "high-touch" experience for their guests, but there are still many ways to provide a personal touch.

This book will thoroughly explore the different things hosts can do to ensure guests have the best experience possible (and thereby give the host the best review possible!). It will also discuss how important it is to get good reviews.

Spoiler alert: it's important.

High-Touch vs. High-Profit

After operating STRs for years, I've found that, over time, low cost has become a bigger and bigger factor for guests and has begun to trump almost everything. Guests naturally gravitate toward the lowest rates. This is too bad in a way, because when guests want to pay the minimum possible, hosts naturally have to be constantly on the lookout for ways to cut costs, in order to make enough profit for short-term renting to be worth the extra time and effort they put into it, beyond what they could make by renting their property as an LTR. Rental income, referring to LTRs, is called "passive income" for a reason. You rarely have to do anything except cash the checks.

If you are not yet operating an STR and imagine that you will invite guests into your lovely home, treating them like family, offer them fresh-baked muffins in the morning, and even take them out on the town or give them tours of your city, this may be an awakening of sorts.

But unless you, somehow, do not have to compete on cost, and are willing to accept low rates with a smile, you will find that the extra time and money you want to spend does pay off in high ratings. When guests get more than they paid for—most of the time—that equals a high rating.

But when you find that you can't get bookings at the rates you need to make a healthy profit, and find that you make a few hundred dollars less per month than you did last year, and you keep getting hit by unexpected big bills (it is inevitable), baking muffins and giving tours are probably the first extras that will go. Especially when you feel like your last three groups of guests were paying pennies for your place, but still blast your A/C with the windows open even when they leave for the day, make an insane amount of noise at all hours, treat your property disrespectfully, and leave a huge mess of dirty dishes when they finally check out two hours late on their final day

Now, I'm not saying all guests are like that. They are not. And three in a row like that would be extremely unlucky. But those are the groups that will make you seriously ask yourself—if you are not making a healthy profit above what you'd make as an LTR—is this really worth it?

What Can Be an STR?

An STR can be virtually anywhere, and come in virtually any form.

Though it varies by location, the majority (about 75% in the New Orleans area, where I live and work) of STRs are "whole-home rentals," with "home" defined as an entire space to which the guests have sole access. It means not just whole *house*, but also whole apartment, whole in-law unit, whole floor of a house, or any entire, self-contained space that the owner does not access to during the guest's stay.

It excludes any place where the guest must share a kitchen, bathroom, or any other interior space with the owner or guests from another group with whom he or she is not staying. Those are "private rooms" or even "shared rooms" (dormitory-like spaces where guests may share a room with one or more strangers). You get to choose how to advertise your space; just make sure that your guests know exactly what they are getting so they aren't misled or disappointed.

It's a particular problem when a guest rents a "whole home" that really isn't. If a guest rents an apartment where you live, but you plan to stay in your own bedroom the entire time except maybe for occasional trips to kitchen, that isn't a "whole home" rental.

But if you are renting out the furnished basement and you live upstairs, and you never need to enter their space, and they don't need to enter yours (i.e. no shared kitchen, no shared anything) that is considered a "whole home." It's best if the guest is able to lock you out. Female travelers, in particular, can feel unsafe if unable to lock all entrances, which they will expect to be able to do in a "whole home" rental.

While many travelers are looking for a "normal" place to stay while in town on vacation or business, many others are looking for truly different experience they cannot get anywhere else. Consequently, quite a few STRs are non-traditional, and that is part of their appeal. Some are school buses parked in a back yard. Some are yurts. The most popular Airbnb in the world is a cabin in the woods.

Such rentals are actually some of the most prized and frequently booked. As of this writing, the most-booked STR in Atlanta is a [treehouse](#).[6] Many travelers are seeking adventures and love the idea of staying in a place that's odd or unique. Four of the [top ten Airbnbs in the world](#) are actually treehouses, one is a "seashell house," another is a "Pirates of the Caribbean Getaway," and another is an "off-the-grid house."[7] Not one is a run-of-the-mill house or apartment.

All of this means that if you have an extra space that someone could sleep in, as odd as a treehouse or as mundane as a spare bedroom, you can most likely rent it out on a short-term basis to travelers.

Especially if your price is right.

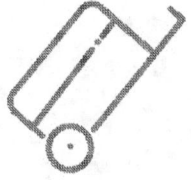

How Much Can You Make?

Like all good questions, the answer is easy—it depends.

Do you have an extremely desirable location?

Is your rental highly appealing for one reason or another (excellent view, right on the beach, walking distance to popular shops and restaurants, close enough to the bars so that guests can stumble home drunk)?

Or, is your rental far from the city center and other attractions?

Does it have significant drawbacks, such as no private bathroom? Or no bathroom?

Is it run-down, not charming, or in a rough location?

And, importantly, do you have good reviews? Do you have any *bad* reviews? You shouldn't—more on that later.

As you can probably guess, rentals the in first few categories I mentioned will be in demand, and will command premium rates. That is, unless some other factor, such as too much competition, pushes down prices a bit.

Rentals in some of the other categories, and I'm sure you can tell which, will not command premium prices.

But it's quite possible your proposed STR does not need to command a premium price in order to make it worth your time and effort.

If you live in a "bad" area, in a nothing-special apartment (that you can easily spruce up at minimal cost—more on that later, too), you may only need to bring in a relatively small amount, in STR rental terms, for your rental to make you more as an STR than it would as an LTR (long-term rental).

In other words—*it depends.*

Real-Life Examples

In the following sections, I will describe my own experiences operating two STRs in New Orleans, Louisiana for several years, including detailed financial information. These are both properties I own.

We will look at both revenues (money coming in) and expenses (money going out), and compare what I made renting the properties on a short-term basis to what I made on them when I had long-term tenants.

One of my places is a whole-house rental, and the other is a whole-apartment rental (half of a duplex, in which I occupy the other half).

The house is on the fringes of a popular area, and the apartment is in a quiet neighborhood on the opposite side of the Mississippi River from most of New Orleans' attractions. It is quite near a ferry that takes you right downtown, but nevertheless, the location is not optimal.

This section of the book will be primarily on *revenues*, which is the money you can expect to bring in (similar to gross income). The next section will be on *expenses*, which are the costs you will have to pay to keep your business running.

The Bywater Bungalow

The Bywater Bungalow is a 900 square-foot Craftsman style house, built in 1908, that most everyone says has great curb appeal. It is often called cute and charming. It doesn't hurt that I have hanging flowers at the front of the house and potted plants on the porch, all of which I keep trimmed and in good shape. This gives the property great online-photo appeal, which is an excellent quality to have in an STR.

The Bywater Bungalow was recently renovated, and has a modern kitchen and bathroom, but retains numerous historic elements. I actually bought it to live in, but decided to use it as an

STR after I purchased the Duplex. Here is an artistically Photoshopped photo of the Bywater Bungalow:

The Bywater Bungalow has a spacious master bedroom with a view onto a back deck, which is 9' by 12' and has a tin roof, and a back yard with a large, New Orleans-style patio of antique, mossy bricks, lit by string lights I strung up. The entire yard is ringed by banana trees for privacy and I have a few random decorations nailed to the fences. I have a small café table on the deck with four chairs, as well as four outdoor chairs and a metal table on the brick patio.

The Bywater Bungalow has a second, much smaller bedroom that had previously been a walk-in closet. Because the closet was not directly off the master, it has its own door into the hallway, making it usable as a separate (though very small) bedroom, which contains a queen bed.

The queen bed takes up almost the entire room, except for a foot or so on each side. The room has two small nightstands with lamps on them. A small princess-style chandelier, probably intended for a girls' bedroom, adds a touch of fun, and it has a wall-mounted, 32" TV. (There would be nowhere to fit the TV if it weren't wall-mounted!)

In short, the second bedroom is not really big enough to be a true second bedroom for a long-term tenant, but it's big enough for a short-term tenant to sleep in for a few days.

The master bedroom has a king-sized sleigh bed which was my most expensive STR-related purchase. It is black and gold (the colors of the New Orleans Saints) and is upholstered with faux-alligator black leather. This is something I would never have bought for my own residence, but I chose it for the STR because it is fun and a little bit crazy. Plus, alligators.

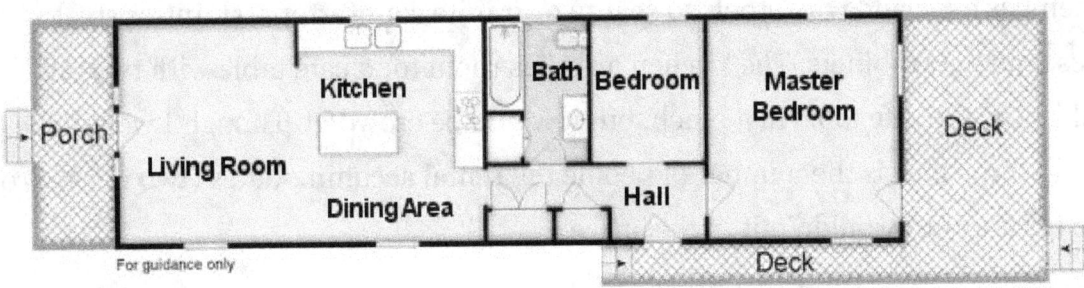

Next to the bed are antiqued gold nightstands I painted myself (I bought them unfinished), and on each nightstand is a lamp from Target with sky-blue shades. There are also two comfortable chairs in faux gold velvet, a bench at the end of the bed that matches the bed itself, and a smallish desk/table with a 32" TV on it. This TV has cable. A full-length mirror completes the room. I also have some 2' x 3' canvas prints on the walls, photos of New Orleans attractions I took myself and had printed on canvas.

The Bywater Bungalow has one bathroom, which has a combination bath/shower, and there is a stacked washer and dryer in the bathroom as well.

Throughout the house are original heart pine floors, which is a big plus in terms of making the house feel historic and truly "New Orleans."

I have furnished the living room with modern-style furniture, most of which I bought fairly cheaply online. It has two lounge chairs, a fairly small (but very modern-looking) couch, and a 50" Smart TV with cable. It has a black and white zig-zag pattern rug that is an attention grabber (some people call it the "Twin Peaks" rug, though I am not that familiar with the show). The walls have pieces of art I picked up fairly cheaply, or made myself by having my photos blown up and printed on canvas. Most of the photos are of sights around New Orleans.

When I chose the furnishings for the living room, I kept in mind how they would look in photos, even at the expense of comfort.

While most seating in the living room *is* comfortable, there are a couple of plastic, tomato-red Herman Miller-knockoff chairs that really aren't. But I keep them, because photos are critical. If I replaced them with comfortable-but-ugly chairs, I would have to re-photograph the living room with those instead, and my online pics wouldn't look as good.

The kitchen has an island with stools to seat two, granite countertops, stainless steel appliances, and new cabinets. The kitchen area has room for a café table with two tall chairs. Four could sit at the café table in a pinch, but it would be crowded. Though I would like a table that seated four, which is the number of people the rental accommodates (two per bedroom), a true table for four just wouldn't fit in the space.

Design tip: one expensive piece in a room can make everything else look more expensive, as long as everything goes together. If you see a pillow that would be perfect on your couch, but it's a little pricey—buy it! If a guest notices you spent a lot on one pillow, they will assume you spent a lot on everything else as well.

Bonus: if guests think your furniture is expensive, they may be more careful with it. Either because they innately want to be respectful, or because they don't want to be charged if they damage it.

When decorating or furnishing your rental, always keep in mind—at the risk of repeating myself—*how things will photograph.*

This is one case where shopping online, where all you can do is look at photos of the product but can't actually touch it before you buy it, can be a blessing. Overstock.com has been great for my needs (cheap stuff that looks good) and I recommend them, though I feel like their prices have been creeping up. Wayfair, in contrast, used to be overpriced but seems to have come down. There is no IKEA in my state (weird, I know) but I have a feeling their furniture, lamps, and décor items would make a significant contribution to my décor if there were one. Just make sure you don't make your place "too IKEA." You know what I'm talking about.

When furnishing a rental property, you have one thing working in your favor: you do not have to live in it. And neither do your guests, except for a few days. If the desk chair photographs really well and is okay to sit in, but not amazingly comfortable, so what? Buy it. A guest might sit at it for an hour on a couple different days, and that's it. Then the next group comes and nobody uses the chair at all. And so on.

Can you get a good deal on some chairs that are not your exact taste, but are a bargain, look good in the rental, and photograph well? Buy them. *You don't have to live there. Nobody does.*

Is there a rug for the hallway on clearance for 75% off at World Market that fits the décor you've chosen, but that you aren't personally crazy about it? You know what I'm going to say.

It's surprising how much less money you can spend on things when you don't really have to love them. And even if your guests don't exactly love them, that's okay, as long as the overall impression is clearly positive.

You will find that many of the rentals you will see on STR sites look sparsely furnished, and the furniture (in particular, the bedding), looks depressing and cheap.

I decided I did not want my rentals to be in that category. I can't really say if the people who decorate their rentals in obvious hand-me-downs, garage-sale finds, and thrift store bargains do well financially. But I can say for certain that they have to charge less than they otherwise could, and are thereby probably going to attract a lower-quality clientele. This is a double-whammy of *less*: less money, and less quality (guests).

Because spending the money up front to decorate nicely is not possible for everyone, you may wind up having no choice but to furnish with the hand-me-downs and thrift store/sidewalk finds and do your best. This is where having a good sense of design, and the ability to take a milk crate and paint or shellac it into what looks like an expensive designer piece, can come in handy.

Plus, as you make money from your STR, you can plow some of that back into the rental and buy better things. Make sure to also update your photos when you add a new piece so prospective guests can see the improvement.

But back to revenues: how much do I make at the Bywater Bungalow?

For the first nine months of a recent year, I took in an average of $2659 per month, before expenses. This compares to $1650 per month I made from long-term tenants in the preceding year.

A couple key differences: the long-term tenants were responsible for their own electric, gas, cable, and Internet bills. I only had to pay the water/sewer and trash pickup.

And, of course, for the long-term tenants, I did not have to spend anything on furniture, kitchen implements, sheets, towels, pillows, or outdoor furniture. I did not have to clean the place once or twice a week (as I do between STR groups of guests), or provide coffee pods, condiments, soap, laundry detergent, dishwashing liquid, and the like.

We will talk about these and other expenses in more detail in the section on Expenses.

Duplex

I bought the Duplex because I thought it was undervalued, and I happened to have enough saved up to be able to afford the 20% down. One side of the Duplex (the "tenant's side") was decrepit, and I decided to move into that and fix it up. A long-term tenant already occupied the other side, at $1050 per month.

After I was done fixing up the formerly-decrepit side of the Duplex, my tenant left, and I moved into her side, and the newly-fixed-up side became an STR. Luckily I had some money saved so that I could buy the necessary beds, sheets, towels, kitchen implements, furniture, and so on. That is, the things I could not use from my own living quarters.

And scavenge from my own apartment, I did. I went quite a while without many of the things one would consider basic, like a microwave, coffee pot, blender, pots and pans, chairs, side tables, and pretty much anything else that could be put in the STR. I think it was a year before visitors to my side of the Duplex had anywhere to sit but my bed, the floor, or a collapsible New Orleans Saints chair that previously had been used mainly to watch Mardi Gras parades.

The Duplex is in a less-desirable location for short-term renters than the Bywater Bungalow, though it has the benefit of being considerably larger, with three good-sized bedrooms and two bathrooms. It has higher ceilings and is across from a park. Because the other side of the street has no houses, there is always easy street parking. It is also in a quieter and safer neighborhood, which are good selling points, particularly for families.

Nevertheless, it is not a premium property for short-term renters, and tends to rent only after many reasonably-priced properties nearer to the French Quarter and other attractions have rented.

It rents for less per night than the Bywater Bungalow, ranging between $85 per weeknight in the summer ($105-ish on weekends), and about $110 per weeknight ($130 on weekends) in busier seasons, with periodic slowdowns that are not entirely predictable.

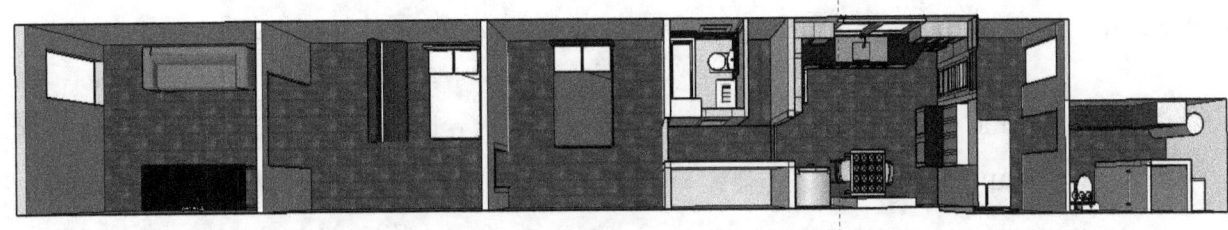

One negative about the Duplex: a large, but relatively low-priced, STR means not only less money, but more work.

The less-than-ideal location results in extra work pre-booking. People who don't know the area will glance at the listing's photos, hardly read the listing, and message you, asking you to explain where the property is (even if you explain all that in your listing, and provide a map of the city with your location and other key attractions specifically pointed out).

When prospective guests find out the property is not in a location where they think they would like to be, they usually don't book it. That means your time has been wasted because your prospective guest was too lazy to look at a map, or do any other research about the city they will be visiting. This is a common problem we will talk about later.

Nevertheless, as with the Bywater Bungalow, I bring in a lot more on the Duplex as an STR than I would from long-term tenants. In the first nine months of a recent year, it has averaged $2765 per month before expenses. (And yes, I realize that is a weirdly similar amount to the Bywater Bungalow. I don't have any good idea as to why they wound up being so close.)

There were quite a few pluses in having a long-term tenant (though she only paid, as I said earlier, $1050 per month, plus utilities, except for water/sewer and trash pickup):

1. Only one person was living in the apartment (reduced noise, reduced wear-and-tear).
2. I knew the tenant; there was no new set of personalities to adapt to and accommodate every week.
3. The neighbors knew the tenant; there was no ebb and flow of strangers coming and going.
4. I spent absolutely no time fielding questions from guests and prospective guests over email and by phone, trying to get bookings, coordinating arrivals and departures, and the dreaded cleaning and laundry (more on that later).
5. I did not have to buy or replace worn or broken furniture, dishes, glasses, small appliances, sheets, towels, etc. My LTR tenant had her own furniture and everything else.

6. I did not have to carefully track expenses all the time so that I could write them off. I *did* keep track of my expenditures for maintenance and repairs for the LTR, but they were minimal, and it was not a daily chore, as it can be when operating an STR.

So, the Duplex as an STR grossed (and continues to gross) approximately 2.6 times as much as it does as an LTR, and the Bungalow grosses approximately 1.7 times as much as it does as an LTR.

But the Bungalow, because it only sleeps four (two beds), only has one bathroom, and is 218 square feet smaller (all of which adds up to less laundry, less cleaning, and less wear and tear), is less work.

Though we have not yet gotten deep into the details of why STRs are a lot of work (if you do your own cleaning, which I do, that's a big part of it), a person with two rental units might consider renting one STR and one LTR, just to make life a little easier. LTR tenants are mostly "set and forget," where STR tenants require daily attention of one sort or another.

If I were to rent the Bungalow STR and the Duplex LTR, I would gross $3809 per month ($2759 + $1050). If I were rent the Bungalow LTR and the Duplex STR, I would gross $4415 per month ($1650 + $2765). The latter is clearly more profitable, based solely on gross revenues.

Why, in a book about short-term renting, am I considering scenarios where I am STR-ing one property and LTR-ing another? Lots of reasons. Amount of work and time I have to put into each property if operating it as an STR vs. what an LTR brings in. Location of the properties, which may make it inconvenient to visit one or the other as frequently as is necessary when running it as an STR.

Regardless, we can't truly conclude what kind of arrangement is more profitable yet. There is a hugely important topic hiding just around the corner that may turn any conclusions we come to upside-down.

Expenses

Expenses for my STRs have always been high. This is in contrast to many hosts who claim to barely spend anything. It's particularly true of hosts who rent out just a bedroom in their home, some of whom claim to only spend $20 per month.

One factor in some hosts thinking they hardly spend anything is that it's likely that many hosts do not notice or track their expenses as carefully as they should, particularly hosts who rent out single rooms in their apartments or houses.

If you are renting out just a room in your home, and your toaster breaks, it is *your* toaster, so you just buy a new one. When a towel gets stained, it's one of *your* towels, so you just retire it and buy a new one. You are probably not tracking these as STR expenses, and in fact, it is difficult to even determine what is an STR expense and what isn't. But it's certain the extra wear and tear, and breakage, is adding up to something more than the $20 per month that you are aware you spend on STR guests, buying things like coffee and toilet paper and so on.

In contrast, when you operate a whole-home STR, you are more conscious that the replacement toaster or towel is a pure STR expense, requiring a trip to the store and a swipe of the debit card *because of your STR*. And, of course, you save the receipt and notate the expense, so you can deduct it from your revenues at tax time.

Many hosts are lazy about this, and do not save receipts for small purchases. In my experience, these expenditures add up to real money over the course of a year.

Tip: save those receipts, log them, and make sure your total expense number at the end of the year includes every cent you spent on your STR business that you are allowed to deduct.

Buying one $6 item you need for the STR on a trip to Walmart where you are spending $192 on your own personal purchases may seem pointless to track.

But if you spend $6 every couple of days, that's $1395 per year. Suddenly it's real money you may be able to write off on your taxes.

Plus, you may be able deduct 54 cents per mile (the current IRS rate as I write this) you drive to buy those items. Check with your accountant to what travel expenses are deductible for you.

If the store where you are buying these things is five miles away (on average, because you will most likely be buying things at multiple stores), that's 183 trips, at 10 miles ($5.40) per round-trip.

If you were permitted by tax rules to write that off that would add up to a $988 deduction for mileage.

So, all those piddly $6 purchases may add up to a total tax deduction of $2383 per year!

If your overall tax rate is 25%, a deduction of $2383 would save you about $595 in taxes. That's real cash that the government doesn't take out of your pocket that it normally would.

This is why I recommend tracking every cent. But again, check with your CPA to find out what you legally can and cannot deduct. These are merely illustrations about how you may be able to save money in places you never realized you could.

STR vs. LTR Expenses

One important negative about STRs as compared to LTRs when it comes to expenses is that, in the STR business, money must often be spent *immediately*, or on a very short time frame.

And, particularly if you are renting a whole-apartment or whole-house, there are just *so many* expenses, many of which you could let slide for a while if you had an LTR tenant. For those of us living on a tight budget, this can sometimes make running an STR stressful and difficult.

In an STR, every time a bedsheet gets stained, and you can't get the stain out, you have to throw it out and buy a new one.

Every time a guest breaks something, if it's a key amenity (like the microwave) you have to buy a new one. Immediately. (Of course, you can buy used sometimes, which saves some money. But if you don't have time to go and find a microwave on Craigslist, and drive around to the seller's house and pick it up before you next group arrives, you have to go and grab a new microwave from Wal-Mart at the lowest price you can find.

You have cleaning supplies you are constantly using up. Paper towels and toilet paper you are constantly buying (and toilet paper, as you have probably never noticed unless you've bought several 24-packs at once, is expensive).

Plants can suddenly die, and you have to replace them right away, because dead plants look horrible. Either that, or leave empty pots. Flowers, by their nature, are always having to be replaced. And it's not just money, but time and work (planting, potting, getting dirty, cleaning, washing).

When you are operating an STR, every group that arrives is new to your rental. With a long-term tenant, if the washer breaks down, you can put off buying a new one for a month or two, and the tenant will grumble, but tolerate it.

If you are running an STR, and are offering a washer-dryer as an amenity, and it breaks, you need to replace it—fast. If not, you will have to explain to every new group that the washer-dryer is out of service, so they will have to go use the laundromat during their stay. You may choose to reimburse them for wash-and-fold service. (They will love that, and be sure to use it.)

Plus, if a guest arrives and a key amenity is unavailable, they may even decide to cancel their stay, and will probably be given a full a refund by Airbnb or whichever platform you are using. After all, your ad promised something important you did not deliver, and it's your fault, not theirs. For a family with small children who may have planned on washing dirty diapers, going to the laundromat may not be a compromise they can live with, and you may not be able to offer a solution that will be acceptable for them.

In my experience, guests rarely choose to relocate, and I've never actually had one do so, though one guest messaged me that she was going to leave early due to "bugs," but decided not to. She may have been seeking a refund or partial refund, since she had already stayed four nights, and that does not quite add up if she was leaving because an intolerable bug problem. I did not offer a refund, and she stayed on without bringing it up again.

But then again, I try to do everything in my power not to give guests a reason to try their luck somewhere else. If just one thing goes wrong, odds are guests will not find the nuisance of having to relocate to be worth it. But if it's multiple things? They might.

A washing machine breakdown in a unitized machine did happen to me at the Bungalow, which was probably the only time I've had to tell guests upon arrival that a major amenity was not available. I probably should have informed them before arrival, but every day I was hoping the new washing machine and dryer would arrive before my next guests. And it kept not doing that.

As mentioned earlier, because I was running an STR and not an LTR, I had little time to shop around and try to find a used washer/dryer or fix the broken one, and was forced to buy machines at a non-sale price through an online company just to get the problem resolved. (Which then created another problem when the company took 3 weeks to deliver.)

During that time, I had to explain the problem to every incoming group and hope they were okay with it, or that I could offer something to make them okay with it. As I recall, nobody really seemed to care that much, so I got lucky in that regard. There probably would have been more pushback or even cancellations had it happened at the Duplex, which sleeps six and is more likely to be booked by families.

To summarize, short-term guests expect everything to be as advertised, and don't like to be told anything they paid for is not available.

But back to the Benjamins: My expenses for the first six months of a recent year for the Duplex have been $194 per month, and for the Bungalow, $328 per month. (If you were to exclude that washer/dryer I had to buy, it would have been $132 per month Bungalow, but I'm leaving it in because it's realistic; this kind of thing does come up regularly, and excluding it would be the kind of denial of actual expenses that I was just accusing other hosts of doing.)

This reduces my income to $2566 per month for the Duplex (down from $2765 gross) and $2431 per month for the Bungalow (down from $2759 gross).

Here's a breakdown of how much I spent on each category of purchases:

Expenditure	Duplex	Bungalow
Appliances maintenance/repair	$0	$146
Appliances (replace washer/dryer)	$0	$1176
Cleaning supplies	$165	$166
Door (replace)	$248	$0
Decorative/seasonal items	$105	$114
Electrical/Electronics	$215	$11
Food (gift baskets, misc.)	$343	$362
Furniture*	$578	$228
Hardware	$33	$88
HVAC (air filters)	$11	$11
Membership in STR advocacy group	$125	$125
Insulation supplies	$43	$204
Landscaping (plants, irrigation, etc.)	$126	$246
Permits	$51	$154
Linens*	$466	$233
Miscellaneous	$215	$221
Office Supplies	$10	$10
Painting	$47	$7
Pest Control	$10	$10
Plumbing supplies (self-repairs)	$0	$31
"Smart" thermostat/smoke detectors	$0	$645
Supplies for guest use (soaps, TP, etc.)	$187	$209
Website	$2	$2

*Includes a new double bed and new linens since I added a double bed in place of a sofa bed at the Duplex.

Those numbers still represent $1516 and $781 more—per month—than I would have made from long-term tenants. Quite a bit of extra money, so definitely worth it. Right?

Yes…except for that whole "tons of extra work" thing I promised to talk more about.

Had I used a house-cleaner instead of doing the cleaning myself, I would have had to subtract $100 per cleaning from each of those figures. This would be, approximately, four cleanings ($400) per month at each property. That makes the Duplex $1116 more profitable per month and the Bungalow $381 more profitable per month than I would have earned from long-term tenants.

Using a cleaner if you have more than one STR is probably the norm (unless the two STRs are just single rooms you are renting out in your own home). I like to do the cleaning myself, for reasons discussed later in this book, but you may want to consider the cost of house cleaning as pretty much a given if you don't want to drive yourself crazy cleaning your rentals once or twice a week each.

Though I wish it weren't the case, it's fair to say that I essentially have a part-time job as a house cleaner, at which I earn $800 per month.

Add to that being on call 24/7, having to answer guest queries any time of the day or night (you are rated by Airbnb on speed of responses, and your response time is prominently displayed in your profile, so guests are encouraged to consider it). A "Less than an hour" response time is certainly preferred to a prospective guest than a "Less than one day" response time.

Buying supplies and making gift baskets (the costs of which are already included in the monthly expenses amounts quoted) takes time out of your week.

Not to mention spending long hours on the phone quarrelling with Airbnb and Vrbo, over damage claims and other issues, as well as the stress of having groups arriving and having to be sure everything is perfect, handling issues that come up (which, in my experience, is too often at inconvenient times like Friday nights, early morning or between 9pm and midnight) and of having to constantly worry about reviews. I find that short-term renting causes me to have considerable extra stress in my life, and there are periods when I feel absolutely run ragged. And, of course, I also have a full-time job.

Also, in the analysis of my own expenditures, I left out something that was a significant pain in my pocketbook in the first part of this year, but that you won't have to deal with if you are just starting up.

In order to be more competitive, I decided to get larger beds, so in the Duplex, I upgraded one of my double beds to a queen bed, and in the Bungalow, I upgraded a double to a queen and a queen to a king. So, I had to buy one king bed, mattress, and linens, and one queen bed, mattress and linens. Total costs were $717 for the Duplex and $1549 for the Bungalow. This comes out to $80 and $172 extra in expenses per month, respectively).

If you factor in the bed upgrades, I made $2045 extra per month than I would have made with long-term tenants (that's doing my own cleaning – it would be $1245 if I paid someone). And that doesn't include ordering and setting up the beds, reinforcing them with extra slats (you have to anticipate all the different types of guests you may have, including the occasional guest of size), buying all the linens, and moving all that furniture.

But for me, the amount I would make from long-term tenants ($1050) in the Duplex doesn't come close to covering my mortgage/tax/insurance, let alone utilities. The LTR rental amount ($1650) on the Bungalow *does* cover my mortgage/tax/insurance, as well as the water and trash bill. And LTR tenants pay the other utilities. But the LTR rental amount certainly doesn't cover all the other homeowner expenses for repairs and maintenance that are always cropping up.

It is not necessarily logical to compare what you pay on your mortgage/tax/ insurance bill to how much you bring in from a particular type of tenant. Your mortgage is based on what you paid for the house, which in turn may be based on how long ago you bought it, how well you negotiated the purchase, what interest rate you are paying, whether you inherited the property and therefore have no mortgage at all, and other factors.

But it's human nature, I suppose, to think about it when one type of tenant will pay your monthly mortgage with money left over, and another type of tenant will cause you to have to dig into your pocket for $300 a month to pay that bill.

Who Can Start a Short-Term Rental Business?

Anyone with a room to spare. Or a couch. Or a yard. Some travelers are happy—even delighted—at just being able to rent your yard so they can put up a tent, especially during music festivals.

You, the host, may even choose to provide the tent. Just make sure there is a hose for water and somewhere for your guests to go to the bathroom (not entirely mandatory, but, well—kinda mandatory, or your flowerbeds might suffer).

In other words, if you have a home any more spacious than a cardboard box (no offense to those living in cardboard boxes) you can probably operate an STR.

But the more precise answer is a little more complex.

Here are some things to consider when you are trying to determine whether you can or should start up an STR business. You probably also have some thoughts based on your particular situation.

Are you in an area where out-of-town visitors would like to stay?

If you answer, "Well, I am located in the densely-populated center of my city," the answer is a resounding yes. Unless STRs have been made illegal or are highly regulated in your city, in which case...it depends. More on that later.

Are you near somewhere tourists regularly visit or business travelers frequent?

If so, then your answer is again yes. Law providing, of course.

Are you in a not-quite-attractive area that is not-quite-convenient to the things most people who come to your town want to see?

The answer is still yes—of course you can start an STR business—but you need to consider whether you will get enough guests to make the project worth your while.

You might. Or, you might not. You might have to lower your nightly rate enough to make your place worth the inconvenience travelers experience being further from the areas they will be visiting or working.

Of course, if you lower your prices too much, you might attract a lower quality clientele than you would like.

If you are in an iffy situation, I would recommend keeping your startup budget low until you see whom you attract and whether you want to continue. More on this subject later.

Are you near public transportation?

This is a huge plus for visitors. Often, they don't have cars. The Millennial generation is particularly enamored of not having or driving cars. They prefer Uber, bicycles, or any kind of public transit.

And, it probably goes without saying, since Millennials are in their 20s and 30s right now, they are at the age when they are doing a lot of traveling. (Millennials also are very fond of traveling, period.) If you are near transportation that goes to the city center or other attractions, maybe your far-flung location will work.

Is it legal?

This has become an issue in more and more cities, particularly large cities that are also tourist destinations.

A fair number of large cities have enacted ordinances regulating STRs, as has been widely reported in the news. And the ordinances vary—greatly.

Some limit the number of days per year a host can rent out his or her property on a short-term basis.

Some ban almost all short-term rentals, and levy stiff fines for any violation. Some can even hand down jail terms for scofflaws with multiple violations. Make sure your town is not one of these. Or, if it is, and STRs are allowed but with restrictions, make sure that you are fully informed about the restrictions and follow them scrupulously.

Rules governing STRs are usually specific to each city, county, and state, meaning you have to research them on your own (or consult a knowledgeable local attorney or other person experienced in STRs who can point you in the right direction). Local rules are one thing it would be impossible to cover in the space of this book. Every city, town, and county has them…or doesn't, but may soon.

You need to research your local STR laws carefully. Pay attention to local news stories on the subject to keep up with proposed changes. Go to city council or neighborhood meetings where STRs are on the agenda and make your voice heard (or just listen).

Aside from medium-to-large sized cities that are tourist destinations, my general impression is that most cities across the US have not yet enacted rules about short-term rentals. Many cities probably have ordinances stating that you can't rent rooms by the hour. But I don't think most of those rules would cover rentals of multiple days.

Most cities *do* have zoning laws designating certain areas residential, which would forbid "hotels" from operating in such places. For enforcement purposes, your city may consider STRs to be hotels, even if the ordinances on the books weren't initially written to address the STR concept. It can vary from jurisdiction to jurisdiction whether the powers-that-be consider STRs hotels or not.

Zoning laws can also include rules about the maximum number of unrelated people who may occupy a residence, though I have never heard of this being a major point of argument in any STR fights. You will have to check the rules in your city/county/state.

But Who Would Even Know?

Just in case you are naively wondering how anyone would find out you were operating an STR, trust me—they will.

The hills have eyes. Even if you don't know it, you have a nosy neighbor who watches everything. There is a stereotype of a retired man or woman with too much time on their hands who trims their hedges just as an excuse to spy on their neighbors. Who gripes about people walking on their lawn and all the problems with "kids today." And they report cars for parking violations that nobody else would even care about.

The stereotype is true.

A neighbor could notice you are running an STR and report you, and odds are, if you do it for a while, they will. Notice, at least, even if they don't report.

I have had more than one nosy neighbor confront me at each of my rentals and tell me "they know" I am running a short-term rental. Really. One warned me that "there's gonna be problems" if I have any guests who make noise outdoors at night. Another didn't make any specific threats, but asked me to police the guests' parking on the street so none of them parked in front of her house. Neither of them seemed aware that STRs had been legalized in New Orleans and that I was operating within the law; I think they thought they "had something" on me, so I'd better do what they said.

In a way, they do, because if they chose to complain that my guests were violating local laws, truthfully or not, I could probably get cited or even shut down.

And just to be clear, if the city did cite me, it would be because I am the homeowner. The homeowner--not the tenant who may be renting on a short-term basis—will usually be the one who is cited, because it's their property and the city knows who they are. Think about this before making an agreement with a tenant for them to rent out part of the property they are renting as an STR. The fines and jail terms would quite likely be applied to *the owner*, not the tenant, even if it was the tenant's name on the Airbnb account and the tenant managed everything.

Europe

Some cities in Europe have incredibly punishing laws against STRs—almost unbelievably harsh. If you are in Paris, Berlin, or ANY city in Europe, you need to research your local laws before you even THINK about starting an STR.

You may think I am using too many capital letters. Well, in Berlin, while some STRs are actually legal, on May 1, 2020, the STR law was revised to allow fines of up to **$616,000** for running an illegal STR.[8]

Now, since I used all those capitals, if someone in Berlin reads this section and doesn't pay attention, it's off my conscience.

Fines in Paris seem to max out at about $56,000 for people renting out a secondary residence, if they don't follow the rules.[9] That's not *too* bad.

Jail

Violation of a local rental ordinance doesn't seem like it should call for jail—but it can.

Needless to say, if you are a tenant operating an STR out of your rented apartment or house, and your landlord receives a citation for it, and the punishment for violation carries a chance of jail time, you will probably be receiving an eviction notice.

Can Renters Operate STRs?

Yes, they can—sometimes. Local law has the final say on the matter, but where STRs are allowed, it may be that a renter can operate an STR with permission of their landlord.

I know of numerous cases where renters are operating STRs with the landlord's blessing. I assume the tenant is somehow splitting the STR income with the landlord, either by giving them a percentage, or by paying a higher monthly rent.

Can STRs Be a Full-Time Job?

Yes. I say that because people definitely operate STRs as their sole source of income.

Can *you*, specifically, do it as a full-time job? It depends.

(For this chapter, I'm going to assume that you have investigated the legalities of STRs in your location, something which we will get into in more depth later, and have concluded that your plan is legal where you are, and any restrictions will not be so burdensome as to make operating STR(s) as a full-time job unworkable.)

Property Owners

First, we will discuss scenarios where you own the properties you will operate as STR(s).

I will assume that, starting out, you have only one property you are preparing to make into an STR. If you already have multiple properties you have been renting out long-term, you should have a good idea of how far the rental income you currently collect, minus expenses and costs of property ownership, goes toward supporting you. Going through the sections on Revenues and Expenses earlier should have helped you to estimate how much more you might make converting your LTRs to STRs, and therefore, how much closer you might be able to get to being able to support yourself on STR income alone. However, it's important that you research your local STR market to determine what you will be able to charge for your property. The expenses may be similar to the examples, but your revenues could vary wildly from the amounts I used.

The question of whether you can support yourself operating STR(s) is highly individualized for each property owner, because the biggest expense is usually cost of ownership. Specifically, your monthly mortgage payment(s).

To keep things simple, I will use "monthly mortgage payment" or "mortgage" to refer to the total of principal, interest, taxes, and insurance you pay each month, usually all together in one payment. You will have a monthly mortgage payment on each property that you do not own outright.

The owners of two houses on the same block, of the same size and in the same condition, may have radically different mortgage payments. One owner may have bought fifteen years earlier at half the price of the other, so his or her mortgage may be a fraction of theirs. One person's may be higher because they chose a 15-year mortgage instead of a 30-year. Your mortgage payment is a big part of determining whether you will be able to support yourself by operating STR(s).

Do you own your house outright? Then, other than costs we have already talked about in the Expenses section, all you are paying is insurance and property taxes. So, the amount you have to make from operating an STR in order to support yourself will be a lot lower than the amount someone has to make who has a large monthly mortgage payment. You still may need to operate more than one to support yourself on STR income. If you need to purchase more properties for that to happen, you will need to consider cost of ownership on the properties you purchase.

When thinking about having STRs be your full-time job, there are two basic routes to getting from here to there. The first is to *buy* properties to use as STRs. (The other is to rent—see Rental Arbitrage section.) This requires that you have some cash for a down payment for each property you buy; usually 20% of the purchase price is required for investment property.

Though the myth of the "no money down" mortgage always seems to be floating around, I'm not sure those exist in the real world. If you have good credit, or are a first-time home-buyer and want to go through FHA for your loan, you can purchase property with 3.5% down (more on that later—it's not as great a deal as it may sound). Discuss with your mortgage broker how much you need to put down to get the loan you need.

I prefer to deal with local mortgage brokers (as opposed to trying to get a mortgage loan over the Internet) for just this reason: you have an actual person you can negotiate with about important questions like how little you can get away with putting down, and the decision will be individualized. It can benefit you if your situation does not fit neatly into the boxes on a web page, or if you are self-employed. I find that the Internet is often not kind to self-employed people (and lenders aren't always, either). Because you may not have a pay stub and an employer, you need to show tax returns to prove income, and many lenders seem to under-value that.)

You should talk to multiple mortgage lenders in your area to determine what you can qualify for, how little they will allow you to put down, and what interest rate they will charge you. Talk to at least three. The interest rates they offer you will probably vary, and negotiation is allowed. Do not accept "the rate" you are told. The mortgage broker can probably get a lower rate if he or she tries, even if only slightly lower. They want your business because their business is making loans.

Even a small difference in your interest rate, like a quarter of a percent, can add up to a large amount over the life of a mortgage. If you borrow $400,000 and pay it off over 30 years at 3.75%, you will pay $14,874 in interest during the first year. Borrowing the same amount at 4.00% interest, you would pay $15,872 during the first year. That's $997, or $83 per month, extra interest in the first year. Over the life of the loan, you would pay $20,591 extra. And that's just for a *one quarter of one percent* difference!

But let's back up. Before you seek out mortgage brokers, spend time browsing properties in your area that you think would make good STRs, and run some calculations. Many websites have mortgage calculators where you can input the cost of the property, the amount of the loan (i.e. purchase price minus whatever you put down, plus any fees), interest rate, and term of the loan (15, 20 or 30 years). These will tell you your monthly principal plus interest payment and, sometimes, will also estimate your taxes and insurance. Definitely include property taxes and insurance in your calculation. You can get your property tax rate from your city's assessor ,and get quotes for insurance from several different companies. Their rates, like mortgage rates, will vary.

To get the best interest rate on your loan, you need a credit score of 740+. Interest rates go up as your credit score goes down. Pre-Covid-19, a score of 620 was about the minimum needed for a home loan. As I write this, the bank industry is still full of uncertainty, and banks have tightened lending significantly. In April 2020, some of the larger banks stopped making jumbo loans (those over $510,400) and refinancing, period. This is very extreme. I believe that things will settle down by the end of summer, 2020, though you may still need a higher credit score than 620.

If you are a first-time home buyer a primary residence for the first time, you may be able to get a loan through FHA with a score of 580 and just 3.5% down, or 500-579 if you put 10% down.[10]

(There are drawbacks to FHA loans, like the fact that you need to pay 1.75% of the purchase price up front for "mortgage insurance," called the "upfront premium," *and* make monthly mortgage insurance payments equal to 0.8% of the outstanding loan amount annually, or 0.85% if you put down less than 5%. The monthly mortgage insurance cost—even excluding the upfront premium—is quite high, about $167 a month if you borrow $250,000, which is approximately four times what you would pay for private mortgage insurance under a non-FHA loan. And with FHA, the upfront premium is essentially just another fee, which if you borrow $250,000 will equal $4,375. What if some life event comes up and you are forced to sell the house after one year? If you borrowed $250,000, you will have paid the upfront premium of $4,375 plus $2,000 in monthly mortgage insurance payments. That comes out to $531 a month! This is awfully steep, since PMI on that amount under a non-FHA loan would be only $40 a month. This is an extreme example, since holding your house for only one year is not the norm and is a bad idea.)

If you kept your house two years, your total would be $350 per month, $285 if you kept your house 3 years, etc. And you are not actually *paying* that amount each month—it was probably added to the amount borrowed, and you are only paying the 0.8% part out of pocket, which, as I said, is about $167 per month to start, going down as your loan balance goes down. The $531/$350/$285 numbers are just to show you how much more an FHA loan will cost you in mortgage insurance costs than a regular loan would.)

If you want to determine whether you can actually support yourself via operating an STR, you need to include your monthly mortgage payment under "Expenses" when you do your net income calculation.

You may find that, unfortunately, after subtracting your monthly mortgage payment, your net income is not very big.

Long-term, this does not mean that operating an STR (or LTR) is a bad idea, because part of the way you make money owning property is through its appreciation over time. Real estate has generally been a good investment over the last century (if you avoid buying during a bubble, but even then, it can be a fairly good investment if you hold it for a number of years).

But real estate is illiquid, and generally you need to buy and hold for several years before you cash out to make up for the transaction costs of selling—5% to agents and 1% closing costs, not to mention possibly capital gains tax. Talk to your CPA about how to minimize capital gains tax.

So, your earnings on real estate ownership are not all coming in the form of a regular income stream (rents). They come partly in the lump sum you get only when you actually sell.

What all this means is that real estate is usually a good long-term investment, but at the level we are talking about, usually does not throw off a lot of cash after you take all the costs into account. If you want to live off the cash you make from your STRs, you need a critical mass of properties that generate enough cash that you can not only keep them going, and even buy more, but take some of the profit to support yourself.

Buying more will be key if your current property will not make enough to support you. If your goal is to support yourself owning and operating STRs, the cash you are making from your current property probably needs to be saved up for a down payment to purchase your second property. Once you get that going as an STR, you need to save up cash for your third property. During this time, you probably want to take out as little money as possible from what you are saving, for things like, say, *trying to live off the income from your STRs*. Taking out cash to support yourself defeats the goal of buying enough properties to run as STRs to generate enough income to support yourself.

Make sense?

There are other options for coming up with cash for a down payment, such as doing a cash-out refinance if you have accumulated enough equity in any of your properties. Talk to your mortgage lender to see if this makes sense. Doing this will increase your monthly mortgage payment for that property, which needs to be taken into account when calculating your income.

Depending on your particular situation, supporting yourself entirely through operating STRs is probably something you should view as a long-term goal, not something you can achieve in a year or two, unless your circumstances are especially favorable—like, if you have a low mortgage payment and are willing to live off almost nothing, and can charge healthy rates for your STR.

Rental Property

Another route to making STR operation your full-time job is by renting or leasing property from others and then renting it out. There are two main versions: you rent one property, where you live, and rent out a room or rooms.

The other version, which is scalable and can allow your business to grow very big, is when you rent out one or more properties where you do not live, and STR them. This is called rental arbitrage. This has become a popular method for some entrepreneurs to start generating large revenues quickly, and you will see a lot about it on YouTube, but there are risks. It is a form of leveraging assets to make money much quicker than you otherwise might. But it can also lose you a lot of money, very quickly.

You will, of course, not make any money on the appreciation of your propert(ies), because you will not own any property. But the upside is that *all* the money you make comes in the form of an income stream (revenues minus expenses, of which a mortgage payment is not one). You have zero costs of ownership, and lower maintenance costs.

(Again, for purposes of this section, I am going to assume you have investigated all legalities and determined that you can, as a renter, legally operate an STR in your location, and that any restrictions on you will not be so burdensome as to negate the possibility of your making a living at it full-time.)

It's critical that if you want to rent a property and use it as an STR that you get your landlord's written permission. Though you can try to sneak the fact that you are STR-ing a property past your landlord, this is not a good idea, if you are serious about being in this business. Landlords will very likely be able to cancel your lease and throw you out for operating an STR, because most leases have a clause that disallows subletting, or having any tenants not approved by the landlord, or both.

Rental Arbitrage

Everyone's favorite new subject in the STR industry is rental arbitrage, where you take out leases on properties and STR them. Some *arbitrageurs* will rent out a whole floor in a new building, or even the whole building.

(Again, for purposes of this section, I am going to assume you have investigated all legalities and determined that you can, as a renter, legally operate an STR in your location, and that any restrictions on you will not be so burdensome as to negate the possibility of your making a living at it full-time.)

You will, of course, need to sell the landlord on the idea of allowing you to STR units in his or her building. Ideally, you want a landlord who is hands off, and just tells you, "Do what you want as long as you pay me my monthly rent."

You may find a landlord who owns a property that you think would be excellent as an STR, and he or she will rent you the property for a cut of the income you make, or rent to you at an above-market rate in exchange for permission for giving you use it as an STR.

Don't get caught up thinking you shouldn't have to pay above-market rent for the apartment(s). Realistically, the landlord deserves more than what they would get from a long-term tenant because the problems, the wear-and-tear, and the risks to the landlord are greater if the property is being STR'd than if he or she rented to a long-term tenant.

Plus, if you are making all the profit and he is making none, he may decide, when your lease ends, to cut out the middleman. You. Then you'll be stuck with a whole lot of furniture you will have to move into a storage unit, and your STR business, at that property at least, will abruptly end. Hope you don't have any future bookings, since you will have to cancel them, or convince your guests to stay at another of your properties instead, if any.

For this reason, you really need to get a multi-year lease on a property of you want to arbitrage it. Even if you *are* paying above-market rent or giving the landlord a share of the profit, he may realize how much you are making (perhaps by finding your property on Airbnb and seeing much you charge per night) and want all of it. Landlords are like that. They won't know or care how much work an STR can be once they see those dollar signs. You will explain that you really only get 20% or so of that amount once you take into account the platform's fees, all your expenses, and so on, so the landlord's cut of the STR income really is more than fair. Good luck with that.

The plus of building an STR empire on rentals is that you can do it much faster. It is certainly not as capital-intensive as buying buildings to rent them out, and does not tie you down to a property for years in order to capture a reasonable amount of appreciation from the asset.

There is a lot that is fundamentally same about running multiple STRs through rental arbitrage as running them in your own properties. Except dealing with landlords and leases. You still need to market your properties, meet the standards of guests, clean your rentals between stays, furnish them, and most of all, get the five-star reviews you need to stay in business.

But I would suggest not going all-in on rental arbitrage from day one. As a first step, try running one, or maybe two, STRs for a year. You can cut that down to half a year if you are really eager. Running a big operation is not easy. Many things you will need to do are time-sensitive, such as same-day turnovers. And you will probably have multiple same-day turnovers more often than you think, especially if you are in an area where people tend to book mostly weekends, or mostly weekdays, or mostly the same days. Can you manage that with multiple units?

A good way to look at the risk involved in doing rental arbitrage with multiple units is to consider the concept of *leverage*.

Sometimes you hear leverage discussed as an unalloyed good. In rental arbitrage, you are leveraging the comparatively low cost of leasing versus buying to expand your number of rental units much faster than you could if you had to buy them. But it's not always an unalloyed good. Sometimes, it can lead to disaster.

We have the perfect illustration of an utter disaster that exposed the weaknesses of leveraging yourself too highly: Covid-19.

If you were not following the STR or travel industries closely during the Covid-19 crisis, travel fell almost to zero. Air travel was down about 90% and at one point, Airbnb bookings were down 95%. There were literally no guests for several months, though a few hosts were able to scrape by hosting first responders, housing the homeless under local programs, or housing people who wanted to social distance in their own rental rather than wherever they would otherwise be staying.

It depended a lot on where you were and what you had to offer. Some beach rentals or rentals characterized by low-human-contact, like cabins in the woods, were more likely to continue to get bookings. But most properties didn't get anything.

If you were a homeowner, it was possible to get mortgage forbearance for up to a year, though there were hoops to jump through. If you had a dozen leased rental units that you were arbitraging…well, it was up to you to figure something out.

Many hosts who owned their properties had to sell some of them. Those who rented their properties had to get very creative, which mainly involved working with their landlords to see if they could figure something out.

Luckily, if you can call it that, landlords were over a barrel as well. There aren't that many people looking for a new apartment when an area is under a shelter-in-place order. So, losing tenants during such a time could be bad for them. They had an incentive to work with existing tenants who might be having financial problems.

The Best Thing to Do

If you are doing rental arbitrage and are having trouble making your rents due to Covid-19, the best thing to do is **contact your landlord and work out a mutually beneficial arrangement.**

Your landlord holds the cards, since not paying rent is usually reason enough for the landlord to evict you, unless the lease contains some kind of language preventing that. Don't make the assumption that rent control laws will protect you when it comes to properties you are using for commercial purposes and where you do not personally live. Read up on local laws in that regard.

The best thing to do is put on your salesman hat and turn on the charm when you go talk to your landlord(s). Sean Rakidzich of the [Airbnb Automated](#) YouTube channel has an excellent approach to negotiating a mutually-beneficial arrangement with your landlord. Watch the video [here](). [11]

One of his ideas is that if your landlord is able to get forbearance on his or her mortgage (which they may be able to, though they may not have known that was possible) offer to *pay them to take a forbearance*. Offer to pay them just the interest on the mortgage (the portion that applies to your leased units, anyway), plus 10%, so they will continue to have positive cash flow. And let them know you will begin paying the normal amount again as soon as you have guests, as well as paying them back for the portion of your rent they did not collect during the time your payments were interest-only (plus 10%). [12]

Will your landlord go for this? It depends.

I don't know exactly what it depends on, though. In part, the landlord needs to understand the arrangement from a financial point of view, and not think you are just trying to scam him since you are out of options. If you happen to know another landlord who has made this kind of arrangement with his tenants, and you can put your landlord in touch with that person so they can discuss it, that would be a good idea. Your landlord may not trust you—in this dire situation, at least—but he may trust another landlord. Or maybe your landlord will trust you, since he may be feeling desperate, and the forbearance idea may be extremely appealing if you can walk him through it. Not that he really needs you for that, but he may appreciate the assistance, and be favorably inclined toward you afterwards.

But…just to illustrate how tough it became during the height of the Covid-19 outbreak, large rental arbitrage companies laid people off almost immediately—Sonder, which has about 5,000 apartments ("doors") laid off 33% of staff. Lyric, which is partially owned by Airbnb, laid off 20%. Waanderjaunt laid off 15-20%. The Guild laid off 22%. [13]

It is hard to get numbers on private companies such as these, since they are not required to report them, nor are they governed by SEC rules. The numbers above were reported The Real Deal less than two weeks after stay-at-home orders began in the U.S. The companies' financial problems may have gotten worse as Covid-19 crisis went on. Time will tell which survive and which do not. The only certainty is uncertainty.

How to Survive Covid-19

In my opinion, travel will bounce back from Covid-19 faster than expected. Here are some things you can start doing right now to attract travelers:

Emphasize that you use "enhanced cleaning methods" at your propert(ies). Airbnb has created The Airbnb Cleaning Handbook[14], "based on CDC guidance and in consultation with industry leaders (such as Ecolab and Dr. Vivek Murthy, Former US Surgeon General)." Follow it—and make sure Airbnb knows you are following it, because otherwise they will automatically require 72 hours between bookings rather than 24. Commit to the cleaning protocol here, where you will be given a 10-question, open-book quiz[15] (based on the contents of The Airbnb Cleaning Handbook) to ensure you understand everything required.

Once you have passed the quiz, you can press a button saying you commit to follow the cleaning protocols, and choose which listings you want to commit to them for. Then you have the option to add a 24-hour buffer between guests in order to have time to clean and follow the guidelines, rather than the buffer defaulting to 72 hours.

You can also download a Committed to Clean sign[16] to put in your property. I recommend taking a photo of it and making it one of the photos on your listing on Airbnb's and/or Vrbo's websites, so guests can see it while they are browsing for a place to book. If you just put it in the living room of your rental, it might be reassuring to guests, but it's not going to get them there in the first place.

Advertise your listing on every channel you can. I write elsewhere in this book about how it can get complicated to manage your listings when you get on numerous platforms, and you create more opportunities to double-book, which is generally a disaster because you either have to cancel on a guest or convince them to cancel. But during the Covid-19 recovery, until a regular flow of guests come back, you need to sacrifice convenience in order to get your listing in front of as many people as possible.

Post your listing in Facebook groups, in message boards on Reddit—anywhere. Post your listing in your news feed on Facebook for friends and family to see. Post on Linked In describing your place as a "perfect corporate rental." Register with Traveling Nurses (or don't—they charge a fee of about $100 per year, and from what I have heard, many people are not sure it is worth it. We are probably past the point in the pandemic when nurses are looking for housing, anyway.)

Sign up for local programs housing the homeless with Covid-19. Look on the website of your local county or city.

Sign up through Airbnb to host Covid-19 first responders. You are required to choose either "free" or "at a discount" for their stays. Choose whatever discount you think is fair. I would request documentation from the "first responder" showing that they are, in fact, a first responder. Airbnb says they verify that, but do your own check anyway.

Lower your rates—but not too much. Low rates, in normal circumstances, attract guests who don't treat your place as well as full-price guests do, and tend to leave worse reviews. And keep in mind that whatever you lower your rates to, guests in these times tend to request discounts, often 50%. They do not seem to be aware that your rates are already heavily discounted. Be prepared for almost everyone to play the "essential worker" or "first responder" cards. "Essential worker" is a near-meaningless term, anyway, since if your job allows you to leave your house during lockdown for a work-related purpose, you are "essential" (in many places).

Temporarily convert your property to a long-term, furnished rental. If you don't think obtaining enough bookings from STR guests in the next 3-6 months is realistic, and you do not have enough saved to ride out the slower-than-slow period (or don't want to) look for longer-term tenants.

Some people try to simply do this through Airbnb, but I don't think that works. People looking for a 6-month rental aren't looking on Airbnb. They are looking on Craigslist, talking to friends, looking on Apartments.com, or elsewhere.

Make any new leases 3-6 months rather than the usual 12. Be careful, though—some areas have strict laws protecting tenants, and once a tenant is in, they may be protected by rent control, meaning it may be difficult to get them out when you want to go back to STR-ing. In states with rent control, or which allow only for-cause eviction, carefully read up on your local laws. The

National Multifamily Housing Council has a helpful map of which states/jurisdictions are likely to give you the most trouble (California, Oregon, New York, New Jersey, Maryland, and DC).

Save up for a rainy day. This advice is probably too late, but save up enough money to cover 6-12 months of your business' expenses. You never know what catastrophe is just around the corner. If it's not a return of Covid-19, it will be something else.

Have business interruption insurance. Also probably too late to help for this particular crisis. And I have had a number of people tell me that their business interruption insurance did not cover their economic losses for Covid-19. But look into it.

Is Short-Term Renting for You?

We have already talked about types of short-term rentals and some urgent questions like how to get through Covid-19. But let's step back for a moment and look at operating an STR from a different angle.

As you have seen by now, STR income is not really passive income. It takes time and effort, compared to LTR income. I have already broken down my own revenues and expenses for my two properties, both in New Orleans, LA. But those aren't necessarily as applicable to your own situation as they could be. You want as much relevant information as possible about running an STR, of the type you want to run, in the area in which you want to run it, before you start looking for a place to rent or buy, or spending any money

If you are lucky, you may know someone operating an STR near your location, similar in size, condition, amenities, and desirability to the one you are proposing to start. Pick that person's brain to figure out what works for him or her and what doesn't. He or she will have done a lot of trial-and-error already. Having a person with a successful STR similar to yours whom you can quiz about everything is really the Holy Grail of preparing to operate an STR yourself.

One thing that is *not* the Holy Grail is throwing questions out to Reddit or Facebook groups and asking people to do all your most important research for you. I'm always amazed by people who post questions like, "Where in the country is a good place to buy a short-term rental?" or other questions displaying what an utterly lazy approach they are taking. Asking an anonymous audience who doesn't know you or care about you may not be the best way to get advice about big financial decisions.

Think about it: suppose I am in an area with unexpectedly high demand where I am one of only a few active STRs, and we are all always booked. Am I going to tell this person about it so I can have more competition, from a clueless out-of-towner? Doubtful.

Or suppose I am a troll who is angry because he is in an area that is becoming totally overrun with STRs to the point that he can't make money anymore. Will he tell the poster to invest in his area, just to mess with her? Maybe.

There are also a lot of people online who are just, well, not that smart. Those people always seem to be the most eager to give advice and share their "knowledge."

Here are some ideas to help you get through the initial, tough period.

Study the STRs in Your Immediate Area

This is very important. **Don't be lazy and skip this step**, and figure you will just try your luck. If you do that, you will pay for it. You will make less money for a longer period of time.

I should have put **STUDY** in caps. That means, don't just skim. Notice the small differences between properties. If someone is charging 20% more than most people with similar properties for the same thing, don't just latch onto that and decide you can also charge 20% more. Figure out why he thinks he can get away with it.

By being careful, may notice something you didn't before—like he has some amenity or amenities that guests love. Maybe off-street gated parking plus a fabulous view. A private hot tub right off the master bedroom. Or he has 100 reviews raving that staying with him has been the best experience of peoples' lives, particularly the champagne breakfast in bed and the fresh-baked croissants.

Pay particular attention to STRs that have been up and running for more than a year (check the number of reviews – if they have twenty-five or so on any platform, they've been going for a while). This means they have probably gotten it down to a science, and are making enough money to make their STR worth their while. They would have quit long ago if they weren't.

Read the Reviews of Comparable STRs in Your Area

Most people who have visited an STR will be very positive in the reviews they write. (I am talking about Americans here—Europeans are usually more measured, and certainly more stingy when giving out stars.) However, by reading between the lines, you can see what was lacking and displeased guests, and what was appreciated by guests.

When guests openly complain, that makes it easy. If you see complaints repeating, either on the same property or across multiple properties, be aware that you pay special attention to that in your own property. For example, if people complain about cockroaches. You may know, or think you know, that your area has cockroaches and eliminating them all is impossible. This is the wrong position to take. Try hard to make sure your place is without cockroaches, even if you, and your neighbors, view them as inevitable. Have a pest control company come out and spray regularly. Seal up your home and apply roach killing bait in places like the kitchen.

Be on the lookout for things that guests says were "fine, but I wish I had known in advance…". This may alert you to things that, again, you see as common or inevitable, but guests may not. For example, in my city, a large proportion of the housing stock is shotgun houses (or double-shotguns, which are duplexes essentially made of two shotgun houses pushed together and sharing a wall). A shotgun house is long and narrow, and has one room following another, without hallways. Consequently, the only room that people do not need to walk through to get to other rooms is the room at the very back of the house.

In New Orleans, it's very common to live in a shotgun house, or one half of a double-shotgun. In other places, it generally isn't. This means people from other areas usually expect private, "normal" bedrooms, and not to have to walk through other peoples' bedrooms to get to the bathroom or the kitchen.

I learned by experience that prospective guests prefer to be "warned" that the rental is a shotgun. This way if the concept bothers them, they won't book, and we'll all be happier.

In short, take my word for it, reading the reviews of your competitors will give you a world of information you can use to improve your rental before you even host your first guest.

Honestly evaluate how other nearby rentals ("comps") compare to yours

Now that you've looked at your "comps" and read their reviews, make a conscious effort to objectively compare their offerings to yours. You have probably been doing that the entire time, at least subconsciously, but now, really focus on it.

Is the comp designed with an obvious effort to host a traveler, or is it dust-covered and jammed full of the owner's stuff, with the owner's dusty doll collection taking up space on the chairs and piles of outdated LPs stacked in multiple rooms, to the point that in places there is barely room to walk? (Is this how *your* place is going to look? I hope not.)

Is the furniture attractive and new(ish), do the beds look comfortable, are there decent-looking, semi-fashionable bedspreads and decorative pillows on the beds? Or are the beds made up with bedspreads that look like a grandmother's hand-me-down, flower-print, polyester ones from the 70s? Are the pillows flat and worn-out? A surprising number of hosts do use these ragged old relics in their rentals—bedspreads that would probably otherwise spend the remainder of their lives in the bed of a truck.

And, how will *your* STR look? Be honest.

Dusty dolls and a hoarder-like environment are considered a negative by guests, as are old and uncomfortable looking beds. What overcomes a negative is generally a lower price. If your rental is going to look similar to those kinds of comps, their prices will give you an idea of what you can reasonably charge.

Similarly, look at what your comps offer in terms of appliances (coffee maker, blender, toaster, microwave, dishwasher, washer/dryer, etc.). Do most of your comps have full kitchens? That's a big selling point. Even though, in my experience, most renters hardly use the kitchen, or just use it just to scramble eggs for breakfast, people on a budget like the option of preparing their own meals.

Remember that if you offer a full kitchen, guests won't be able to use it unless you provide them all the things they need to cook and eat with—pots and pans, knife set, cooking utensils, plates, bowls, silverware, glasses, mugs, etc. If your listing makes it appear to guests that you have a full kitchen, but then they get there and discover there are no plates, no cooking utensils, no pots and pans, and no silverware, they will be disappointed. A gas range, an oven, and a dishwasher are great, but most people don't travel with a box full of pots and pans, cutlery, plates, glasses, etc. A surprising number of hosts don't take care to provide all these things in their "full kitchen." Don't sell your property as having a full kitchen that guests can't cook or eat in due to lack of the essential tools for cooking and eating. Many can be found at dollar stores for low prices.

Do the comps have features you don't?

Be honest with yourself. Does a comp have an amazing outdoor space, with a slate patio, a redwood hot tub, comfy lawn chairs, sparkling lights, nice landscaping, and lots of privacy? If you don't, and know you are not going to any time soon, you might be tempted to think, "Well, renters in my town don't really care about that stuff." Don't be so sure.

Does the comp have its own entrance? Off-street parking? Cable TV? If your proposed rental is short on features that the comps have, consider which rental a traveler is going to book if both are priced the same.

Which would YOU choose? I'd take cable TV over no cable TV. I'd take a luxurious outdoor space over no outdoor space, even though I probably wouldn't use it. That is, unless the rental without the amenities were charging a price that was low enough to balance out the reduced offering.

Set your prices a bit lower at first

When you first put your listing online, you may have found a comp that is almost exactly the same as your proposed STR, in almost exactly the same location. *Bingo!* you think. Now you know what to charge—the same!

But, no. Before you have positive reviews, lots of people will be hesitant to book your rental. Prospective guests have very little to go on other than reviews and photos. On many sites, people cannot see your exact address. They do not know your full name. You are in a faraway city where they don't live or know anyone. Guests know that your photos may be putting a positive spin on your rental. In fact, your photos could even be fake! You could be a scammer for all they know. It does happen—and people have read the stories. (More on scams later.)

So, until you are established, you will need to charge a bit less in order to attract travelers to take a chance on you and leave you some reviews. Even still, travelers will be wary. When you first start out, you will get more inquiries where people ask you questions than you will bookings. You will need to patiently explain to the people who inquire about the property why you have no reviews yet, and try to make them feel comfortable enough to book the property without being afraid you will abscond with their money. Even if they do book it, they may still fear you will abscond with their money. Paying less helps balance the perceived risk with their desire to save.

Point: you need to make an honest evaluation of where your proposed STR will fit into the marketplace. You don't want to overshoot and make renovations and improvements and spend money you won't get back. But you also don't want to be the worn-out, unattractive place that sits on the shelf and doesn't rent unless you lower your price enough to make it worth it for people to hold their noses and stay there.

Legal

Probably the most important background you should do before you get serious about operating an STR is researching the legal landscape in your local area (city, county, and state).

Start with an Internet search about the legality of short-term rentals in your area. Since most laws governing STRs are set at the city or county level, start there. (There are, however, some statewide laws today—find out.) Your city or county government website probably talks about STRs and whether they are allowed in your jurisdiction, and under what conditions. Read these rules carefully, and make sure your proposed STR will be operated so that it meets all the conditions. A license or permit may be required, and there may be other conditions you must meet before you even apply (like, working smoke detectors in all the bedrooms, a fully-charged fire extinguisher, etc.). **Consult a local attorney for assistance in ensuring you know and are following all the rules!**

If you can't find anything on local government websites, don't assume STRs are legal. Call or visit your city or county's property bureau and ask for any information they have. Remember, this is the government you are dealing with. They may be less than conscientious when it comes to posting important information on their website(s) or keeping it updated. That doesn't absolve you of the responsibility of knowing it.

Talking to a real person should turn up something. But because laws and ordinances around STRs tend to be in flux these days, also look for local news stories on the subject. Many localities are currently debating whether to allow STRs, or have recently banned them, or have hearings coming up on them. It's a moving target, so tune in to local news outlets, among all the other sources I have mentioned.

Also, find out if there is an STR advocacy group in your area, and attend their meetings. If there isn't one, there may be anti-STR groups. They will probably have current information on the laws governing STRs as well. You don't need to tell them you are thinking about starting an STR to go to their meetings. Just go as a concerned citizen—concerned about whether you should open up an STR of your own.

Neighbors

Your neighbors are a very important factor in whether hosting an STR is right for you.

Are they organized into groups strongly opposed to STRs? Are they the type to confront your guests and say horrible things to them? I have one like that. Luckily, she is old and gets out of breath easily, so even when she gets worked up, it is primarily hand-waving, not speech. (This is also the neighbor who asked me to police my guests' parking on the street. Unfortunately, that conversation was not the extent of her negativity.)

Or, is your area urban and transient, where people come and go frequently, and neighbors do not know or even acknowledge each other? These neighbors may notice you are operating an STR and not be happy about it, but they are probably not going to actually take any action against you. I say this based on the fact that I lived in San Francisco for 14 years in small apartments. People don't like neighbors being noisy, but usually, they don't bother complaining to the landlord, who wouldn't care anyway, because he would prefer that his longer-term tenants move out (due to rent control) so he can replace them with market-rate tenants.

Do you have a busybody in your building, or next door, who watches every move of everyone on the block?

Do your neighbors have the power to report you to the city, and would you be cited for operating an STR? (This goes back to "Legal," of course.)

Some of the above questions are easy to answer, but some of the important ones are difficult.

It's hard to ask a neighbor whom you know, but not well, whether they will care if you rent your place out short-term. Asking them will alert them that you are thinking about doing it, and if they are opposed to it, you are giving them an opportunity to batten down the hatches and prepare for war. At minimum, they will begin gossiping about it with other neighbors.

I'm putting this section right after legal because your neighbors and their attitude become more important if short-term renting is illegal or in a legal gray area where you live.

If STR-ing is legal, and you follow the rules, there is little your neighbors can do unless you are violating those rules. Except, of course, watch like hawks for violations, or even lie to the city and say you *are* violating the rules, which humans have been known to do.

If STRs are not legal, or in a legal gray area, then…you may put a lot of time, effort and expense into starting up your STR, only to be shut down by a busybody neighbor who makes it his or her mission in life to shut you down. "Not on my street!"

If that happens, your only option may be the rent out your place long-term to someone with a passel of dogs who bark constantly.

Here are a few tips:

- ✓ Long before you start operating your STR, make friends with your neighbors. If they are older (or even if they are not), offer to pull weeds for them near the property line, since, heck, you are doing your own side anyway. Be friendly and offer to keep an eye on their place when they are out of town. On garbage day, drag their can back into place after the trash service comes, since, heck, you are doing yours anyway. This way, when your STR is up and running, despite their desire to shut you down, they may stop themselves because they think you have a good heart.

- ✓ If STRs are legal in your area, know and follow all the rules to a "T."

- ✓ Don't allow too many guests to stay in your rental at one time. It's okay to set your rental's maximum at less than your jurisdiction's allowed maximum, or less than the property could actually sleep if you put a bed in every room with a sofa bed or two in the common spaces.

- ✓ Ensure your guests are firmly told, and that they obey, any ordinances or association rules about noise and quiet hours. Or even your own rules that you made up, which you are allowed to do, though you must put them in your House Rules in your property listing. Additionally, make sure your guests follow the unspoken rules of the neighborhood. There are probably more of these in the South, where I live, than in some other places.

- ✓ Do not allow your guests to throw parties or hold events at the rental. Ban guests from having other guests over to the rental entirely (I do). Tell guests in your House Rules that the rental may not be used as a meet-up place, or for parties, gatherings, events, or commercial activity. Enforce that.

- ✓ Emphasize to guests that they are in a residential neighborhood, not on Bourbon Street or the Las Vegas Strip. The rules of behavior are different, and if they choose to stay at your property, they have to fit in. Again, this should go in your House Rules (more about House Rules later—they are important).

- ✓ In a nutshell: control your guests!

Some Types of Short-Term Rentals

Here are some examples of the ways your property, or the spare room you would like to rent out, can work as a short-term rental. This is not an exhaustive list, but hopefully it can give you some ideas.

Room Rental, Urban Setting

If you are renting an apartment in a densely-populated urban setting, and you live there, you may have an extra bedroom you want to rent out short-term. If the apartment is small and your neighbors are close, they will quickly figure out what you are doing. They may also be sensitive to noise. While many city-dwellers put up with noise as the price of living in the city, and many also have an I-don't-care-what-you-do-as-long-as-you-don't-murder-me-in-the-hallway attitude, the closeness and the likelihood of your guests making noise may make your neighbors more likely to report you to your landlord.

This matters because, even if it is legal for you as a tenant to operate an STR, with or without the permission of the landlord, it's likely he can get you shut down if your STR is generating complaints. Any time you, as a tenant, are creating a nuisance, and the landlord has evidence showing it's not a one-off but a pattern, good luck prevailing in court.

But as I said, often landlords don't care what their tenants do and don't want to hear their complaints. Anecdote: I had a landlord in San Francisco who I called late one night to tell him that one of his tenants—call her "Apartment 12"—had had a fire, the building had filled with smoke, and the fire department had to come put it out. *Again.* Yes, this was Apartment 12's *second fire in the space of a couple months.* The landlord yelled at me for bothering him.

If you are not renting, but own, an apartment (condo) in similar circumstances, many of the above advice will apply, just substitute "condo association" for "landlord." Condo associations are more likely to have clear-cut, written rules about STRs than your typical landlord. And while a condo association may not have the power to kick you out, they may be able to fine you or take some other action if your STR violates any rules (possibly just by existing).

Tip: if you are renting out a room in an apartment, do not allow guests to have anyone over. Similarly, only allow one guest, not two, in the room you are renting. If you have two guests, you have talking, and the noise level vastly increases.

Another Tip: if you are able to charge a high nightly rate, you may be able to rent out your spare room or couch just a few days per month and make a decent amount of extra cash. Your neighbors will take longer to figure out you are STR-ing (they may assume that your occasional guests are just friends in town), and you can be choosier about guests, only taking the ones you think will be quiet and discreet.

Another Tip: if the above applies, and you can charge a high rate, don't get greedy! If you take in guests too many nights per month, or if you start taking multiple guests at once so you can charge more, your neighbors will notice, and the bad things already mentioned could ruin a good side-hustle.

Room Rental, Suburban or Rural

I have to admit, I don't know much about the market for suburban or rural rentals, particularly rentals of single rooms in occupied homes.

If you live near a special attraction of some kind, and it happens to be suburban or rural, then it's possible you could do well with a single-room STR, particularly around special events or specific draws like specialty hospitals, which are often found in suburbs.

You might also do well if you live in a location with seasonal activities—people will pay to stay in places they normally wouldn't when everything else is booked.

Also, if almost nobody is offering an STR in your area, you may do well by virtue of the fact that, even if there are very few people seeking to stay at an STR in your area, if you are the only game in town, you will get the business. It's all about supply and demand, and while demand may be very low, if supply is even lower, you have a business opportunity.

Just make sure not to talk about it too much, or people will start copying you and ruin your thing.

Tip: Think about whether and when people would find renting a room in your home to be an attractive option. A long-term tenant might be better for you financially, because that person will be a source of income month after month, regardless of season. But on the negative side, they will be in your house 365 days a year, creating more wear and tear, and you'll rarely get a break where you have the house or apartment to yourself.

Whole-House Rental, Tourist Destination

Whole houses are not usually available for rent in densely-populated city centers, which is why I did not address them above when I talked about apartments. But some major tourist attractions or vacation spots have whole house STRs available. If you have a whole house to rent out (which you are not occupying), and are thinking about doing it as an STR, you have a lot to consider.

Supervision. If you are renting out a whole house, unless you live next door, you don't know what your guests are doing at any given time. (This is true of whole-apartment rentals too, but the potential for problems is even greater in whole-house rentals, since there is probably an outdoor space, and in my experience, in a whole-house rental people just feel more "unsupervised.") They could be blasting music all night, having a house party with 300 people, or worse. While most guests are respectful and don't cause problems, there is a small minority who seem to have been raised by wild dogs. These are the guests who get the cops called and push your neighbors over the line from grudging acceptance of your STR to making the decision to complain to the city.

So, of course, have exterior cameras you can view at any time, and make sure to disclose them in your listing online. Also consider a Minit noise sensor that will alert you when the decibel level gets too high.

Tip: Screen your guests as best you can. (More on screening later.)

Maintenance. You will probably want to maintain the exterior of your house and your landscaping in good condition. You won't attract top-quality guests, or be able to charge top rates, if there are weeds growing up through cracks in the front porch and the wind has blown a big pile of trash in front of your front gate.

Maintenance costs money, as well as time and effort (unless you pay someone to do it, then it just costs money). You will find that, if you do everything yourself, you will frequently need to be replacing something and maintain plants, pull weeds, and shovel up waste from the dog your next-door neighbor won't restrain.

With a house, there are also the big expenditures that fall from the sky, sometimes one after another. A house is a house, they call them money pits for a reason.

The above considerations apply whether your house is used exclusively as a rental or if you live in it yourself and vacate when it is being rented. (If you do not vacate when it is being rented, then it is not a whole-home rental.)

If You Normally Live There, But Vacate When You Rent

Many people live in places where they can make a lot of money renting out their home just a few times a year for festivals or in certain seasons. Here are some considerations if this applies to you:

Keep a portion of the house lockable and make it a no-go area for guests. This can be anything from a closet to a whole room, or maybe a store room in the garage you build out of plywood. But you need a place to put non-shared things where guests cannot get to them, especially when you are renting out your whole home and will not be on the premises.

I have found that it is human nature that guests will snoop. If you have a locked cabinet, they will pull on the door.

So, not only have a lock on your closet or room, have it deadbolted so that the guests will try once and give up. I am not saying your guests will steal anything, but they will snoop. They cannot help it.

Tip: Don't try to use your powers of logic to predict what guests would and would not be tempted get into. Your powers will fail you.

Separate Towels, Linens, Etc.

I have never had a property where I lived part-time and occasionally rented out. But I am pretty sure I would keep my own sheets, towels, blankets, pillows, and other linens separate from the ones I used for my guests. You may even consider having separate plates, glasses, cups, silverware, and so on, depending on how you feel about visitors using your stuff.

If you have a special dish set or a special set of wine glasses and you decide to leave them available for guests, be prepared for something to break sooner or later. If in doubt, save yourself the worry and buy a cheap set of dishes or glasses at Wal-Mart for guests to use (wine glasses at Wal-Mart are either $4 for six, or $6 for four, I can't remember which) and put your good ones in that locked room.

Just to save you some heartache, I want to drive home again that logic does not work when trying to forecast what guests may get into. Do you have a china closet full of mementoes that a visitor would have absolutely no reason to open up? Is the topper on your wedding cake in there on the top shelf? If you don't want it used as a child's toy, put it somewhere behind lock and key.

Note: if you have an upscale rental and you have pictured crystal decanters and expensive leaded glasses in the photos in your listing, you can't just take all that stuff and lock it up, leaving your guests with a stack of Solo cups. If you featured something in a photo in such a way that a guest might reasonably believe it would be available to them, they need to be given access to it. You can't deliver your guests a house that looks like it's just been stripped of everything of value and expect them to be happy about it.

Do Not Leave Your Pets!

I wish I did not need to say this, but DO NOT leave your pets behind in the rental for your guests to take care of. Even if they agree to do so, and sound happy to do it. Assume that guests, no matter how nice they seem, will not take good care of your pets.

Guests are looking to rent a place to stay. A surprising number of people are *not* animal lovers.

Your guests may very well have agreed to take care of your pet(s) because they felt they had to in order to secure the rental. If you gave them a *discount* to take care of your pets, keep in mind that their sole concern may be the discount, not the pets.

Unless you want to come home to missing, escaped, malnourished, or abused pets that may have been locked in a room (or closet!) the entire time you were gone, don't leave strangers to take care of your pets. Make other arrangements.

Whole-Apartment Rental

In certain places of the country it is common and expected that people will rent out their entire apartments during certain seasons. Florida beach condos are a prime example. This section is not really about those, though some of the advice may apply. It is more about when you want to rent out an apartment in a regular, non-tourist neighborhood where most apartments are housing long-term tenants. In other words, the classic "Airbnb" that allows a visitor to "embed" in a real community.

STR guests generally want to live like a local rather than spend all their time among other tourists. Whole-apartment rentals allow them to do that.

As with whole-house rentals, unless you live next door or nearby, or have a neighbor who is on your side and can report back to you what's going on, you don't know what your guests are up to. We will talk later about some ways to help address these concerns.

If you live in the apartment part-time and vacate when you rent it out, the same advice applies as applied to whole-house renters: have a space that you can lock things you do not want guests getting into.

Apartment in a Building

If your proposed STR is in a building with a single entrance that everyone must enter through, like a lobby with a locked door, and everyone needs either a key or a code to get in, this is a hurdle to short-term renting you need to think through in advance.

Will you need to meet all guests and give them a key, and is that feasible? Or do they need a code to get in, and is it okay for you to give that code to STR guests? I have a feeling residents would be leery if a stream of STR were being given their building's door code.

The ideal STR apartment has a door directly to the street, but you may be able to make it work the other way.

Upshot: some apartments are better than others when it comes to STRs.

Non-Traditional Space

Non-traditional spaces are some of the most fun when it comes to STRs, and from one viewpoint, are the STR ideal. They allow people to experience spaces where they would never otherwise be able to stay.

If you have a non-traditional space, you are probably already aware of it. And, you can probably also throw all the rules for traditional houses and apartments out the window.

But here are some basics that apply to all rentals, traditional and otherwise:

Humans need clean water. They like to drink water, and some use it to bathe.

Humans go to the bathroom. You should have an idea about where they can do this. They will ask.

Humans often find electricity useful. Sure, your non-traditional rental may be the type that any fool should know does not have electricity. However—if possible—you might want to provide an electrical outlet or an outdoor-safe extension cord your guests can at least plug one or two things into. You might even decide to be super-nice and provide guests an LED lantern or some other helpful device they may not have thought about, and wait for the good reviews to pour in.

Humans get cold. If your non-traditional rental is a drafty barn in Montana (fun fact: the original use of now-trendy shiplap, in which the boards have rabbets so that they overlap at the top and bottom, was to keep wind from blowing into drafty barns, making them less drafty) and the forecast is for -40 F, and your visitors are a bunch of young stoners hitchhiking across the country, you should probably have a backup plan in place that will give them a decent chance to avoid dying.

Humans overheat. Similarly, your "Death Valley Oasis" needs to come with a fallback survival plan, even if the plan is for you to go and pick up your guests up and bring them to your air-conditioned house, otherwise… well, you know. Death. Too many deaths on your property, generally speaking, is frowned upon.

Upshot: you know a lot more about your non-traditional rental than your guests do, and you will probably have guests at times who make assumptions that are very wrong. When you say in your listing, "Only true survivalists and experienced wilderness adventurers need apply," some guests may read between the lines, "…but, I've put this property on Airbnb, so obviously I don't mean that for real, ha ha." If you *do* mean it for real, and you know that anyone who cannot catch and kill a rattlesnake, filet it, and roast its flesh over a fire made from sagebrush twigs will likely not survive, make sure your guests are on the same page.

Humans are liable. This refers to you. If people are on your property, for any reason, invited or uninvited, you may be liable for their injuries or damages. (Or, maybe you won't, depending on circumstances and your local laws.) We will talk more about that perpetual bugbear, insurance, later. But if you have any concerns about your liability for things that happen at your non-traditional STR, talk to your insurance agent and/or local attorney.

Does Operating an STR Fit Your Lifestyle?

I know the word "lifestyle" has a flaky connotation these days, but we need to talk about it.

The answer to the question is probably "yes"—but you, or your guests, might have to make some compromises.

As we have already talked about, there are myriad varieties of STR properties, and there are also myriad types of hosts and guests. But there are a few key things that are universal:

- Guests have to arrive, and be able to get into the rental.
- Guests have to leave, and you need to be able to inspect the rental for damage shortly thereafter, sometimes with a window of just a few hours.
- The rental has to be cleaned between guests.

You could argue that some of the above are not absolutely, positively universal (cleaning? what's cleaning?), or that there are other things that should be added to the list. But the above all have to happen for the vast majority of STRs, so let's talk about them.

Guests Have to Arrive

Guests have to arrive, and sometimes that process can feel like an hours-long cat-herding hell. One of the biggest headaches for many hosts, and a big source of complaints by guests, is arranging the meetup with the guest where the host physically gives them the key.

Another source of problems and misunderstandings occurs when the host lists the check-in time of their rental as "Flexible." I would advise against doing this. Just pick a specific time that generally will work for you, like 6pm. Then, if you and your guests want to modify it by mutual agreement, you can.

Here's why: hosts, if their property requires that they give their guests a physical key, may have to sit there and wait for the guest to arrive in order to give them the key. So, hosts tend to believe "Flexible" means, "I am flexible about what time we decide upon for you to check in. Could be 4pm, could be 9pm. But once we decide on a time, that's the time I will set aside to meet you. You are agreeing to be there at that time, unless unavoidably detained, in which case you, like any person with a speck of decency, agree to notify me immediately, as you would do for any appointment."

But guests may think "Flexible" means something different. They may think it means that, even if a specific time is discussed for them to meet you and get the key from you and check in, the time remains "flexible," because you are just naturally a "flexible," go-with-the-flow kind of groovy person, as your listing states.

Judging from Reddit threads alone, this misunderstanding happens A LOT. Though I think logic (and common courtesy) are on the host's side, why not avoid the problem? Don't list your check-in time as "Flexible." Put it at 6pm, or 4pm, or 4pm to 6pm, or whatever works for you. Don't worry, if the time isn't good for the guest, they won't be shy about suggesting a different one. But at least they won't think they have a "flexible" window of time to show up, that may well stretch beyond your breaking point.

Early Check-in

There is another issue around check-in time separate from the key-handoff issue. I call it the "What's the earliest I can check in?" issue.

Whether you have put a specific check-in time in your listing or have made it "Flexible" (gah), guests will often ask, "What's the earliest I can check in?"

Another variant is frustratingly common: "I'm thinking about taking a redeye flight that arrives at 7am. Would it be okay if I checked in early?"

Well...it depends.

Many guests do not understand, or care about, the logistics of STR turnovers. As the host/owner, you know that you quite possibly have a guest checking out at 11am, and need some time between guests to clean, change linens, and maybe even fix or replace something.

This means that if check-out time is 11am and check-in time is 4pm, and you have people leaving and arriving on the same day, your window to get absolutely everything done between guests is five hours. *Those specific five hours.* And this is assuming the departing guests leave on time, which sometimes they don't.

If you have a guest checking out at 11am on the day the group who is thinking about taking the redeye will be arriving, your first instinct might be to snap at them that you can't very well start cleaning at 5am just to get the place ready for their 8am arrival when you have guests that won't be departing until 11am.

Luckily, you don't need to do that. What you need to do is practice saying "no." Practice saying it in the nicest way possible. It's a mandatory skill if you want to be in the STR business.

I think one major reason for all the troubles about check-in times is that when guests hear the words "check-in," they think "hotel." And other hotel-related terms quickly enter their minds, like "early check-in" and "late check-out" and "I need you to store my luggage after check-out or before check-in." Or both.

As a host, you would think an STR guest should know that they are renting a single property, not a hotel room, of which you have 100 spares you could slot them into if they felt like arriving ten hours early.

You would think. But you need learn how to politely explain that 4pm is the earliest you can have the rental ready for your guests.

Do not offer to allow them to drop off their luggage. (Do you want to be liable for it when they come back later and say things are missing?)

Do not bend over backwards for them and make the fact that they booked a flight to arrive at 7am is your problem. It's not. Or as the workplace sign says, "Don't make your failure to plan my emergency."

This brings us to one of the tricky (and frustrating) parts of being an STR host: Guests often expect you to provide all the amenities, services, and flexibilities of a hotel, even though you only have one apartment/house/room to rent, have your own job, and clearly cannot do everything a hotel concierge/manager/maintenance person can do as promptly as they can do it.

(Actually, you do kind of wear all those hats as an STR host, but there are limits grounded in the laws of physics that put boundaries on what you can physically do, and when you can do it.)

And, naturally, guests don't figure in the fact that they are only paying $125 per night for a 2-bedroom, 2-bathroom apartment near the city center when they stay at your place. How much would a 2-bedroom, 2-bathroom hotel suite cost? Twenty times as much. Which is why you also have a full-time job in addition to your STR business, and guests need to accept that.

Sorry, guests, but if any of this makes you unhappy, you need to plead your case to Isaac Newton: it's not personal, it's physics.

Set Firm Rules and Stick by Them

Now, in most circumstances, it is perfectly great to be accommodating to guests when you can, if their requests are reasonable. All guests are different, and they all have needs. If you can help them out, at little inconvenience to yourself, they will be appreciative and give you better reviews. That's a win-win.

However, when it comes to check-in and check-out times, accommodating them is often not possible, so permit yourself to be strict: the times are firm. Bend them only when *you* think it makes sense. When you haven't had anyone in the rental for a week, and it's perfectly clean, you may decide to let your guests go ahead and check in at 7am, because why not?

Well, one reason is insurance. The platform's insurance may not go into effect before your stated check-in time. Airbnb's "Host Guarantee" does not. If something happens before check-in time or after check-out time, Airbnb's Host Guarantee will not cover it. It's on you.

Another reason: in my personal experience, a guest's request to check in early or check out late will often set the tone for their stay. Whether consciously or not, they are testing the boundaries to see how flexible you are, or, to put it bluntly, how much they can push you around. This is an argument for not letting people check in early, ever, *even if it's no problem to you whatsoever.*

You will find that the guest who asks to check in early is often also the guest who also asks to check out late, who wants to leave their luggage at your place until 6pm because they scheduled an 11pm flight (who does that?), and who treats your place disrespectfully and leaves it a giant mess.

It's not a coincidence.

Make Your Life Way, Way Easier.

Schlage and Kwikset should both put me on their payroll, so highly do I recommend that you put a lock with a keypad on the door of your rental. Give guests the code before their arrival, and they can check in whenever they want after check-in time. You can change the code any time you want, ideally between each guest. Make the new code the last four digits of their phone number. That makes it easy for them to remember and for you to easily look up.

Counterpoint: some hosts I know say you should *always* be present when guests arrive in order to give them a tour and, importantly, to let them get to know you personally. When they see you as a real person rather than a series of emails and text messages, they will be more likely to treat your property with respect. You've heard the expression, in regard to cars, "drive it like a rental." You want to do what you can to avoid having guests drive your property like a rental.

Side note: Ring doorbells with two-way video and audio have become the new thing. I have not installed them, but they sound like a great idea. If you can't be at your rental to give your guests a tour is person, you can at least greet them by video phone (doorbell) and answer any immediate questions.

My gut feeling is that I'm a little doubtful that this would substitute very well for an in-person meeting. But if you live far from your rental or simply can't get there for check-in, it's better than nothing.

You need to be reachable— or it may cost you

One of the biggest complaints you will ever hear from a guest is not that there was a problem, but that when it happened, *they couldn't get ahold of the owner.*

People have different views on what is a minor problem and what is a major problem. For one guest, not being able to find an ironing board is reason for a Defcon Level 1 meltdown. Other guests meet a clogged and overflowing toilet with a shrug. Human beings—the variety is near-infinite.

You may forget to leave any clean towels for the guests, and they may simply make do with what they have. I have one group who did this. I didn't find out until after they left that I had forgotten to leave them clean towels. They just made do. Wow. Talk about low-maintenance.

Another guest might go nuclear at such an outrage. I wouldn't entirely blame them, though I am not the type to go nuclear. The point is, you never know.

You need to be available at all times, just in case you have the second type of guest when something bad happens.

You may have noticed I said it could cost you. How? A bad review. Guests who feel they need to reach you but can't may get more and more wound up, and not being able to reach you can become a worse problem than whatever they were trying to reach you about. It may even take up more space in their bad review than the problem itself.

This is not good for business. All travelers dread the unreachable host, who drops off the keys and disappears, not caring when something cataclysmic happens that the guest has no reasonable way of resolving. And some travelers really, really freak out about this. It seems to happen a lot to Americans traveling in Europe.

I've realized that a host being unreachable when problems occur is disturbing to guests because it is not just an administrative snag, it is something worse: a violation of trust.

Guests have to trust the host from the moment they book your listing all the way through their trip, and even after, until they get back their security deposit and their whole experience is wrapped up in a bow and their last selfie has been Insta'd.

Reading a review (hopefully not two!) about an unreachable host will trigger prospective guests' thoughts to immediately jump to their own worst fears.

I'll be a single female traveler in a foreign city, what if I get locked out at 2am and I can't reach the host?

It'll be my first time in Canada, what if a moose attacks the house and I can't reach the host?

What if the ironing board is stolen while I'm out, and when I get home, I can't reach the host?

The last one sounds funny and stupid but it's actually the most likely scenario. Guests will call in the middle of the night because they saw a bug or they think the water pressure is low. That feeling of your brain tying itself into knots is normal. The solution is not what you might expect—calling a 24-hour exterminator or plumber. It's talking the guest down off the ledge and convincing them they don't need to worry about it until morning, when you can actually do something.

Having to be available at all times will change your life, particularly if you have more than one STR going at the same time. You will have to get used to answering your phone at any time, day or night. That means numbers you recognize and numbers you don't. Weird numbers that don't look like real phone numbers (could be European). During dinners or evenings out, after you've had a few drinks and don't feel very professional. But you have to answer. Your house could be burning down.

I don't particularly like talking on the phone, and I don't like having to pick up the phone when I'm with a friend or out to dinner.

But I have to. To be a good STR host, you have to realize that whenever you have guests, you are on call, 365/24/7.

Cleaning

Cleaning is my least favorite part of short-term renting. I hate it, especially when I am doing it myself.

Guests are paying to stay with you, and though it's usually not spelled out, they expect to stay in a space that's clean. Airbnb's rules for hosts, which we will review in detail later, do explicitly state that cleanliness is required.

In fact, it's pretty common that guests expect the space they're renting to be not just clean, but spotless.

While a house that's not spotless may be okay for many guests, those people can't be the benchmark by which you set your standard.

Because, once you get one bad review from an overly fussy traveler who makes your place sound filthy and rife with vermin, you will regret your failure to clean to a high standard from day one. Don't give people something to complain about in an area you can actually control.

Removing Cigarette and Pot Smoke Smells. I am sticking this here and breaking the flow a bit because smoke smell from guests smoking indoors (when they are not supposed to) seems to be one of the most serious and difficult cleaning issues that hosts encounter.

If you have reinforced that your property is non-smoking in all the usual ways (House Rules, signs, including it in your thank-you-for-booking message and other communications with guests) but your guests still smoke indoors, many hosts swear that the best way to get rid of the smell is by using an ozone generating machine.

Ozone generating machines, which cost a few hundred dollars, are not the same as air purifiers that ionize air to create that alleged after-rain smell. An ozone generating machine's purpose is just to generate ozone, and turn over the air in your space multiple times per hour.

Ozone is a reactive form of oxygen that many hosts have said is the best way to eliminate smoke smells. The EPA says that ozone "is believed to react with acrolein, one of the many odorous and irritating chemicals found in secondhand tobacco smoke."[17] It may also "inhibit the growth of some biological organisms" at .50 to .80 ppm, the amount generated by some ozone generators.[18]

Though ozone is naturally present in the air we breathe in small amounts, larger amounts can irritate the mucus membranes or even cause more severe problems[19], **so your rental must be empty of people and animals when the machine is running.** I am told the machine should be run for a couple of hours, after which the property must be aired out. (Ozone, being an unstable molecule, does naturally break down into normal oxygen in a period of anywhere from 30 minutes to 4 hours, depending on the concentration, so technically it will break down whether you air the place out or not—but I would air it out anyway.)

You will read multiple and conflicting things online about whether or not ozone can remove smells, and whether it is harmful. The problem is that there aren't too many other methods available to get smoke smells out of your rental, especially if you only have a short period of time in which to do so.

One option is to wash everything, not just linens, but, if your guests have really smoked a lot and for a long time, walls and floors, and clean fabrics and upholstery. That's a lot of work. You can also try to mask the smoke smell with lots of Febreze or Lysol Neutra-Air and see if that helps. Opening all the doors and windows and letting the place air out is also good.

General Cleaning. Setting aside the enhanced cleaning requirements related to Covid-19, which we will address shortly (I am hoping Covid-19 has gone away by the time you read this, then you can just skip that section and not think about it), your rental needs to be thoroughly cleaned between guests. This regular cleaning includes:

- ✓ All bedding washed and changed.
- ✓ All garbage containers emptied and liners replaced.
- ✓ Towels, hand towels, and wash cloths clean and nicely folded.
- ✓ Bathrooms cleaned from top to bottom—bathtub/shower scrubbed, toilet spotless, sink/vanity spotless, mirror Windexed, toilet paper refilled, and numerous spare rolls provided.
- ✓ Rugs clean and shaken out. Carpets vacuumed.
- ✓ Floors swept with no crumbs, dust, etc. in the corners or anywhere else.
- ✓ Everything dusted.
- ✓ Counters, tables, and all other surfaces wiped clean.
- ✓ All kitchen and bath cabinets wiped down.
- ✓ All mirrors throughout the house Windexed.
- ✓ No crumbs under couch cushions.
- ✓ No dust under beds.
- ✓ No dust or cobwebs on light fixtures, in ceiling corners, or anywhere else.
- ✓ Supplies replenished (toilet paper is critical, so I'm saying it twice).
- ✓ Dishes, pots and pans, etc. clean and put away.
- ✓ All kitchen appliances clean.
- ✓ Refrigerator wiped down, inside and out.
- ✓ Outdoor areas appropriately tidied up so they resemble your photos.

These are the minimum things that I believe need to be done between guests or groups. Some are obvious, some may not be. I talked to a host once who was irritated because a guest complained that there was dust under the bed. Guess what—the guest was right, there should not have been dust under the bed. If there is, you should expect that at least some guests will notice it and be unhappy about it.

Sure, there is dust under my own bed at my own home, and probably a decaying half-sandwich and a nest of spiders. But that doesn't matter. Your STR should not have dust under the bed. The shelves inside the refrigerator should not have gunk on them—even a tiny bit. Guests should not arrive to see any garbage in the garbage bins—even a few things. It's not *their* garbage. They are not familiar with that garbage. They don't know where that garbage has been. The rental needs to be a blank slate for each new group of guests.

The preceding, of course, does not apply to *all* rentals. You, of course, have the option of only getting your place semi-clean between guests, with dust under the bed, crumbs on the counter, a less-than-sparkling bathroom, smudges on the refrigerator doors, etc.

But guests will notice. Your overall rating will go down (or never get that high in the first place), and so will the prices you can charge.

Of course, depending on what you are renting out, this may be OK. The reduced income may be worth it to not have to clean so hard (or spend on a house cleaner). Maybe you are renting out a garage for $29 a night and sparkling cleanliness is not included in that price. And if you only get a 3 on cleanliness, guests will rent anyway if your place is what they can afford and it sounds tolerable.

And despite what I said previously about Airbnb giving people warnings that they could be delisted if their overall rating fell below 4.5, which other hosts have testified to me is true, I have also seen some run-down places (one right around the corner from me, in fact) with overall ratings in the 3's, and they seem to be surviving. I believe this may be because they offer bargain rates that keep them booked despite the low ratings. I speculate that if you continue making money for Airbnb, and guests are not complaining to them—which likely means you are being very honest in your listing about what guests will be getting, and not getting, for your low, low price—you may be given a pass for lower ratings.

A Positive Note

Ideally, I would like guests to walk into my STRs and feel like they are starting off their trip on a positive note. I don't want them to feel like they just walked into someone's house where the person just walked out the back door and left everything as-is. That is part of why I always try to ensure that my places are spotless. The guest is on vacation, and is in a new place they've never been before. They are paying money to stay there. Walking into a really clean place starts everything off on a positive note.

Also, seeing everything spotless and smelling very clean, guests can relax. They have not spotted a spiderweb shortly after entering, which would then prime them to keep their eyes pealed for more disappointments they can make a mental note to complain about later.

The Secret to a Clean

Smell is a big part of "clean." Use a bit of bleach in the bathroom, even if only to swish around the toilet. Use some Murphy's Oil Soap or Spic-and-Span, even just a tiny bit, in some of your wash water when you damp mop, or do some dusting with a damp rag.

For many people, a house is not clean unless it *smells* clean.

Hiring a Cleaner

For me, when I am done cleaning the place, it needs to have a sparkle to it and everything needs to be perfect. It's hard, but not impossible, to get a cleaner to understand that. You need to stay on them, which they always appreciate (not). This is why I pay my cleaners more than I have to, so they will hopefully do as good a job as possible. I need my cleaners to know that if they discover a stain on a sheet on a bed they've just made, they need to unmake the bed and replace the sheet. And so on.

Of course, there is another big issue involved with STRs that may necessitate paying your cleaner a bit more: timing. It may be tough to find someone who can be at your place at exactly 11am so they can be done doing their highest-quality work by 4pm. Particularly if there is laundry involved. Personally, I do some of the laundry to take that burden off the cleaner.

One way to reduce stress all around is to always have a spare day between guests. It will reduce your income, and is not guaranteed to prevent all problems.

Check-Out

It's best to check your rental immediately after guests leave for damage or other problems. Though it can be tempting to let a few days go by before you check on the rental, I highly recommend you don't.

Most of the time, after guests leave, they will leave the place looking decent. Of course the sheets and towels will be dirty and the beds will be messy. This is what your cleaning charge is for. Of course there will be things here and there you will need to throw out (used coffee cups, a takeout container on the kitchen counter, an empty bottle of tequila under the bed).

But occasionally, there will be issues that require immediate attention, and you will thank your deity of choice you didn't let the rental sit for five days before checking on it. Here are some that have actually happened to me.

- Guests have left the thermostat at 68 degrees, even though it was the dead of summer. This is actually a more-often-than-not occurrence. Guests who are vacating aren't usually thinking about the thermostat. To avoid this particular problem, I would recommend you install a thermostat that you can set to be operable only in a limited range, and which you can adjust remotely. I have Nest thermostats for my rentals and set the minimum temperature to 72 during the summer months. I put this in my House Rules so guests know that's how it's going to be when staying at my rental. Guests aren't paying enough to have the thermostat at 62 degrees during a New Orleans summer (I don't specifically say that part). The Nest also allows me to turn the temperature up to something energy-saving, like 82 F (28 C), remotely, as soon as guests check out. I love it.

- Guests have left the front door wide open. Scary. Again, guests have a lot on their mind when they are vacating. The last person out the front door may have been a child who ran back in to use the restroom and failed to pull the door all the way closed. If you don't come by for a week, then people have spent a week looking through your wide-open front door. And, to reiterate, *this has happened to me*.

- ➢ Guests left the water running.

- ➢ Guests left spilled liquid puddled on the hardwood floor.

- ➢ Guests left dishes, pots, and pans half-full of food all over the countertops and stove. That's a great way to ensure your neighborhood cockroaches and rodents are well fed.

I recommend that every time a guest checks out, you stop by the rental either on your lunch hour or after work, just to strip the beds and gather the towels, bath mats, and anything else you need to wash. Set the thermostat appropriately, make sure everything is locked, collect and throw out all food the guests have left behind, and set the security alarm if you have one.

This not only keeps your rental safe and secure, it also gives you immediate feedback on whether your guests took good care of the place, and whether there is any damage, which you should photograph and note immediately. Under Airbnb's rules, you must report any damage and make any claims *before the next guests check in*.

If everything looks good, you have the information you need to leave your guests a review quickly and refund their security deposit (guests love that).

Bathtubs

I don't really know why, but at both of my rentals, I have had an ongoing problem with the coatings on my bathtubs chipping or peeling off. Both of these rentals, as I have said, are over 100 years old, but I suspect that the bathtubs from the 50s or 60s, based on the bathroom tile. I believe the tubs are both the porcelain enamel variety.

I have had them "reglazed," where that specially-trained person comes out and spends several hours doing a bunch of things to the tub, then spraying it with a coating that has to cure for three days (lesson learned!) before it can be used or gotten wet.

"Reglazing" costs about $300 per sink or tub, and in my experience, it doesn't work very well. It chips. And the chips grow into little patches where the edges sometimes even come up and allow water underneath them, so the coating bubbles up and stays that way for a while, with the bubbly texture looking a skin disease, before peeling off.

It's possible that my reglazer just didn't know what she was doing. But I don't think that's the case, because I had two tubs done by *different* reglazers at different times. Both looked perfect after they were done, but both degraded over time quicker than they should have, for $300.

In one case, after 48 hours, I was touching the reglazing and it seemed completely cured, so I decided to, stupidly, try scratching it with my fingernail. It peeled right off. I called the reglazer and she said she had told me 72 hours, not 48. However, that incident is not what led to the failure of the reglazing, because patches of the "glaze" in totally different areas of the tub later chipped and started to come off, even though I did wait well over 72 hours before anyone used the tub. I just didn't wait 72 hours before I decided to scratch it with my fingernail.

I have also tried the "Tub & Tile" spray paint that they used to sell at Lowes and Home Depot but no longer do, probably because it doesn't work. Same issues. Plus, it leaves a rough coating, like sandpaper. But if you sand it down, you quickly find yourself at the bare metal or acrylic or whatever it is.

I then took when I think will stand as my final shot at tub-coating repair, using an epoxy patching kit. The epoxy mix is like a smooth putty you put into the bald patches on your tub after sanding the edges of the "bald" area. You let the epoxy cure for four hours, then sand it off. It's really hard to sand, and, in my case, I wound up sanding some of the non-damaged areas surrounding the patch.

As I sanded, I noticed that the epoxy had dried a cement gray rather than white. I definitely did not buy cement gray color, I bought white. So, now my tub has a bunch of oddly-shaped, large, gray spots scattered around it. It basically looks like it's been prepped for some kind of work that has not yet been done. Maybe I will go spray it with some of that Tub & Tile spray paint. It never ends.

My point: unless you are flipping a house and don't really care what your tub or sink looks like in six months, don't bother with reglazing, just replace it.

Analyzing Your Market

The title of this chapter will cause some people to experience a hit of excitement, and others to experience a hit of drowsiness.

If you are suddenly drowsy, get a cup of coffee. And while you're getting that coffee, remember: analyzing your market helps to ensure you bring in the maximum amount of money you can from the day your STR opens for business.

Some may find words like "analyzing" and "market" boring because they sound like school or business-talk. So, let's talk about it another way: you need to know where your STR fits into the bigger picture. Analyzing your local market helps you figure out things like:

- What mistakes you're likely to make, so you can avoid them.
- Where to spend money on your rental, and where not to.
- What your customers want, including things you wouldn't want yourself or didn't consider.
- What amenities are standard in your area, so you can offer them too.
- What kind of traveler will show up to your STR—and what type won't.

I could go on.

Measure Twice, Cut Once

You've probably heard the adage "Measure twice, cut once."

It refers to, for example, measuring the length of something *twice* so that, when you go to cut the piece, you will be certain to cut it correctly. Making a bad cut and ruining your piece of wood is a much worse outcome than the extra time it took you to measure a second time.

More broadly, "measure twice, cut once" is about preparation. It implies that doing twice the preparation you think you need results in the best chance of success when you actually execute your plan. It is the opposite of just jumping in and presuming you will learn from trial and error.

There are times when just jumping in and learning from trial and error can be a good approach. As I said in the Introduction, I would argue that setting up an STR is probably not one of those things. The time and dollar amounts at stake are too high.

Vacancy Costs Money

If you have a house or apartment you are thinking about short-term renting versus long-term renting, and you have a mortgage and carrying costs on that home (electric bill, water bill, cable bill, property taxes), and you "just jump in" to short-term renting, the financial impact of any mistakes you make could be large.

You may mis-judge the market and find yourself without many bookings in a key season, and then discover (too late) that your target guest does not generally book last-minute, so you can't fill the vacant days, even by lowering your prices.

You may put your place up for rent and not understand why nobody is booking—because you did not take the time to study what guests expect (things that they know they can get somewhere else, for the same price you are charging)—until it's too late.

Vacancy costs money.

If I had to sum up in three words why analyzing your market is critical, those would be them. So, keep reading and we will analyze your market.

Legalities

The first thing to know about your market is whether STRs are explicitly legal, explicitly illegal, or in some kind of gray area.

In some municipalities, short-term renting is clearly illegal, and subject to fines or even jail time. In other places, it has been legalized for those who meet certain criteria and follow the rules. Usually this includes, but is not limited to, giving the city or county money.

But because of the newness of short-term renting, I would venture to say that most municipalities do not yet have ordinances specifically addressing STRs, and I know that only a few states have passed statewide laws at all on the subject.

In many places, particularly cities that attract a lot of tourists, there has been endless discussion among citizens and their elected representatives about the subject of STRs, but not all have reached any final resolution.

There's a good chance that you are living somewhere where short-term renting is either in a legal gray area or where the local ordinances are in flux. If this is the case where your proposed STR is located, you should pay attention to the conversation going on in the local news and online, and get up to speed on what direction your town is heading.

Tip: if your locality has taken the time to pass any ordinances or laws regulating STRs, chances are that they will get only get stricter over time, not looser. I say this because it parallels the tough-on-crime trap that legislators fall into. Once they increase the penalty for a crime, they can never vote to reduce it, because if they do, their challenger in the next election will shout from the rooftops that "Candidate Y voted with the Crime Lobby to reduce penalties for violent crime, sending hardened criminals back out onto our streets. Is that what you want for our state?" Similarly, "Candidate Y, backed by short-term rental advocates, voted to loosen restrictions on short-term rentals [video of a huge party at a house on a residential street, with cars parked on the lawn and hundreds of teens drinking from Solo cups while disco lights flash and music blares, while nearby residents look on and shake their heads helplessly]. Candidate Y lives in a cushy gated community, where short-term rentals are strictly banned, but that didn't stop him from voting to turn every house on *your* block into a hotel! [Teen stumbles to the curb and vomits, then looks up at residents, shrugs, and wipes his mouth.]"

You know, stuff like that.

Another reason is the simple fact that once anti-STR people have organized, it's likely they won't be satisfied with whatever compromise measures have initially been passed. Sometimes referred to as the People Against Everything, they don't tend to give up, and are likely to be back in a year or two, hectoring the city council to pass more restrictions.

If you have read up on the STR situation in your area and it looks like your locality is headed in the direction of regulation, you probably don't want to make expensive improvements targeted toward operating an STR. Maybe you'd be better off just getting a long-term tenant and calling it a day.

If it looks like your city is headed toward legalization, you need to pay even closer attention. The trend nationwide has been for cities to come up with schemes that create categories of different types of STRs (whole-home rentals, apartment rentals, rentals of one apartment in a building where the owner lives on site, rental of a room in a house where the owner lives), as well as other rules that apply to some types of rentals and not others.

I take a dim view of these schemes, which can be complicated and seemingly designed to frustrate and annoy. Not to mention, of course, cost you and your guests money and time in the form of fees, taxes, administrative work, and other costs.

That is how political compromise sometimes looks, unfortunately. You need to consider where the chips will fall…and when they may fall.

Enforcement

Part of operating in a legal gray area is that, when the rules are not clear, enforcement is the key practical matter an STR host needs to worry about.

Does short-term renting arguably violate some existing ordinance, but the City Council is publicly bickering over whether that ordinance actually applies to STRs?

Is the city's code enforcement department holding off enforcing the ordinance until they get clarity? Or have they taken other action, such as announcing a date on which they will start enforcing the ordinance against STR hosts?

Hopefully you live some place where things are more clear-cut and not so complicated. But the more complicated your city's regulatory scheme is, if they have in fact created on, the more attention you have to pay.

As I have advised before, keep in close touch with fellow STR operators. Join groups where you can talk to people who are in the know about what is on the horizon. If you have a local attorney knowledgeable about the STR landscape, check in with him or her.

Marketing Your Property

If you are brand new to short-term rentals, you may not be aware that Airbnb basically committed suicide in terms of its relationship to hosts at the beginning of the Covid-19 crisis, by overriding all hosts' cancellation policies and refunding all guests automatically. They even proactively sent guests messages informing them they could cancel and get a full refund, ensuring that any guests on the fence would be pushed over to the refund side.

But then, when a guest did go to cancel, Airbnb tried to convince them to accept a credit for a future stay (with any host, not just the host who was cancelled upon) instead of a refund.

This means that, though hosts would lose all their bookings and income for the period of March 15 – April 30 (later extended to May 31, then to June 30), except whatever they got from the very few guests who did not cancel, *Airbnb would end up holding onto almost all of the money.* That is, the money paid by guests who accepted a credit for a future stay. Airbnb helped ensure that guests chose the credit option because the refunds offered were based, if I understand correctly, on the host's actual cancellation policy. So many guests saw two options, a refund of $0, or a 100% credit toward a future stay.

In other words, in a time of crisis, Airbnb threw hosts under the bus—then backed up and ran over them a few more times, yet did everything it could to hold onto as much cash as possible to hedge against what was coming.

This caused such vocal antipathy for Airbnb on the part of hosts that it began to make national news, and thereafter became part of the story of Airbnb's response to the Covid-19 crisis in all further reporting. It even, in my opinion, played a part in triggering the wave of stories speculating that Airbnb might not survive the crisis[20], since the media, unlike Airbnb, seemed to realize that hosts were an integral part of Airbnb's business.

As the late, great Grumpy Cat might have put it—"Good!"

Airbnb Attempts Damage Control

Airbnb responded to the bad publicity by creating an alleged $250 million fund to pay hosts 25% of *what they would have received had guests cancelled their stays without Airbnb's involvement,* for reservations made before March 1 with a start date between March 15 and April 30.

Calculating the payment a host would have received is complicated by the fact that Airbnb has changed their cancelation policies multiple times over the years to make them more guest-friendly. The following is based on the policies in effect on May 31, 2020.[21]

The stated way of determining a host's payment from the "fund" meant that if the host had a flexible cancellation policy, under which guests could have cancelled up to the last minute and receive a full refund without Airbnb's involvement, the host got nothing.

If the host had a moderate cancellation policy, under which guests could cancel up to 5 days ahead for a full refund, the host got nothing, unless the cancellation was, in fact, made within 5 days before the date the guest was to arrive. In that case, the guest would still be eligible for a 50% refund, so the host got 25% of the 50% they would normally have gotten, or 12.5% of the total they would otherwise have gotten.

If the host had a strict cancellation policy, under which a guest would get a 50% refund if they canceled 7 or more days before the start of their booking, the host would get 12.5% (that is, 25% of 50%) if the cancellation was made 7 or more days ahead of the date they were to arrive, or, if the cancellation was made less than 7 days ahead of the date they were to arrive, an actual 25% of the booking total they would have received if the guest had stayed.

That is, until the $250 million fund was depleted, after which nobody got anything. (I'm not sure if the fund ever was depleted, or how much Airbnb actually refunded. As a private company, they are not required to release that information, and as far as I can tell, they haven't.)

This whole system allowed Airbnb to talk a lot about "25% payments to hosts" during the Damage Control Era, while giving out very few actual 25% payments to hosts. Ingenious. Of course, when hosts started getting payments that were much, much smaller than they had imagined they would be getting, a whole new round of complaints started that Airbnb was screwing hosts.

And then, Airbnb extended their full-refund cancellation policy for guests through May 31, and again through June 30—but did not extend any payments to offset hosts' losses beyond April 30. So, hosts got zero for anything cancelled with an arrival date of May 1 through June 30, even though Airbnb would only give guests actual refunds based on the host's cancellation policy, but would give them a 100% credit for a future stay, with any Airbnb host, if they agreed to that.

This part has not gotten much publicity at all, diabolical as it is. Hosts, of course, are all highly aware of it, because guests send us messages complaining that Airbnb offered them either some minimal dollar amount as a refund, or a full credit for a future stay.

The guests probably think we are getting part (all?) of their money when Airbnb tells them they can either have a $0 refund or a 100% credit toward a future stay. No, we are not, and no, we cannot help you by telling Airbnb to give you a refund. It's their platform, we just try to survive it. We are getting $0 regardless of what you do. Airbnb holds onto the cash.

What about Vrbo?

Homeaway/Vrbo became a favorite of hosts during the Covid-19 crisis because they did not force hosts to give refunds. Naturally, hosts liked this (even though many, if not most, did give refunds of their own free will, including me).

Over time and because of public criticism, Vrbo began to pressure hosts to give refunds. A few weeks after the crisis began, a notice from the CEO informed hosts that Vrbo "expected" hosts to give guests who had to cancel due to Covid-19 a minimum 50% refund. Hosts who gave 100% refunds would receive a bump in search rankings equivalent to one 5-star rating. Hosts who did not give at least a 50% refund would receive an anti-bump in search rankings equivalent to one zero-star rating.

I am pretty sure everyone preferred this method. At least we had a choice in the matter.

What Did That Have to Do with Marketing?

That was background as to why many hosts who, before Covid-19, were perfectly happy listing their properties solely on Airbnb, now want to take some of their eggs out of the Airbnb basket, and either use different platforms or market their properties directly to guests.

I have been using multiple platforms all along, which is why both editions of this book have discussed both Airbnb and Vrbo.

Booking.Com

The third large platform to consider is Booking.com, and it is in fact the largest platform in the world, but it was not originally designed for short-term rentals, and initially treated them as an afterthought. I tried using it several years ago and was put off, in large part because (1) they "hide" their fees from the guest, and (2) at the time, they did not process payments. The guests paid upon arrival, leading to a lot of no-shows and no-pays.

A few years ago, I listed one property on Booking.com as a test, before I was fully aware of these things, and decided to take down the listing shortly afterwards. It was not easy. I called and asked to have my listing taken down (at the time, you could not do that through the website). I was told it would be taken down, but it wasn't. I called back, and the same thing happened. I think it took at least three calls, maybe four, before my listing was no longer on the site. I received two or three booking requests over the couple of weeks this dragged on, then had to explain to those guests that I had actually cancelled the listing, several times, and yet it was still on the site. This felt ridiculous and unprofessional.

Once my listing was actually down, an onslaught of calls began from Booking.com reps trying to get me to reactivate my listing. Clearly a call center somewhere was given a list of canceled listings and were offered a commission for any host they could get to start back up again. The calls felt much like collection agency calls, if you've ever been unfortunate enough to experience those—high pressure, clearly from people paid on commission.

My listing got restarted at least once, even though I clearly said no, I definitely did not want to restart my listing. They just did it. There was a lot of hard-selling and salespeople refusing to take "no" for an answer, until finally I would have to hang up on these callers. This experience makes me leery of getting entangled with Booking.com again, even years later.

But putting that aside, while Booking.com still hides their fees (they let you set your prices, then they take 20% of whatever you've charged the guest), now they process payments. So, today, they are not too different from Airbnb and Vrbo, presuming the hard-sell system to keep you from taking your listing off the site is no longer in effect. I don't know whether it is or not.

A couple tips about Booking.com in case you decide to take the plunge: in search, Booking.com shows the guest your nightly rate, excluding any fees, and it seems that most hosts use fees to make up for the 20% that Booking.com takes. This makes your price, while guests are browsing, look significantly cheaper than it's going to be once fees and taxes are added. I recommend you play the game, which is to keep your nightly rates on the low side and make up for that in fees as well.

Booking.com hosts seem to add a lot more fees than you generally see on Airbnb or Vrbo, like "Property Fee" or "Home Association Fee," which both sound made up, especially when the rental is just a regular single-family home clearly not part of a neighborhood association. Many listings state "cleaning included," and do *not* charge a cleaning fee, which almost all Airbnb and Vrbo listings do. It's a different culture.

Which leads to another thing about Booking.com: it's complicated. I mean, the site itself, as a property owner. You may have thought Airbnb or, even more so, Vrbo, were complicated to use. Try Booking.com. This, again, probably goes back to their history or being designed for hotels, not STRs.

As one example, when you log in and go to the main page of your listing, you will see a Rates & Availability tab. Sounds straightforward. Click the tab, and you will see these options (erratic capitalization from the website preserved):

- Calendar
- Adjust rooms to sell
- Copy Yearly Rates
- Open/Close Rooms
- Rate Plans

- Rate plan optimization
- Sync Calendars

Some, like Calendar and Sync Calendars, have clear meanings. Others, well... there's a learning curve. And that's just one of the tabs.

One thing I can say for Booking.com is that it is heavily used by European travelers. If your property targets European travelers—or if you happen to be fluent in a non-English European language that allows you communicate with potential guests in their native tongue—you may want to more seriously consider listing on Booking.com than if you are in North America and cater to mostly North American guests.

Since I am neither recommending Booking.com nor *not* recommending it, I have decided not to go down the rabbit hole of creating a chapter about navigating it and its strange and confusing options. There exist whole websites that already do that (search "guide to booking.com," without quotes, and you will see many). They can show you the ins-and-outs and tricks to optimize your listing for that site.

Other Sites

Airbnb, Vrbo, and Booking.com are not the only three websites on which you can list your property. Some other big ones are Expedia, Tripadvisor, Homeaway, Travelocity, Kayak, CheapTickets, Trivago, Orbitz, and TravelMob.

But those, like Vrbo, are all owned by the same parent company. Together, with some others, they make up what they call the Expanded Distribution Network. Your listing will be automatically be put on all those sites if you are on Vrbo and you offer online booking/online payments, are in "good marketplace standing," and have "integrated listings" enabled on Vrbo.[22]

It seems like there might be some consolidation going on in the STR and hotels markets.

There are also innumerable STR websites that are trying to get off the ground, such as Houfy.com. Houfy claims to not charge any service fees or commissions. It seems that they are still trying to build a critical mass of property listings; if you search your town, you probably will not see too many.

I would suggest giving them a try, but one thing to remember is that you always need to keep all your calendars sync'ed so you don't double book. You also need to keep your room prices updated on all the sites on which you are listed. I use Beyond Pricing for this, but it only works with Airbnb and Vrbo (and thereby all the Expedia Distribution Network sites). Beyond Pricing dynamically determines prices for each night for your property and automatically pushes those prices out to Airbnb and Vrbo and updates them. You can, and should, go to BeyondPricing.com and manually override any of their prices you don't agree with, which can be done on an individual day basis. It's certainly not perfect and the prices it generates are sometimes ridiculous. But I have used it and it's OK.

There are numerous property management services/softwares out there that you can use to manage your STR properties as well. But it's important that whatever you choose, you be able to update prices and availability across all platforms quickly and reliably.

In other words, branching out from Airbnb and Vrbo may make you a less dependent on Airbnb, but you need to consider the possible complications.

I personally am still on only Airbnb and Vrbo, despite brief ventures onto some of the smaller, niche sites. The problem I run into with them is that I get very few inquiries or bookings, but generally have had to update them manually whenever I get a booking through Airbnb or Vrbo. Not worth it, unless I were to come across software that was versatile enough to update everything. Oh, and cheap enough.

You may want to talk to other hosts in your area and see if there is a particular platform or means of reserving properties that people use for that area, and consider joining. For example, the Hamptons (New York) is a very different animal than other vacation rental markets, and properties are generally rented out through real estate agencies. If you don't know the peculiarities of your property's market, ask around.

Direct Booking

Everyone who wants to reduce their reliance on Airbnb wants to know about direct booking, meaning the guest books directly with the host and there are no platforms or intermediaries involved.

How to Attract Guests. A big issue with direct booking is where to get your guests. One way is to give current Airbnb or Vrbo guests your card and tell them that if they want to book your place in the future, contact you directly. Airbnb and Vrbo may not like you doing this, though I am not aware of their taking any action against hosts who have. What they mainly do is try to scare you to stay on the platform by reminding you that they are not liable for anything that goes on off-platform, such as payments, insurance, and so on. They have a point.

To get guests, other than the ones to whom you have given your card, in this day and age, you will probably need to have your property online somewhere, and should probably have a website for it.

It is not hard to create a website for your property. There are myriad tools out there to help you create one. Once you have done so, you can either put your phone number and email address on it so prospective guests can simply contact you and book, or you can use what's called channel management software that will allow guests to actually reserve your place on your website, and pay.

Guesty

Guesty seems to be the biggest player in channel management software. They are not open about their pricing, asking you to schedule a "live demo" (that means giving them your name and contact information and they will contact you) to "discuss the product" and learn "more about pricing."

I think we all know that when a company doesn't want to publish their pricing, and will only reveal it if they can talk to you one-on-one, it means there's a bigger price tag involved than you were hoping.

I heard through the grapevine that they charge an initial setup fee, then from 2%-5% of your total rental amount plus fees, per guest/group. The lower number is for high-cost stays, so expect to pay closer to 5% if you have only one, or a few, properties that don't command premium prices. I doubt any credit-card processing fees are included in that, so I'm conservatively assuming you will pay 3% for that on top of the Guesty's other fees.

Guesty has a cool website and they offer a lot of features, such as a website building and hosting tool, through which you can build your own website (with or without a domain name you have procured) and guests can make reservations and book through the platform. They offer pricing suggestions, a unified inbox, and support the major platforms (Airbnb, Vrbo, Booking.com, TripAdvisor, Agoda, and MisterBnB.)[23]

They also offer a "native mobile app," and features such as Analytics, Automation Tools, Reporting Tools, Revenue Management, and Task Management. For an additional cost, they offer 24/7 guest communications.[24]

Most Airbnb hosts already offer that—it's called our cell phones.

One thing that looks intriguing is that their payment processing tool[25] "allows you to open a running tab for your guests so you can offer them concierge goods or services that they can enjoy now and pay for later"—also known as **upselling**!

Guesty also allows you to collect the guest's money up front, or break it into two payments of 50% for their convenience, with the second 50% collected upon check-in or at any other time you specify. There may be extra fees for breaking up the payment.

They also offer their own in-house APIs,[26] useful if you are a programmer type.

They also offer a "free custom website building tool and website building guide,"[27] and claim that their "software run[s] automatic processes…to increase search rankings and encourage more bookings."

Guesty, once you join, *does* charge you its fees for any existing reservations you have on your calendar through Airbnb and all the other platforms. Their "policy for cancelled bookings," as described on their website, sounds a bit ominous—it depends on the channel through which the reservation was made (Aribnb, Vrbo, etc.) and "whether the guest or host canceled the reservation."

Kind of makes you hope they don't meddle too much in how you go about cancelling your reservations. I don't really need my channel manager doing that. Perhaps this just refers to whether they refund Guesty's fees or keep them (i.e., if you, the host, cancels, you get charged, but perhaps they do not charge you if the guest cancels.)

Lodgify

The other major player in channel management is Lodgify, and it seems to me like the better choice for small operators. The cost will very likely be lower for you, and though it has fewer features, the ones it lacks seem to be things you don't need.

Lodgify interfaces with the major platforms (Airbnb, Vrbo, Booking.com, and the Expedia Group sites) and has a tool for creating a website for your property on which guests can book directly.

Their [Website Builder][28] tool, which includes "SEO-friendly templates," helps you create a website through which you can accept direct bookings, including taking credit card payments as well as bank transfers, checks, and cash payments (I have no idea how that works). They also "integrate with" payment processors such as PayPal and Stripe.

Best of all, as soon as the guest pays, Lodgify "send[s] the funds directly to your bank account."[29] Woot!

They currently have two plans: a Starter plan at $12 per month for the first property, plus a 1.9% booking fee (not just for direct bookings, but *all* bookings, including those made through Airbnb, Vrbo, etc. if Lodgify's software is used to manage them); and the Professional plan at $32 per month for the first property, with no booking fees. With the Professional plan you get a few more features, such as the ability to pre-authorize a damage deposit against a guest's credit card.[30]

Prices go up as you add more listings (your second listing is an extra $5 per month on the Starter plan, or $18 per month on the Professional plan). This pricing seems pretty reasonable to me if you expect to get at least a couple direct bookings per month. Especially for the convenience of having the service keep your calendars and pricing updated across multiple platforms, including that of your own direct-booking website.

But Wait, There's More: Part I

Unfortunately, creating a website and starting up with a channel manager are the *easy part* about trying to get significant business through direct booking. The hard part is getting traffic. Let's call that Part I.

After you build a website for your property and activate it online, you then have to venture into the wonderful world of Search Engine Optimization (SEO) so people can actually find your property.

And yes, channel management options with website-building tools will say they help you create websites that will be "SEO-optimized," but that means very little when it comes to getting traffic.

If you want your property to appear fairly high on Google, it's a bit of a slog, and the rules change all the time. A general, if brutal, rule with Google is that if your website does not appear on the first page of search results, it is probably not going to get clicked on.

Sure, it *might*, but the chances plummet for every page past the first that a user has to click through.

Google "ranks" websites based on the quality of the websites that link to it (the system is creatively called PageRank). If a Wall Street Journal article links to the website for your property, that is a very valuable link, and Google credits it highly. If the only sites that link to your site are spammy web pages you came across when looking for places to list your site for free, Google does not credit those links highly. The more quality inbound links, the better. The more links from spammy sites, the worse. Your website could, itself, be categorized as spam, and knocked down to page 50 in the search results.

Some ideas about good places to list your property would be:

- In Facebook Groups of which you are a member
- On quality message boards to which you belong
- On your blog, if you mutually link to other quality websites
- Any other quality website on which you can post things (including Craigslist), particularly if the site exchanges links with other quality websites
- In the notes below YouTube videos you publish (Google owns and controls the content on YouTube, so that can't hurt)
- In news articles that happen to mention your property (make sure they hyperlink it!)
- On any other websites that discuss real estate, vacation rentals, or related matters.

Make sure it is okay with the administrators of the sites where you want to post a link to your property (such as the admin of the Facebook Group). Otherwise, doing that may be a faux pas, and your post may be deleted, and you may be kicked out of the group.

Doing the things on the list above might seem like a bit work. Spoiler alert: it is.

But that's how you get traffic to your website—you either pay for it (Google Ads, or other paid placement—more about that below) or find reputable places to post a link to your property so it begins to gain some traction, and better placement, with Google Search.

More: Part II

Part II is making sure your page contains the content that people searching Google are looking for.

If you are offering an Alpine Cabin, Sleeps 10, Walking Distance to Ski Slopes, and that's exactly what people are looking for, your webpage virtually creates itself. Just write some more text, add some gorgeous photos, and voila!

You have probably heard that, in order to show up highly in Google searches, websites need to have the keywords and search terms people are typing into the Google search box. That's still mostly right, but is not the full picture.

Google has gotten much smarter over the years about how it analyzes web pages. Even ones with the right keywords don't get a high ranking automatically. You can't fill your web pages with nonsense punctuated by keywords. Google can tell what your page is about. It can tell if it's computer-generated. It can tell if you've duplicated the same page on multiple URLs (very bad idea, don't do that, duplicative pages will get banned).

Basically, assume Google knows every trick your tiny human mind possibly think up when creating your web page, and many you could not. Just create a web page or pages that honestly represent your property. And make sure to mention all the key things that your property legitimately has that people searching Google may look for. Brand new hot tub with a view of the mountains and the setting sun? Of course put that in there.

Those are the very basics of SEO for Google.

Specializing in SEO consulting and helping people optimize websites is a full-time job for many today, and the quality of their services vary. It's one of those occupations people are drawn to if they "go freelance," and anyone who's worked on a website in any capacity can—probably—legitimately say they have, as part of their job, helped optimize a website for search.

If you decide to use an SEO consultant, try to verify that what you are getting will be useful and of high quality. Some may specialize only in Part II and leave you on your own for Part I. That may seem odd to you if you are encountering this subject for the first time. SEO consulting can be very niche. Make sure that, before you give anyone their first payment, they are able to explain in simple terms what they will do, what results you can expect, and what they may be leaving on *your* plate. And don't give them their second payment until they show you where they've gotten your website placed, and preferably, also after you've gotten some actual inquiries or bookings from their efforts.

To be clear, you don't need to hire someone to do SEO for you. There are a million websites, YouTube videos, and books to tell you everything you could possibly want to know about it. It may just not be something you want to spend hours and hours learning about—though, if you have a business which you are hoping will draw a substantial number of its customers through Internet searches, it wouldn't be a waste of time.

It's an unfortunate fact that when you are outside of the STR platforms, whose most important purpose is putting your property in front of likely renters, you take on that job. But if you do it successfully, you get to keep the 3% or 5% they charge you, and more importantly, the guest does not have to pay the approximately 15% they are charged by the platforms, making your rental much more affordable. Even if you split the difference and give them 7.5% off while you keep 7.5% extra, everyone wins.

Advertising Your Property

SEO is less important if you decide to pay for online ads to attract guests. How best to advertise will differ based on your rental and location. I would look into whatever location-specific options you can find, first.

Second, two of the biggest places for online advertising are Google Ads and Facebook Ads. If you pay for Google Ads, you don't have to worry about fighting your way up to page one or two – you can pay to be there. But the cost may not be worth it.

The pricing on Google Ads is *very* individualized, based on the exact demographic and keywords you want to target. Google will also rank you higher (even the position of your ad on the page is ranked!) if your ad is frequently clicked when displayed. This leads to a virtuous cycle where if your ad is clicked more, it is ranked higher, has more visibility, attracts more clicks, etc.

Of course, once your competitors see that your ad is ranking higher than theirs, which they will pretty quickly, they will copy whatever you are doing, then you need to reevaluate and tinker with your ad some more. To me, this endless cycle is tiresome, but some people really get into it.

You won't know if Google Ads is worth the cost unless you open an account and spend some time trying various keywords and see what, if anything, works. Based on experience, Google

Ads are just a bit too expensive to be worth the cost in many instances—though it does not have to be that expensive to test it out, since you can set any budget you want (e.g. $5 per day, which you can change or stop at any time).

I would be more likely to consider Google Ads if I had a high-value property that I expected to rent for hundreds or thousands of dollars per night, or alternatively, a number of properties in the same area, which I could then advertise on one website to which I could direct whomever clicked on my Google Ad.

A Google Ad campaign might also make sense if you got together several property owners and pooled resources to pay for the ads and the website displaying all your properties. It's possible you could all save a lot of money versus all of the fees you and your guests would otherwise be paying to use STR platforms to get bookings.

But for a standard-issue vacation rental without some special appeal, I would not be too optimistic about Google Ads being worth the money.

I have not yet personally tried Facebook Ads, nor have I heard much about whether they are useful for vacation rentals. I don't think I have ever seen a vacation rental ad on Facebook, so that says something. If you are serious about leaving the STR platforms behind and moving to direct bookings, you might want to at least look into Facebook Ads, but my suspicion is that the same kinds of scenarios under which you would be successful with Google Ads would also apply to Facebook Ads. Both sites are capable of delivering a highly targeted customer, and you'll pay for that, so the dollar value of your bookings would have to be high enough to be worth it.

If your property is very high-end, you may want to consider an agency, and last I checked, they still placed magazine ads in publications like Town & Country. They will probably help you with marketing in other regards as well (they already have their own databases, or Rolodexes, of wealthy clients).

A Few More Notes About Direct Booking

Rental agreement. When booking your property directly, it's best to have a signed, written agreement between yourself and the guest regarding the proposed stay. I have a sample rental agreement posted [here](). Before using it, you will need to modify it for your own property, and verify with a local attorney that it's suitable for your purpose.

Lodgify also has a [Rental Agreement Template]() to consider.[31] Guesty has an [Owner's Rental Agreement Template]() that looks a bit primitive.[32] They also have a page called [What is a Rental Payment Agreement?]() that has a list of things that should be included when creating a rental agreement.[33]

Unfortunately, neither Lodgify nor Guesty seems to have a system where guests can electronically a rental agreement at the time of payment. That would be useful.

Insurance. Make sure you have insurance in place that covers you when you are not covered through one of the platforms (such as when you take direct bookings). Look into vacation-rental-specific insurance, such as through Proper Insurance or CBIZ.

Attracting Guests During the Slow Season

They endless cry of people whose rentals are in seasonal areas is, "How do I get customers during the winter? Or summer?" Or whatever their slow season is?

There is no easy answer. I've talked about most of the options. Get creative. Network. Advertise. If the summer is your busy season, look for long-term customers to rent your place during the winter months. Students could be a good fit if summer is your high season. Maybe consider *before* buying your property what appeal your property will have during the off-season.

The fundamental problem is one of supply and demand. There's little demand in the off-season. Traditionally, with vacation properties, people just accepted that they would make their money during the high season and make next-to-nothing during the off-season. But with mortgages these days, it's become a year-round job.

Here are some ideas:

Up Your Offering

Does your location or rental offer anything at all for guests to do during the off-season?

Think of whatever that is and make your place as friendly as possible for it. Have "toys" that are relevant for off-season activities—kayaks, bicycles, even ATVs (high liability—talk to your insurer), coupons for boat rentals or restaurants, maps of hiking trails, or a guidebook of ideas of things to do. Bird-watching. Bear-watching. Cage diving with great white sharks. Camping.

You could also set your place up so that the property itself provides entertainment. Have a game room with a pool table, a pinball machine, a home theater, and so on. Have a playroom for younger kids. In the yard, have games like a cornhole set or even a trampoline and a climbing gym or swing set (liability again—talk to your insurer). Hot tubs are always highly valued, though you need to keep in mind the need to clean them between groups. Grills and outdoor kitchens are excellent. Take photos to show your ideas in action. Buy some disposable, season-appropriate décor and plates, napkins, cups, etc. and take photos of scenes of outdoor fun for your listing.

A fellow host gave me some good advice: generally speaking, groups of less than 6 will go out a lot, but groups of more than 6 will spend a lot of time hanging around the rental.

If you have a large enough place for more than 6 guests, then what I wrote above goes double: add features or amenities that make it fun to hang around the rental. Your pinball machine and pool table and hot tub may seal the deal and get your place booked even if there are 20 other more-or-less identical places—without those amenities—sitting vacant nearby.

Cage the Snowbirds!

Marketing to snowbirds is a good way to get your place booked for a couple of months in the off-season. (They go south in the winter and north in the summer.) You need to start well in advance, and probably offer your place at a significant discount. But put something in your ad like "SNOWBIRD DISCOUNT!" Let the wording sit there all year long and people will probably inquire. Make sure to be very welcoming and flexible on price. If your place is highly seasonal, you need them more than they need you.

And, since snowbirds are often retired, push any amenities you have that you think may be appealing to older people.

Make Your Rental Handicap-Accessible

This is good general advice to make your rental more appealing to a broader number of guests at any time of year, but during the slow season, it could be the reason you are booked while your neighbors are not. It's surprising how few rentals are set up to be fully accessible to disabled people.

Airbnb has a number of filters that disabled people can use to find places that meet their needs, and it is a good guide as to what they may be looking for when choosing a rental. The more you can offer, the better you will look to these travelers:

Entering the home

- Step-free access
- Wide doorway
- Well-lit path to entrance
- Flat path to front door

Getting around

- Wide hallways *(at least 36" (90cm) wide)*
- Elevators (i*f needed, contact hosts about the width)*

Bedroom(s)

- Step-free access
- Wide doorway
- Accessible-height bed
- Wide clearance to bed

Bathroom(s)

- Step-free access
- Wide doorway
- Roll-in shower with chair
- Bathtub with shower chair
- Accessible-height toilet
- Wide clearance to shower, toilet
- Fixed grab bars for shower, toilet
- Handheld shower head

Common areas

- Step-free access
- Wide entryway

Parking

- Disabled parking spot *(city-approved parking spot or a parking space at least 8ft (2.4m) wide).*[34]

Discount

Does discounting help you attract guests in the off-season? Probably…but are you sure you want them?

In the off-season, quality guests will often opt for a nicer rental at a price they can afford rather than scooping up a too-good-to-be-true deal on a place they might normally rent, in season, for much more

In other words, if they can only afford a 2-bedroom condo in season, they may decide to treat themselves in the off-season to what would otherwise be unaffordable to them.

You never know, of course. Some good guests will be perfectly happy saving a bundle. And some people just need to be in town for business or family reasons, regardless of season. Make sure to publish your listing far and wide. Ask your local Chamber of Commerce if there is a particular place you can advertise to target business travelers.

What you hope to avoid when you heavily discount is being booked by the trailer park denizens who will treat your place disrespectfully because they are getting it for only $39 a night. Or people using it for hookups or drug binges (it happens).

Festivals

Slow seasons are a perennial problem, and sometimes big problems require big solutions. Maybe even at the town or city level. Some cities (New Orleans and St. Louis come to mind) put on festivals that draw travelers at times when there is no real reason travelers would otherwise think about making a trip to those destinations.

Want to put together a festival? It takes some work, but once it starts to draw attention, you get travelers, at least for the week or weekend the festival takes up. After that one is up and running, create another. It sounds like a ridiculous amount of work just to get your rental booked, and it can be. But cities really do this to increase tourism, and they all start with someone with an idea who was willing to get the ball rolling.

The New Airbnb Guest

There is a not-so-new development in travel that keeps getting more pronounced over time, so we need to talk about it: the line between STRs and hotels is blurring.

When the first edition of this book came out in 2016, STR guests (and hosts) had a bit more of a feeling that we were all part of the "sharing economy." And though this was already on its way out, guests came into your property with the sense that they were getting something special and doing something a little outside-the-box.

In my opinion, both guests and hosts were simply nicer, and more open to new experiences. Expectations were flexible, and everyone gave everyone else more slack, since we—both hosts and guests—were all kind of making it up as we went along.

Now, that is becoming more the exception than the rule.

STR guests are becoming hotel guests. Both Airbnb and the Expanded Distribution Network that includes Vrbo are now advertising hotel rooms right alongside STRs on sites like Expedia, Booking.com, and new entrant Google Travel, which can make STRs seem just like hotel rooms to guests, particularly guests who have never stayed at, or thought of staying at, an STR. Sure, if your listing is an entire house, and your photo shows an entire house, and lists the number of bedrooms and bathrooms, prospective guests will know this not hotel room. But they may not know exactly *what* it is.

Is it a hotel-like house? Or is it like when you rented a house by the lake or by the ski slopes twenty or thirty years ago, where clean sheets were plopped on the beds—which often were packed into rooms, lofts, or wherever they would fit—and hopefully you could scrounge up pillows and towels? You certainly didn't *expect* A/C in those days, except maybe a grumbly window unit or two. I could go on recollecting all my childhood vacations, but you get it.

Most guests who find a place on Expedia are probably thinking more along the lines of "hotel-like house." They were looking for hotel rooms on Expedia, and they found a house. They have no idea how STRs work, probably. They don't know what to expect, and almost no STR listings explicitly say, "There is no maid service, we do not change your sheets every day, we do not pick up dirty towels from the floor every day and replace them with clean ones, we expect you to do your own dishes, and you are supposed to leave the place looking as you found it." But those things are true of almost *all* STR listings.

Sure, the House Rules may mention some of these things, like *please do your own dishes*. But this does not fully explain STRs to the new-to-STRs traveler who books your place, having only known hotels in the past.

In short, some inexperienced guests will probably expect that your rental meets the general standard of a hotel. Your personal touches may go unappreciated. And, if you gave the guests a great rate, they may value your place even *less*. A weird quirk of human psychology makes humans value things they got for cheap less than things they paid a lot for. And they value *free* things least of all.[35] Yes, it's weird. But you will see it in action when, as happens, your generous discounts or thoughtful freebies go utterly unappreciated. The guests view the rental as entirely transactional, and whatever they get is what they paid for, so there's no gratitude for little touches. The gift basket wasn't thoughtfully put together for the guest by a human who made an effort to think of what that particular guest might like, it was stamped out by a robot.

There are still guests who are nice, appreciative, and just all-around cool people. Probably more than you might think as I warn you of pitfall after pitfall to be avoided when hosting. All of us still in the business know this, because if a significant number of guests weren't at least appreciative, we wouldn't be in it.

Are Hosts to Blame for Newer Guests' Behavior?

Yes.

Well, sort of.

As a culture, we—both guests and hosts—continue to move further away from the "sharing economy" ideal. This has happened in other industries as well, such as ride-sharing (Uber, Lyft) and delivery (Uber Eats, Door Dash, PostMates). If anything, those industries have become much less about "sharing" than STRs. Fun fact: 60% of Uber riders have never tipped a driver, and only 1% tip every time. An Uber driver gets a tip on only 16% of rides, and the average tip is 50 cents. Meanwhile, Uber takes 30% of the fare right off the top. Not a whole lot of sharing going on there.[36]

Back in the STR industry, a feedback loop is well underway where hosts have begun to run their STRs less personally and more as businesses. Particularly those rental arbitrage companies with rooms by the thousands.

In my opinion, many hosts have become too inflexible, and don't establish a personal connection with their guests. They are all about getting paid, and actually having to deal with guests seems to be a bigger inconvenience than they want to take on. (I do get like that sometimes. Meditation can help.)

As I've mentioned before, as competition has increased and profits have consequently gone down, many hosts have dropped the little touches that used to differentiate an STR stay from an impersonal hotel stay. When guests have more and more choice, they tend toward cheaper options, requiring hosts to cut costs to stay competitive. Profit shrinks, and jars of homemade jam are no longer made or gifted.

When this cycle goes on for a while, the uniqueness that differentiates STRs from hotels starts to disappear, it's no surprise if guests start to treat STR stays more transactionally.

Do Guests Game the System?

Another result of the impersonal, transactional nature of more and more STR experiences is that guests are more likely to game the system in order to get a fully or partially free stay. The more they view you, the host, as a faceless entity, the more justified they will feel in trying to get some or all of their money back. After all, without a personal connection, you become just the representative of a $50 billion or $18 billion dollar company (depending on your valuation that day). After all, it's not like the money you're being asked to refund is coming out of your kids' college fund (even though, yes, it is).

You will see a lot of complaints on message boards about guests who offer a long list of petty complaints ("I moved the dresser in the bedroom and there was a spiderweb behind it"), then ask for a partial refund.

But the host can do a lot to prevent guests from asking for discounts or refunds for stays that are already underway.

One of those is cleanliness (and with Covid-19 in the picture, guests will be focusing on this exponentially more). I talk about cleaning a lot elsewhere in this book, so I won't rehash it, but hosts often do not "get" how clean guests expect the rental to be. Cleaning your rental to the standard you clean your own home is probably not good enough. On message boards, I have seen photos—posted by hosts—that guests have taken of dirt, cobwebs, dust bunnies, spills on cabinets, and so on, which guests have sent the host to request a refund of their cleaning fee, arguing that they did not receive the place in clean condition, so they should not have to pay a cleaning fee for the benefit of the next guest. It does make sense. The hosts who post these photos are invariably indignant, complaining that the guests are "looking for things to complain about," using what the hosts say are inconsequential problems in order to get money back.

I often don't agree. In many cases, the guest is right. The place should be cleaner.

Personally, if I were the guest, I don't know if I would take photos and go to the host and ask for money back. It would depend on the cleaning charge and the cost of the rental. I'm a believer that you get what you pay for, and if the place was cheap and the cleaning fee was low—well, I got what I paid for.

But if I felt the place were on the expensive side, and had been advertised in such a way as to make me expect excellence, the host is asking for complaints if the rental isn't spotless. If a listing is $400 a night and advertises itself as "spa-like," I would expect it to be as clean, sanitary, fresh and spotless as a "spa," whatever that means to me. The host is the one who chose to use the term "spa-like," rather than "finished-basement-like," so it's up to him or her to live up to the expectation created.

Similarly, using your photos to make your place look better than it is can get your guests asking for partial refunds. It is understandable that, as a host, you want to present your place looking as gorgeous as possible. Many of us are used to looking at real estate ads, and that is what they do in the real estate business. Real estate photographers are wizards at making a dump look like a palace.

But the STR industry is different, so don't follow real estate's example. Real estate listings are designed with one goal: to get people in the door, so the agent can personally sell them on the property's positives and explain away its negatives.

Prospective real estate buyers are not going to live in the property for a week and rate it. A real estate buyer may feel cheated by the photos and annoyed that their time was wasted. Then they will drive off, probably never think about the place again, while the agent awaits his next prospect. No star ratings are given. There is no impact on the agent or on the listing's search rankings. In fact, the number of views a property gets, and the more time it gets favorited, probably improves its search ranking. That means all that really matters is how good the photos look!

Most STR guests will never see their rental until arrival, and driving away is not usually a realistic option. So, don't borrow the idea from real estate business that you should use Photoshop to make your photos sparkle in a way that the actual place does not. Doing this is a bait-and-switch, and in the STR game, will result in bad ratings and disappointed guests. Who maybe even have the chutzpah to ask for some of their money back.

Under-Promise and Over-Deliver

There are few concepts more important when it comes to satisfying guests than *under-promise and over-deliver*. Use honest photos, and allow your guests to be pleasantly surprised. I can't count how many guests have told me, "The place looks even better than the pictures!" It's so common that I no longer even absorb the compliment. But it certainly gets the guest's stay off on the right foot.

I can sense your objections. Not using the best possible photos can lead guests not to book your rental in the first place. You'd rather have them actually book and hope they're happy with what they get. A booking is a lot better than no booking, right? In fact, it may mean the difference between your survival and failure as a business. And after all, it *is* a nice place, you decorated it yourself!

You may find that by using aspirational photos, you can charge more than the places in your area that look much like your place does in real life, but with photos that reflect that, and still get bookings. More bookings, and at a higher rate—win-win! The problem is, you are charging what the place in the photos is worth, which is too much.

This strategy leads to short-term gains at the expense of long-term viability. And it leads to the "type of guest" who tries to get some kind of refund. They feel deceived and taken advantage of.

Your guest may not be able to articulate exactly why, since it's been a couple months since they actually looked at your listing online and booked. But they feel the listing was *inaccurate*. (They are going to be asked to rate your place on "accuracy," remember? So, there's that to think about.) And in a way, it was. They are disappointed. The guest paid a premium for less-than-premium. It's natural for people who feel they have overpaid to want some sort of refund.

Compounding the problem, and keeping you from realizing what is actually going on, is that guests are not always honest.

Some will be honest and tell you they feel the listing was inaccurate, which naturally you won't agree with, since the guest saw the photos, actual photos of your actual place. And *everybody* uses Photoshop filters these days, right? So, *caveat emptor,* guest!

But guests may realize that this vague reason for requesting a discount or refund will not get them very far. So, they try something more specific, gather evidence, maybe even lie. The neighbors were too loud. Nearby construction kept them awake. The place was dirty (these are the guests who "look for things" that are not perfectly clean and photograph them). The heater didn't work, and the reason they didn't tell you is because they didn't try to use it until their final night. The place smelled bad. There must have been a pet there because it was activating their allergies, and your listing says no pets. The place was damp and smelled like mold. It smelled like the previous guest smoked. Bad smells are almost impossible to disprove.

A few such experiences will naturally lead hosts to feel there is a type of guest who tries to scam them for a refund, particularly when they go into the rental after the guest leaves and don't smell any mold, smoke, or pets, and there's really no dust or dirt, unless you look under couch cushions or move furniture.

But really, it may not be the guest. It may be your over-promising and under-delivering.

Guests with No Reviews

This is probably the number one discussion topic among new hosts. More and more people are discovering the world of STRs, and we are definitely well beyond the "early adopters" phase.

One result is that you may have virtually no information about people who instant-book your place. I find that more than half of my guests have no reviews and have just joined whatever platform they are booking through.

It's natural when you are renting out a property for which you may have paid hundreds of thousands of dollars to want to know exactly who will be staying there.

On Airbnb, before a guest can book, they must provide Airbnb with a phone number (which Airbnb says they confirm), an email address, payment information, and the guest must explicitly agree to your House Rules.

You also have the option of requiring that the guest provide Airbnb with a government-issued ID, and at least one positive recommendation from a previous host. This means that a previous host has reviewed the guest and answered the question "Would you rent to this guest again?" with a "yes."

Of course, enabling these requirements (particularly requiring a recommendation from a previous host) will reduce your number of bookings. How much? It depends. Guests will jump through more hoops if there are few options in your area, or if your place is special and they really want it. If you are renting an interchangeable condo on a Florida beach, however, and there are thousands of others available just like it, your prospective guests are likely to just move on if you create hassles for them.

Personally, I do require a government-issued ID on Airbnb, and I don't think it reduces bookings much, because the guest does not have to provide the government ID at the time of booking, just sometime before the start of their stay. I think kicking the ID verification down the road reduces the friction of going ahead with the booking. People are more resistant to doing something *right now* than they are to agreeing to do something sometime over the next 3 months.

And I do believe requiring government ID reduces bad behavior by guests. If a guest can rent a place completely anonymously (except for phone number, email address, and credit card, all of which can be acquired in throwaway form), they will feel they can get away with things.

For the guest who does intend to use your place for something bad, like one of those huge parties we hear about in the news, renting anonymously is the obvious choice.

Airbnb, as a result of some horrible publicity, has recently made changes to their algorithm to steer guests away from booking based on criteria which they do not make public, but most people believe include a guest, perhaps on the young side, attempting to book a very large, expensive space (like a house with a pool and a view), for one person, for one night, arriving that day.

Tip: you can greatly reduce the number of guests looking to use your place for a giant party by having a two-night minimum. And not renting to locals.

Vrbo's options for booking are more black-and-white: you can either enable Instant Booking, or not. Enabling Instant Booking means you "automatically accept booking requests from all travelers for dates you have available." The information the guest is required to provide is minimal. I just had a request come in moments ago where the guest's profile had a name and an email address, with other information "hidden for security purposes." Was there even any other information? Who knows.

Vrbo's alternative option is called 24 Hour Review, which gives you 24 hours to accept or deny a guest's request to book, during which you can communicate with the guest and ask them whatever questions you want. With either option, guests must agree to your refund policy and house rules, including number of guests, and whether parties, events, smoking, children, and/or pets are allowed.

As a general rule, and this applies to most guests, Vrbo does not require any kind of verification—email, phone number, or anything else. However, they do encourage guests to become "verified," which requires that they provide, and that Vrbo verify, their first and last name, email address, mobile phone number, physical address and birth date.

Again, requiring verification is going to reduce your number of bookings *a lot*, because it is a process, and there seems to be little incentive for guests to do it. Very few places require verification, so why, as a guest, would you bother? Plus, the guest has to become "verified" *before* they book, so it's not the same frictionless booking as with Airbnb, where the guest agrees to verify their identity with Airbnb sometime before the date of the booking, not necessarily right now.

What I recommend doing instead of focusing on a prospective guest's lack of reviews is to do everything you can to discourage guests from doing things you don't want them to do, and to discourage those guests from booking who are most likely to do those things.

Some thoughts:

Exterior security cameras. These are an absolute must. Make sure to disclose their presence in your listing. They not only deter bad behavior, but allow you to check on guests. I don't have a specific recommendation for camera type, but I do use Blink cameras. I looked at many cameras before buying, and I ultimately bought Blink because they are pretty cheap, unlike many cameras, and I found after purchasing one that they do a good job. (I was leaning toward Nest since I already have Nest thermostats, but at approximately $300 per outdoor camera, no thanks.)

Have a camera over every entrance to your property. This advice was validated for me by a recent group of problem guests. They booked for 8 but had 14 or 15 one night, and were extremely drunk, loud, and hanging around on the sidewalk and front porch. It's a quiet neighborhood, and my guests are told that in advance, so this behavior stuck out like a sore thumb.

The guests possibly did not know that my unobtrusive Blink camera on the front porch not only captures video but also sound (or, they were too drunk to care). I had to text the booking guest after midnight to tell him a neighbor told me (not really) that there were more than 8 people there, and they were being too noisy, and 10pm to 7am were designated quiet hours.

Immediately after the call, the guest went out onto the front porch and drunkenly asked his friends if they could leave *and come back*, but enter through the back door, since "there's no cameras there." He was right, there was no camera there, *but*, the camera on the front porch has a wide angle of view and captures a part of the alley between my building and my neighbor's, which is the only way to get to the back of the house (other than going through the house). His friends, in their wisdom, did not want to do that, and just left. Soon after all this, I did put a camera over the back door, just to deter future bad behavior.

Set your cameras to detect motion and send you an alert when motion is detected (Blink does that, and I assume fancier cameras do it as well). Check for extra guests and inappropriate activities when you get alerts. Nip bad behavior in the bud by calling your guests and reminding them nicely that you don't allow parties or extra guests. Guests don't like to be monitored, even outdoors, so keep this in mind and continue reading.

It is best not to mention that you have seen something over your security camera! Many guests find it creepy to think that you are monitoring the cameras, and they picture you sitting in front of a bank of screens watching their every move, like the villain in the Saw movies.

They don't know or understand that you get a text alert when motion is detected, and you only have to glance at your phone when you get one—or, particularly, when it's 2am and you start getting a bunch of them in succession—to see what's going on.

Instead, tell a white lie and say a nosy neighbor has called you about too many people at the rental causing a ruckus. Tell the guest this neighbor is a real pain but you have to keep her on your side, and you are sorry to bother them. But if some kind of a party is going on, you need to remind them that's not allowed. If the neighbor reports you to the city, you could get shut down. They could even call the cops if the disruption doesn't stop, in which case the guest could be cited or even arrested because, you know, cops here are really strict.

Okay, that was more than one white lie, but it's better than being viewed as the creepy Saw guy.

Motion and Noise Level Detectors. These are a touchy subject, because if I were to use either of these, it would make the most sense to have them inside the house. I have found in my research that a surprising number of guests find exterior cameras and monitoring devices "creepy" (I'll live with that), but that goes up to around 100% for monitoring devices indoors.

You have probably seen articles about pervert-hosts placing monitoring devices in their rentals to inappropriately monitor guests. There are even tips and actual devices designed to detect covert cameras and other devices, as if STR hosts were trying to illegally invade guests' privacy around every corner.

Stories like these make guests even more touchy about indoor monitoring than they naturally would be, and they consider it invasive, inappropriate, and probably illegal by default.

That said, you need to decide what's right for you. If you have a problem with guests lying to you about the number of guests and throwing loud parties, you might want to invest in a device like a Minut Smart Home Alarm, which has a motion detector, sound decibel detector, "alarm recognition" (meaning if the Minut detects an alarm going off, it texts you), and a few other features such as temperature monitoring.

But be sure to fully disclose in your listing that you are using a device like this inside your rental, so guests are aware in advance that it will be there. It may be a good idea to fully explain what it does (detect decibel level) and what it does not do (record, or allow you to listen to any of the actual sounds being made).

I would like to install a Minut inside my rental, but I have not, because I know there are a substantial number of guests for whom any kind of interior monitoring would be an automatic "nope."

Or, they might not read my listing description, and book not knowing the Minut was there, then call you out in the review about your "creepy indoor microphones." The Minut is not that, but touchy guests will exaggerate. Guests who do book, such as if their options are limited, but do not like the idea of interior monitoring, may figure they will try to live with it, but once they arrive, feel like they have to walk on eggshells so as not to make too much noise. You will exacerbate this if you call them every time the decibel level goes too high. My guess is that even if the guests are just sitting around having a few drinks, not a party, a few moments of laughing really loud could spike the sound level, causing you to receive an alert. Even a civilized gathering, not exceeding the allowed number of guests, will be punctuated by group laughter or people occasionally all talking at once and getting louder in order to be heard. In my opinion, you should not consider this a problem in the way that party noise is a problem, and if you do decide to install a Minut or similar device, you should be very judicious about contacting your guests as a result of the noise level.

As with cameras, even if you do feel the need to contact your guests about information you received from the device, try to avoid mentioning the fact that it was the monitoring device that is causing you to call them. Blame it on that ornery old scapegoat neighbor as usual.

Guest-proof your rental. This is a general rule but applicable here. Ask yourself why you are worried about guests having no reviews. They guest should have been ID-verified, email-verified and phone-verified, or some combination thereof, by Airbnb or Vrbo before arrival. They will also have given the payment processor a credit card on which they have probably put $1000 or more in order to rent from you.

I was recently on a message board for hosts where one member was saying a guest had broken one of her collectible plates worth $200 and it was part of a set of six. She was asking whether it was fair to ask the guest to pay just $200 for the plate they broke, or $1200 for the entire set.

That's a hard no. All of it.

Do not put $200 collectible plates in your rental! Don't put an $8000 couch in your rental. Attach electronics like TVs to walls. Don't put priceless original art on the walls, decorate with prints on canvas from Home Goods. Don't spend a lot on sheets and towels; find brands and styles that are comfortable but cheap to replace. Try to limit the damage guests can do in any way. Then, if a guest breaks one of the decorative plates you paid $6 for, you keep your stress level at zero.

I also have a related rule, "nothing with fire." No matches. No lighters. No birthday candles. No sparklers. No grill. No fire pit. No Hibachi. NOTHING!

If I had a fireplace, I would brick it up.

By making your rental as bulletproof as possible, even if your guests have no reviews and are not perfect saints, you minimize the damage they can do if you always keep guest-proofing front and center.

What Kind of Town Are You?

More accurately, what kind of destination is your town? If BuzzFeed had a quiz about your town, would it be…

- Seasonal (ski town/beach town)
- Big City
- Historical Destination
- Party Town (Las Vegas, New Orleans)
- Event Destination (Wine Country)
- Family Destination (Pigeon Forge TN, Branson MO)
- College Town
- Nothing Town

Your town may have characteristics of more than one of the above, or may fit none of them. The main thing is to think clearly about your town and what types of travelers you might expect, whether there are slow seasons and busy seasons, what part of town visitors want to stay in, and so on. Your conclusions may not be perfect, and may even be downright wrong, but at least you will have thought through the subject.

Seasonal

Certain towns are so obviously seasonal that you don't need my input on figuring out when you will be busy. Lake Tahoe is an example. You know that when there is snow to ski on, there will be people. A preliminary question you need to consider is, based on the type of town where your STR will be located, does short-term renting make sense for you?

I used to go to Lake Tahoe as a child, and while we went there mostly for skiing (winter), there are times when I did go during the summer (lake), but it was clear even then that the summer was the slow season. It does have gambling on the Nevada side, which is a plus, but it's not very *good* gambling. If someone in California wants to go to Nevada to gamble, why not go to Reno or Las Vegas?

I'm quite positive that owners of vacation rentals in Lake Tahoe make most of their money when there is snow, and pick up renters when they can during the warmer times of year.

As I write this, it happens to be the middle of August, so why don't we scope out the rentals available in the area.

Searching in the South Lake Tahoe area for the Friday through Monday rental only ten days from now, August 25-28 (Friday through Monday), I do find lots of availability. There are 300+ rentals available for groups of up to eight, at an average price of $468 per night. There are even 199 rentals available for groups of 10, at an average rate of $587 per night. That seems like a lot of availability only 10 days out. Even for Labor Day weekend, Friday through Tuesday, 17 days out, there are 300+ available for a groups of up to eight, though the average price is higher at $536 per night. There are 181 rentals available for groups of up to 10, for an average rate of $665 per night.

Now let's look at this winter. Ski season usually starts between mid-November and mid-December, depending on the elevation. Let's gamble and assume there will be snow the first weekend of December. For Dec. 1-4 (Friday through Monday), there are 300+ rentals available for a group of eight, for an average price of $444 per night, and also 300+ for a group of 10, for an average of $541.

This may not seem to tell us much. But it does suggest one thing to me: *market saturation*. There are a heck of a lot of places in Lake Tahoe big enough to accommodate up to eight or ten people! That's a lot of big places. And, we are seeing that even desirable winter weekends don't book up months in advance.

Why do I assume the first week of December will be a desirable weekend? If you know any skiers or snowboarders, by the time December 1 rolls around, they are so eager for their first trip that they are practically ready to explode. They've been watching the forecasts obsessively since late October to see when it may snow and try to calculate whether it will be enough. They are probably already thinking about it right now, in August. Based on the people I knew growing up in Northern California, booking a cabin at Lake Tahoe in August for the first week of December would seem very rational. Particularly if they could get a good deal on a desirable cabin. Such people *know* there is no other activity they would rather be doing the first weekend in December than being at Tahoe. Even if it unfortunately happens not to snow, at least they could stand there and stare at the mountain, holding their skiing or snowboarding gear, just in case it snowed overnight.

And yet South Lake Tahoe has a lot of vacancies for December 1-4.

I'd also guess that, because prices are skewed in the opposite direction of what I would expect (I would expect low in summer, high in winter, but the prices I'm seeing when I search *available listings* right now, in August, are the opposite) that Lake Tahoe is a place where the cheaper lodgings rent first. Looking at August 25-28 again, there are 51 listings that sleep eight for under $300. For December 1-4, there are 227. Eight people renting a place for only $300 (actually, less) is only $37.50 per person, per night.

This significant number of rentals available on the lower end, for the December 1-4 weekend, pulls average prices down. As the lower priced places book up, average prices climb. This whole picture suggests to me that prices are indeed higher in the winter (not surprising), and the ones we are seeing for August are based on the fact that pretty much everyone who wanted a cabin for the end of August already booked it, and the cheaper ones are gone. I bet if we waited until the beginning of November and did some searches, we would see much higher prices for December 1-4.

Times When Short-Term Renting is Not the Right Choice

Setting aside the South Lake Tahoe example, which has so many listings on Airbnb that you would have to assume that listing on Airbnb works for the people who use it, you have to determine whether listing on Airbnb (or any other STR platform) is the best way to go *for you* and your property.

The longer the period for which you expect to be renting your STR to a given individual or group, and the shorter your season (if you have a season), the more sense it may make for you to find a tenant outside of the STR platforms.

A good example would be if your typical renter rents your cottage on Martha's Vineyard from Memorial Day to Labor Day.

This is, admittedly, an extreme example that applies only to a very wealthy set, but it's a good example for what I'm talking about. For a place on Martha's Vineyard, you may only need to find one tenant for the summer, not one tenant each weekend. By using something like Craigslist or another solution that might work in your local area, you will save a huge amount on fees. That's pure profit. Have the person sign a lease or sublease for the period, get a security deposit from them, check with your insurer to make sure you are covered, and forget about giving Airbnb or Vrbo a percentage.

Of course, being in an area where rentals are done for an entire season puts you in a rather fortunate position (you have more of an MTR—medium-term rental—than an STR). But it's definitely something to consider.

This past summer, I rented the Bywater Bungalow on Craigslist for the entire month of August (32 days, above what New Orleans defines as a "short-term" rental), because I knew that there was a possibility I would only book a few nights if I went through Airbnb or Vrbo. There are simply too few people traveling to New Orleans during August and too many STRs on the market. I only charged about 50% of what I would charge an STR tenant, if that, but it was worth it to get the place rented.

Make Your Property "Findable"

Keep in mind that the first step to someone renting your place is that person being able to find the listing for it.

Putting unusual restrictions on rental dates is one way to greatly limit the audience of people who will see your rental in search results. The STR platforms have all kinds of settings like, "Guest must arrive on a specific day of the week," which may look appealing. But keep in mind that the search results don't show your listing to people and *then* tell them they can only check in on a Friday. If they have entered travel dates, and the first date is not a Friday, your listing will not show up.

Having a minimum number of nights guests must stay also reduces the number of people who will see your listing. A lower number gets you into more searches. Don't be tempted to think, "If I choose a minimum stay of seven nights, and have people always arrive on Fridays, then I just need four groups per month and I'll be booked every day!"

That's not a good idea.

If you have a minimum stay of seven nights, you will show up when a guest searches for a place available for seven nights, sure. But so will *every other* place that meets the searcher's criteria that has seven available nights. You won't get prime placement because you have a special preference for seven-night guests. You'll show up in much fewer searches, and when you do show up, you'll be one of many.

Then add in a Friday-nights-only arrival requirement, and you won't even show up in most of the searches for 7-night stays.

So remember to avoid adding requirements that will result in your showing up in fewer searches. How you ideally want your calendar to look bears little relation to when guests actually want to pay money to stay there, unless your place is so desirable you are fighting off guests with a stick. (In which case, raise your prices.)

Gaming Calendaring

There's more to talk about when it comes to your calendar. Guests who are really obsessed with getting a bargain will attempt to "game" the system to get the best deal possible, even if it means moving between different rentals halfway through their stay.

If you have your place priced higher on Friday and Saturday nights, and quite a bit cheaper Sunday through Thursday nights, you may think people who happen to be coming into town for a Friday-through-Tuesday vacation will have no choice but to pay more for the weekend, since everybody charges more on weekend nights.

Well, almost everybody. Some people don't. Your guests may be tempted to divide up their stay between two places, cherry-picking the cheaper dates at each place. You may find people doing things like leaving on Saturday morning so they can avoid the high-cost Saturday night rate. This often makes it hard to rent the other days of that weekend.

I'm not sure there is an ideal solution to this, except maybe to *not* raise your rates on Friday and Saturday nights. But I don't recommend going that route unless you have discovered that a substantial number of your guests are business travelers and demand falls during the week.

What gets exponentially more complicated is trying to price 3-day weekends where you expect demand to be high. You will probably want to have a 3-night minimum stay for those weekends, if not more and have higher prices on three of the nights.

The way calendars work on Airbnb and Vrbo, you can choose a date range on which you can specify "3 night minimum," but this, confusingly, only means that if a guest's stay includes any one of those nights, it must be at least three days. On Labor Day weekend (Monday is Labor Day), if you put a "3-night minimum stay" requirement on Friday, Saturday, and Sunday, and then raise your prices substantially for those nights, you may think you are covered, and will maximize your income for Labor Day weekend.

But maybe not. Because someone can come along and book Wednesday, Thursday, and Friday nights. They have fulfilled the 3-night requirement, but they paid your cheaper weeknight rates for two of the three nights. Not exactly what you had in mind.

Now you've got a three-day weekend that's all messed up. Hopefully you'll find someone who wants to arrive on Saturday and wants to stay until Tuesday. Because, unless you now remove the three-night requirement, nobody who wants to just book Saturday and Sunday nights (which, at this point, you would be fine with) will be able to book them. Just to be clear, you *should definitely* now remove the 3-night minimum stay requirement, since Friday is now booked.

How to avoid this on the first place? A couple possibilities:

First possibility, you could require guests for Labor Day weekend to arrive on Friday night (and have your 3-night minimum in effect) so the guests would have to rent Friday, Saturday, and Sunday nights, at minimum.

This approach has the appeal of simplicity, but there is a negative: you will not show up in any search results where the searcher wants to arrive earlier than Friday, but still stay through Monday.

Second possibility—my preference, since it does not keep you out of as many search results—is to raise rates for the 3 nights preceding and following the key nights of Friday, Saturday, and Sunday, to whatever your weekend rates will be, to avoid the problem of guests making a cheap/cheap/expensive Wednesday/Thursday/Friday reservation which then messes up your three-day weekend.

It's not a perfect solution; the Wednesday/Thursday/Friday groups will probably not book you (but at least they will see you). But it does ensure that at least three days on or around the three-day weekend will be booked, at your increased holiday rate, and no "cheap nights" will be snuck in.

I prefer this to the frustration of having a group book some weird date range on a key weekend far in advance where they check out on a Saturday, check in on a Sunday, or some other weird arrangement. That makes me want to tear my hair out.

Your Town Type

We talked about "seasonal," which led to other important topics, but let's go through the other town types.

Big City

If you have a property available for rent in a big city where you are legally allowed to STR it, then you are arguably the best-positioned type of STR host. You will probably have all types of guests, in town for all types of reasons, and through all seasons.

But the first thing you should do if you have a rental in a large city is to look at your precise location and figure out what types of travelers you may reasonably attract.

If you are downtown, you can probably get both vacationers and business travelers. I would suggest deciding which one you are aiming for and designing your property and listing accordingly.

If you are targeting business travelers, emphasize convenience, efficiency, and features enabling the traveler to get work done. Make sure you have a desk or other work area and places to plug in electrical and USB cords. Having a laser printer/scanner would be a huge plus to most business travelers. Make the décor professional and, if you can afford it, a bit luxurious, but not excessively so. Furnish it with things that would allow the guest to have others over for business meetings.

But if you are targeting vacationers, put the emphasis on "fun." People who are on vacation like the place they're staying to seem "vacation-y"—kind of like when you go to a beach house in Florida, you'll find it's decorated with seahorses, life savers, fish netting, bowls full of shells, and summery colored pillows. When you decorate, buy a couple goofy pieces of furniture you might not really want to look at in your own house every day, but that signal "fun" to a traveler.

If your STR is in a rougher neighborhood, or a neighborhood further from the city center, you will probably need to first analyze what you expect to be able to charge. Look at what nearby listings are charging, and make sure to see how full their calendars are. (You may see some that are priced high, but also notice that those aren't being booked very much. Remember, many hosts out there do not have it all figured out yet, either.)

Being in a less-than-desirable location and having to charge less usually means trimming your budget wherever you can, since guests will expect to pay as little as they can get away with. Try to do more with less, and don't over-invest in your furnishings or your rental's contents.

Unfortunately, if you are at a lower price point, you may be more likely to encounter troublesome guests. You may find that more things get broken or "disappear," and that your guests do not respect your property as much.

Historical Destination

By "historical destination," I mean a place that is not a large city and which has one main draw that attracts a consistent stream of visitors: history.

It may be a small town with few places to stay. The key thing to look at is how many rentals are available, and how much demand there is. True, this is kind of what you'd have to do anywhere. But if you happen to have a property for rent in a town with lots of visitors but no places to stay, you may find yourself pleasantly surprised at how much business you can get and how much you can charge.

The first thing to do is search Airbnb and other platforms for available STRs in the target area. Choose a couple of days a few months out which are unlikely to be booked. Also look at some upcoming weekends, and various lengths of time (two nights, seven nights). This should give you an idea of how much competition is out there and what they are charging.

Event Destination

By "event destination" I mean a place that people often go for weddings or similar events. I am thinking of Sonoma/Napa (the Wine Country) as well as Las Vegas, New Orleans, and innumerable other places. Most event destinations are also tourist destinations in their own right, but the reason I bring them up as a separate category is that, if you happen to have a large property that can accommodate ten or more people, you probably should be focused on housing guests who are in town for an event. Perhaps they can even hold their event on your property. In New Orleans, as I suspect is the case in most other event destinations, the more bedrooms a prospective traveler is seeking, the more limited their selection will be. If you are located in an event destination and have a rental that can host twelve or more guests at once, particularly if you also have grounds where events can be held, you are in a category that may be beyond the scope of this book, since you will probably have to take on a bigger role and your rental could be more of a full-time job. And you could rake in a *ton* of money. Talk to people in your local area with similar properties to get some tips.

If you have a property that sleeps only 2-8 people, though, you need to be wary of "events," and make sure that your guests are fully disclosing what they are in town for. Most STR hosts have a "NO PARTIES" rule, including me. If you have a three-bedroom rental in which you allow a maximum of six guests, you do not want your guest using your place for a party or any kind of event.

Preventing your guests from using your property for parties or other events is something you have to constantly be vigilant about. Why? Noise. Excessive numbers of people. Drunkenness spilling out onto the sidewalk. Damage to your property. People smoking indoors. Not to mention the result of *any* decent party...a huge mess.

Guests will almost never tell you they are planning to use your rental to host a party, since they suspect, correctly, that you are not renting it out with that in mind.

One clue that guests have a big party in mind is if your property is on the larger side, and the guest insists on a walk-through before booking. Most guests who just want to book a room, apartment or house as a place for a small group or family to stay can get a good enough idea from the photos and reviews if it will meet their needs. Guests who want to use your house for a party, on the other hand, will want to get an idea of whether the indoor plus outdoor space will be big enough for all the people they plan to invite over.

Another clue is if your prospective guest lives in town. Many hosts do not like renting to locals and I don't, either. If your place is on the large side, there's a good chance they want to use it for some type of gathering. Even if it is not on the large side, local guests know too many nearby people and will likely invite them over. I recommend saying "no" to locals.

Some other guests may not have concrete plans to hold a party *per se*, but they may plan on more wild activities than they let on. Groups of single people, especially groups of four or more, visiting a city like New Orleans, are basically always here to party to some degree. I do not disallow these guests from my rentals, but I make sure they know that they cannot have people over; the partying needs to be done somewhere else. They can come back to the rental to sleep and vomit.

One thing that makes my radar go up is when a prospective guest who is young (under 26) and coming to town with a group of friends offers me, unprompted, an elaborate story whose purpose seems to be to get across why they are *not* coming to town to party on Bourbon Street every night. That's exactly the kind of person who not only is here to party on Bourbon Street every night, but who will end up taking half of Bourbon Street home with them.

Family Destination

A "family destination" is like any tourist destination except a larger percentage of your guests will have young children. These groups may value things like high chairs, changing tables, and dishes, cups and dining ware for infants. A pack-n-play is good as well. (Even if you are not in a family destination, or don't think you are, these things may be a value-add that can help you attract more guests.)

Most STR hosts don't consider the needs of families with small children, which creates an opportunity to target that market. Contrary to popular belief, children don't really break things or dirty everything, at least not in my experience. Of course, part of that is "bulletproofing" your home to make that as difficult as possible.

The amenities you will want to offer will be more tailored toward the needs of families. For example, you might want to put one or even two sets of bunk beds in one of the bedrooms instead of a queen bed. Buying play equipment for the back yard will make your place more attractive to a lot of potential guests. Have a small crate of toys (buying toys is fun) and a video game setup. It doesn't have to be the newest, most expensive kind, because those cost about $400, believe it or not. I bought a Nintendo NES Classic Edition ($39.99) that has old-school video games like Pac-Man and Donkey Kong. This way parents can play along with kids and get nostalgic.

One thing I don't provide is other electronic devices like iPads, computers, or expensive electronics, other than wall-mounted TVs. People will need to bring their own when it comes to that.

College Town

I have been hearing that more and more people visiting children or friends at colleges are staying at STRs, since some college towns are quite small and do not have many nearby hotels. This is a desirable market if you are so situated, and you should be able to charge decent prices, presuming a large number of other people in town have not already jumped on the STR bandwagon. I'm sure there is a seasonality to college towns; this would be a good thing to talk to local hosts about.

Tip: if the college's website has a place that lists lodgings, try to get your property listed there. It's one of the places many visitors will browse when planning their trip.

Nothing Town

Do you live in a nothing, nowhere town? Surprisingly, you may be well-positioned to be an STR host. Short-term renting, like any business, is about supply and demand. You may live in No-berry, USA, and can't imagine why anyone would travel there. But people do visit obscure towns for work or to see family or friends. If everyone in town thinks nobody ever visits, then nobody will ever think of setting up an STR. And if you are the only STR in town, you may be pleasantly surprised at how much business rolls in.

And again, don't tell the neighbors, or they will copy you.

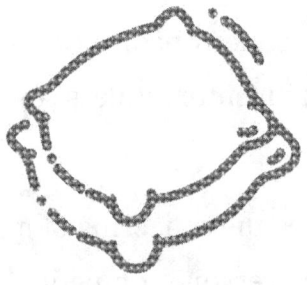

STR Saturation

Back to our Analysis. The STR portion of the "sharing economy" has now been underway for enough years that most everyone has heard about "Airbnbs," and has either railed against them, or thought about converting that spare room or in-law unit into one for extra cash, or both.

(I should point out that even though everyone has heard of "Airbnbs," that somehow does not mean the people on Expedia who rent your STR will understand a thing about them. Knowing they exist and knowing anything about them, or what the expectations will be when you stay in one, are two different things.)

My next-door neighbor is a free-spirited nudist in her 70s who recently evicted her long-term tenant (she owns a duplex like I do) so she could convert the apartment into an STR. Apparently it is going pretty well.

My next-door neighbor at my other property, whose house and its environs resemble a junkyard/pitbull breeding colony, also took a stab at it, badly scaring (scarring?) several groups of European tourists. After some horrific reviews, he de-listed his STR, much to the benefit of, well, the world.

Because everyone is living somewhere, and everyone by now has heard of "Airbnbs" and thought about starting one, something has happened in my town and possibly yours: market saturation.

In other words, there are too many STRs and not quite enough guests.

Short-term renting is a fairly easy side-hustle that so many people can do that it's almost inevitable that markets will become saturated with inventory unless something prevents that from happening.

I fear that the ultimate result, in many places, will be the squeezing of mid-range STRs out of the market. This is because oversaturation leads to everyone competing on price, which leads to hosts trimming budgets as much as possible. At the same time, guests expect more for less, and become more and more demanding even as hosts make less and less money.

So, hosts who previously tried to maintain a certain level of quality in their rentals, and who got used to making a significant premium over what they could make from long-term tenants, will find that they can no longer maintain either the quality or the profit margin, and are likely to exit the business. No-frills places that charge bargain rates while still making decent money will be the only ones left standing, and guests will be stuck with thrift-store furniture and hand-me-down bedspreads, and will have to adopt a laissez-faire attitude about broken appliances, poorly-functioning HVAC systems, and rodents.

But the luxury STRs for price insensitive guests will continue to exist. People who want high quality will continue to be willing to pay for it, and will also continue to have the money to do so.

Those are my predictions, anyway. A lot depends on whether customers really do become obsessive about seeking the lowest price possible, or if they retain a willingness to pay a little more for quality, or other attributes like location or charm.

We shall see.

Know Your Competition

The best way to check if your market is saturated is to go on Airbnb or Vrbo and do searches a typical traveler would do, like we did with South Lake Tahoe. Do a bunch of them, for different lengths of time and at different times of the year.

Search for a one-night or two-night rental for two people for the upcoming weekend. Search for a four-day rental for the middle of a week two months from now. Search for a three-night rental for six people three months from now. And another for the weekend after next. Add some filters to your search, such as "Superhosts Only" or "Instant Book Only."

How often are you being shown 300+ results? On Airbnb, when you do a search that returns more than 300 results, it doesn't tell you the exact number available, it just says "300+

results." If you keep seeing "300+ results," even if you search by narrower and narrower criteria, that tells you something: you have a lot of competition.

Know Yourself

But, in addition to all your other searches, *do* make sure to search for things that *you* have that not everyone does, and that people may want. Views. Direct access to lake or beach. Proximity to Bourbon Street. A certain (large) number of bedrooms. Ability to accommodate 6 or more guests.

Even if your market is very saturated, it's going to be *most* saturated among properties that can only accommodate a small number of guests. If your place is an "entire home" rental that sleeps only two people, your competition is everyone (except single rooms that only allow one person). If your place sleeps ten, your field is about 95% less crowded.

Similarly, true luxury rentals are few and far between. It is an expensive market to target in terms of startup costs, but there will be far fewer properties with which you are truly in competition.

Same thing with permitting pets, and probably most of the other things that most hosts don't allow, like smoking indoors, or musicians.

Know Other Hosts

If you already know some STR hosts in your town, talk to them. Don't avoid the topic out of fear they will be mad that you are thinking about joining the competition. Maybe they will be mad—who cares? They are going to find out anyway as soon as your put up your listing. If they find out by seeing your rental in a search rather than you just telling them, that might make things even more weird.

But my guess is that they will not be mad. In fact, you will probably get an earful about their last rotten guest or the city's latest dumb plan. Like all STR hosts, they will already know what I hope I have gotten across by now—STR hosting is a lot of work. Sure, it is something you can do on the side and still work full-time, but that doesn't make it easy. They may be thinking about quitting (a lot of hosts are—especially those who have been doing it a long time and have become disillusioned with steadily dropping prices and steadily more demanding guests), and the last thing on their mind may be whether you entering the market will tip the scales toward any change that will really affect them.

Any information another STR-host in your area can give you is extremely valuable, so if you get access to an experienced STR host near you, listen up and ask questions. They may say negative things that you, in your youthful enthusiasm to start this new business venture, would like to dismiss, thinking they might be true *for him*, but they will not be true *for you*.

These are likely the kinds of things that you would never have thought of, but might be a fact of life in your area.

For example, say you live in a safe, quiet neighborhood a mile from downtown. Your neighbors are pretty homogenous, and that leads you to assume that you can predict what type of guest your rental will attract: people just like you and your neighbors, of course!

But perhaps not. Your neighbor one block away, who operates an STR much like one you are planning, says most of his guests are considerate and cause no problems, but occasionally, he gets some that just want to use his place to do drugs.

What? This isn't that type of neighborhood! you think. *He must be crazy, or on something himself!*

What you are not considering is that, a mile from your neighborhood, in the *opposite* direction of downtown, is a rough neighborhood where people do in fact buy and sell drugs and engage in other unsavory activities. There's even a prison.

You never go there, and there are no shops there but corner liquor stores and pawn shops, so why would that area even cross your mind? Those don't seem like the kind of people who would patronize an STR, anyway.

So, unfortunately, you remain fixed on the idea that any guests who would be looking to rent a small house in your quiet, boring neighborhood would be quiet and boring themselves. And—as your neighbor did say—you are probably right, for the most part. But what your neighbor is telling you is that you will also get some people whose interest is in the other direction, literally and figuratively.

These are the types of things we overlook before we get actual experience, because we don't want to think about bad stuff, or just don't have the creativity to imagine what some other people (very unlike us) will do in, or to, a rental. So listen to your neighbor.

The second place I would do research would be in online forums frequented by local people.

There may be a message board on Reddit or Facebook where local STR hosts have discussions, and you can pick up a lot from participating or just observing. These groups may be private, so you may need to make real-world connections before you can find out about them. But as time goes on, I see more and more of these groups popping up, particularly on Facebook, and the ones in my area are certainly not all private, so you may not need to worry about that.

People love to vent online, so in an online forum, whether devoted to your local area or not, you will probably get a good idea of all the problems you might encounter. You will also get a lopsided idea of how horrible guests and hosts can be, since people don't go online to vent about considerate, quiet guests who cause no problems, or nice hosts who weren't around much but were perfectly fine, which is like 90+% of them.

On forums that are open to both hosts and guests, such as Reddit.com/Airbnb, you will also hear a lot of guests writing desperate pleas for help with their problems, some of which are indeed awful. While it's nice to have a forum that is just for hosts, in a "mixed" forum, you can learn a lot about what ticks guests off so you can strive to avoid those situations in your own STR business.

Evaluate Your Property

As any real estate agent well knows, it is difficult to evaluate your own property objectively. You know how much work went into things, and how much money you have put into the house. You almost certainly have some sort of emotional attachment to it. Think about it: could you be as objective in evaluating your own property as you could in evaluating a random property that you walked up to on a random street, entered, and started looking through? No way.

Here's a quick example that illustrates why it's hard to evaluate your property objectively.

Say, for the longest time, your property did not have central air and heat, just window units. And you lived there listening to the rattling window units and eagerly awaited the day when you could save up enough money to install central air and heat. Because something more urgent was always coming up, it took you a few years. During that time, you researched HVAC systems. You figured out the best HVAC system, and figured out the best place to buy it. You know your HVAC system was installed by a master HVAC technician and the plumbing was installed by a master plumber. You know your HVAC system is 30% quieter and 26% more energy efficient than the average HVAC system on the market.

Guess what? Nobody cares.

Well, they do care that you have central air and heat, but only insofar as it's a feature among many others swirling around in their heads as they try to decide between dozens of properties they've browsed on Airbnb or Vrbo. It's not at the top of their list. And if 75% of rentals in your area have central air and heat, it's particularly unremarkable. *Not* having central air and heat would be remarkable—in a bad way.

What has happened is that, by spending all those months saving money, researching HVAC systems, and installing an excellent HVAC system, your status has increased to…average.

The $7,500 did not buy you a gold star. It just removed a red "X."

Curb Appeal

Starting at the sidewalk, walk up to the house or apartment you are proposing to STR as if you were a skeptical buyer.

Are there cheery flowers in flowerbeds and decorations like seasonal flags, such as you might expect to see at a beach house or vacation home? Does the place burst with energy and radiate "WELCOME"?

If there is a front yard, is the grass green and lush, or does it have yellow patches and gopher holes? Is paint visibly peeling off exterior walls? Is there trash piled anywhere?

Is there a rat trap with dried cheese on it in a dusty corner of the none-too-clean front porch?

These will be your guests' first impressions, and it's best if they are good.

Walk-Through

Enter through your front door and walk through the property, room by room. Do you see old furniture that looks like it's been used for ten years by the Roseanne Connor family? Is the furniture dated and highly worn?

Is there a 60" Smart TV, or an old junker with a cathode ray tube that's a cubic yard in size and weighs 300 pounds?

Do you have carpet? If you do, does it look very fresh and very clean, or does it look like it could reasonably be featured in a cat litter commercial—the one where the family *does not* use Fresh Step®?

Importantly, is your house cluttered, stuffed to the gills with "things" (you might call them prized possessions, collected over a lifetime of travel and experiences; travelers might call them "dusty old junk")?

In a rental, travelers appreciate a sense of space and openness. Walking into a place with so much junk that finding a place to sit requires picking through piles of newspapers from the 1940s is not inviting. It's much nicer to walk into a room with a sense of airiness where you can breathe. Furniture should not crowd the room or be too big for the space (a good general rule that many people do not seem to understand).

It can be prohibitively expensive to update all your furniture,of course. But here are a few things you should be able to do in any room and keep to a budget:

- *DE-CLUTTER*. Watch an episode of hoarders and pretend (or you may not even have to pretend) that you are the hoarder. Become the determined relative who wants everything thrown out. Even that Princess Diana Beanie Baby you are certain will increase in value if you just hold onto it a few more years. *It won't!* A few tears may be shed, but consider every tear to be extra money in your pocket that you will get from a short-term renter who otherwise would take a pass on your hoarder-trailer.

- *Paint your walls*. Especially if your paint is visibly yellowing or peeling. Fresh paint always makes everything look unexpectedly new and…fresh.

- *Paint or touch up your moldings and door frames, or simply clean them.* Touching up chipped trim or marks in doorways and on moldings takes little effort. Wipe clean the moldings first so that the newer paint matches the old. Do this particularly around doorways. You might be surprised how much nicer your doorframes look after simply wiping them down with 409.

- *Window coverings*. Can, and should, you update them? You can get blinds online for $50-$100 per window, depending on the size. Gauzy curtains are even cheaper, and they let in light but also provide privacy. Are your curtains functional, but relics of the 70s? You may think they work fine, and they may work fine, but what impression do they give? If they are expensive curtains that you want to keep, would having them dry-cleaned make them look more attractive?

- *Existing blinds*. Make sure they are clean. Metal blinds can attract grease and dust. If mere dusting is not enough, take down your blinds and clean them, either outside or in the bathtub. Use a strong detergent to cut any grease. Once clean, dry them to the extent possible to prevent rust. Cheap plastic blinds don't usually attract as much gunk, and usually just need dusting. Other types of blinds—use your judgment. Dirty blinds are gross.

- *Lighting*. Could you replace the boring light at the center of your ceiling with something quirky, antique, or dramatic? A chandelier can make any room seem more exciting, even a walk-in closet or bathroom.

- *Furniture covers*. These can be tacky and ugly, but may be an improvement on your existing furniture if it's stained or just shapeless, old and ugly.

- *Clean any stains on fabric*. Particularly ones that catch the eye as you walk through the room.

- *Buy decorative pillows*. Throw out any pillows that are overly flat or show their age. Or, try refreshing them by dry cleaning the covers or washing the covers in the sink with Woolite.

- *Buy decorative throws*. Drape them over a couch or chair back and they add to your decor. DON'T use a throw or blanket to cover a large part of the seating area of a sofa (like the Afghan draped over the back of Roseanne Connor's couch). It looks grandparental.

- *Put things on the walls*. This is a big one that many hosts overlook. Things on the walls is the finishing touch that every room needs. Bare walls look stark and uninviting. Though framing gets expensive, bargains are out there. Have photos printed on canvas—not family photos, but views of your city and its features and landmarks. Hang a flag or two. A 2' x 3' nylon flag is usually fairly cheap and takes up a lot of wall. Don't use flags from the military, which can be off-putting to some people. Framed mirrors are especially good. And large clocks. Also, in New Orleans, Mardi-Gras masks. You probably have a local equivalent.

Tip: rather than trying to fill whole walls, create a line at approximately eye-height, and make that the midline of every wall-hanging. Hang items all in a row, like they would be hung at an art gallery. This looks good, and you need fewer items.

Tip: pick wall-hangings that are relevant to your destination. It reminds guests that they are on a trip and are there to have fun.

- *Steam clean your carpets*. Renting of a big, powerful carpet cleaner is currently $30 per day, or $21 for four hours, at Home Depot.

- *Clean your hardwood floors*. The best way to clean hardwood floors is by hand, with a very slightly damp rag. Alternatively, mop with a very slightly damp mop, the sponge kind, and mop in long strokes with the grain of the wood. Do not buy one of those stringy mops you see janitors pushing around in movies. And, in my opinion, going against generations of grandmas, Murphy's Oil Soap sucks. If you put even a little bit too much it leaves a murky film. I don't think it really does anything except fill the air with a pleasant scent. A rag dipped in water (with a little bit of Murphy's Oil Soap if you want that clean scent) then wrung out to the maximum amount possible will get your floors clean.

- *Clean your baseboards*. The initial cleaning may require a slightly damp rag or sponge, but after that, you should be able to vacuum or use a "feather" duster (the newer ones are not made of feathers, but a sticky, fluffy material that grabs dust). You should be hitting the baseboards in at least one room every time you do a cleaning.

- *Clean your windowsills, and paint them if necessary*. You may not want or need to paint whole rooms, but painting your windowsills is a small amount of work that can yield a big payoff, especially if your sills have become stained from window A/C units. Use semi-gloss paint on windowsills (and wood trim in general), not flat paint.

- *Clean your fireplace brick*. Does your wood-burning fireplace have a big black semi-circle of soot above the opening? Scrub that with a scrub brush.

- *Paint your fireplace brick*. Those HGTV flippers do it all the time. Though I have a thing for old brick, and usually hate seeing it painted, if your fireplace makes your living room scream "DATED OLD HOUSE!" you might want to take the plunge.

- *Fireplace mantle*. I promise this is the last thing about fireplaces. If your mantle is ugly and dated, replace it with a simple wooden shelf. Again, see any HGTV home renovation show. They always do this.

- *Pops of color*. If a room screams "bland" or "beige" instead of "fresh" and "new," add pops of color. A brightly colored ceramic vase. Small knick-knacks on the shelves. Buy cheap, random small items at thrift stores for $1, then spray paint them with a bright color like robin's egg blue. Use gloss paint for best effect.

- *Fresh flowers*. If not too expensive, have fresh flowers. If your rental is on the higher end and you are able to charge healthy rates, $3.99 on a bouquet of daisies, purchased on the day your guests arrive, may be affordable. It's certainly a touch that shows you go above-and-beyond.

- *Scents*. Guests can be very picky about scents, and many people claim to have scent-sensitivity. So, be careful. If you use any scents at all, make sure they are very mild, almost subliminal. Bowls or glass vases containing pinecones and dried orange peels (or something specific to the season) are good. Glade and Airwick plug-ins or solid air fresheners are too strong. Don't use them.

- *Decorative floor lamps*. While you or I may do our reading under existing ceiling lamps and manage just fine, it's a nice touch to have a floor lamp next to a chair or couch. It feels cozy to read a book in a room where the only lighting is from the floor lamp next to the chair. A nice-looking floor lamp can also add a nice touch to your décor.

- *Lamps in general.* Many people hate overhead lighting and prefer lamps. I have nightstands with small lamps on each side of all my beds. I buy small lamps from Walmart or Target and you can get small lamps fairly cheap (lamp prices seem to be proportional to lamp height and rise on a steep curve).

- *Clocks.* I have a wall clock in my kitchen (you can get decent-looking ones for $5 at Walmart) and a small digital alarm clock by each bed and by each sofa bed. The latter you can get for $2. Bigger clocks can also be found on the cheap and make good wall pieces.

- *Bed coverings.* I see so many bare-bones, old bedspreads on the STR sites it makes me glad—glad that most guests are going to pass right by those listings and keep mine in the running. If nothing else, have nice-looking bed coverlets or bedspreads that look contemporary and spotless, not old. If your bedspread looks like an old hand-me-down, guests will make the assumption that your pillows are old and lumpy and your sheets are old and your mattress is old as well. They will think "dust" and "dust mites" and "I don't want to sleep there."

- *Multiple pillows and a decorative pillow on each bed.* I put two pillows for each person sleeping on a bed (that makes four pillows for any bed other than a twin, which gets two), plus a decorative pillow with a sham for each side, plus a small decorative pillow for the center. This sets the tone for guests to assume they will have a great sleeping experience. Sleeping is important.

- *Mattresses.* Lay down on your mattress. Is it comfortable and do you start falling asleep almost immediately? That's good. Mattresses are not as expensive as you might think-- $250 to $300 online for foam-topped or memory-foam-topped. I recommend making good mattresses a spending priority. If you can't afford them up front, start with a foam topper 4" thick or more, then after you start making some money, buy new mattresses.

➤ *Make darkness possible.* Many guests do not want any light getting into the room when they sleep. Blackout blinds or very thick curtains are appreciated by some guests. Personally, I didn't think of this when I initially furnished my first rental, and I bought translucent blinds which are not really light-blockers. I haven't gotten any complaints, but I did notice that sometimes guests would try to hang a blanket over the window. A not-too-subtle sign. For my second rental, I did get heavy curtains in one bedroom and light-blocking blinds in another.

Dining Room

Do you have a dining table and chairs, either in its own room or in the kitchen? Does the setup look ready for visiting guests, people whom you have never met before, to sit down and eat a pleasant meal? Your guests will most likely be eating at this table often, even if you yourself always eat in front of the TV or computer (guilty).

Do the chairs all match? If not, can you genuinely say that the mismatched look adds a funky vibe and fits with the décor you are going for? If not, and it just looks like you stole 4 random chairs from a church basement, invest in matching chairs.

Kitchen

Kitchen renovations are very pricey, and it's probably not realistic to redo your kitchen, even if your appliances are all relics. But look around at what you could improve at a reasonable cost.

Are your counters crowded with stuff? Get rid of it. Clean counters look best. Only have things out that *guests* will need: toaster, coffee pot, microwave, knife set, and maybe a tray with coffee/tea condiments and a bowl with some fruit. Even if you are living in the home yourself, and your guests are just renting a room, put all your extra junk in drawers or cabinets. Get it off the counter.

Are your cabinets old and ugly? A lot of that may just be dirt and grime. Clean them with 409 or some other strong surface cleaner. You may be amazed at how much brighter and newer they look. Painting cabinets is an option, though that is a project that takes some work. Watch a couple YouTube videos before deciding to do it. You will definitely need to remove the cabinet doors, and may need to sand them in order for them to take paint, depending on the finish.

Buying new cabinet doors is also a possibility, but it is expensive and also quite a bit of work.

Changing your cabinet door handles and drawer pulls is one way to give your kitchen a quicker facelift. Many door handles and drawer pulls are very dated, and drag down the overall look of the kitchen. You can get door handles and drawer pulls that look good at a surprisingly low price. One you get your cabinet doors and fronts really clean, and replace the pulls and knobs with more stylish ones, you may find your kitchen looks a lot more updated than you thought it could.

Most importantly, clean your kitchen—spotless.

If gunk has built up around the range, sink, oven (by the floor), refrigerator doors, or anywhere else, for God's sake, CLEAN IT! Scrub linoleum floors. Their color is probably lighter and brighter than what you have actually seen in a long time.

Wipe clean the insides of your cabinet doors and the shelves, and wipe clean your drawers inside and out. Things that either look like (or maybe are) mice or bug droppings tend to collect in the backs of drawers. You don't want guests to see those. Also wipe clean the tops of cabinet doors (they tend to collect drops of spilled stuff over time), particularly those at waist level or below.

Clean under your sink and remove everything but what your guests may need: dishwashing liquid, Windex, Shout, 409, plastic garbage bags (large for kitchen, small for bathrooms), an emergency flashlight, a fully charged fire extinguisher, extra sponge(s), and a couple of unopened gallons of water for emergencies. Put any other stuff in a box if you must keep it there, so your under-sink is tidy. Clean the inner cabinet doors and wipe the dust off the drain trap.

Replace the metal pans underneath the burners on your stove, if you have those. You can get replacements for a few dollars at the grocery store or dollar store.

To sum it up in one simple rule: there should be nothing in your kitchen that may cause a guest to say, "Ew, gross!"

Bathrooms

The overall concept is the same as for kitchens—bathrooms cost a big chunk of money to remodel, so you are probably not going to do that. So, focus on making the bathroom as clean as possible and do some sprucing up where you can.

One unfortunate problem with bathrooms, especially older ones, is that they can develop little things that are unsightly but not "dirty" per se. Those little screws that hold the toilet to the floor get rusty, and over time, little dribbles of permanent brown (from the rust) can appear, leaking down the side of the toilet base and looking gross.

Same thing with the plumbing fixtures under the sink (luckily, vanities hide most of these, but maybe they don't hide yours). Clean them as best you can. Usually just wiping up dust and cleaning the tile and the porcelain, including scrubbing grout clean and spraying it with mildew-killing spray, will improve the appearance of your bathroom. One of my rentals admittedly has older bathrooms and has these types of problems. If anything would make a guest say, "Ew, gross!" treat it as a must-fix.

And hide whatever's too ugly behind strategically-placed decorative items, a nice-looking trash basket, hamper, etc.

Changing light bulbs to a lower wattage never hurts, either.

Bedrooms

The general rules I've already talked about regarding wood furniture, wall hangings, lamps, and of course, bed linens, all apply.

Make sure to DUST the bedrooms, and sweep the ceiling and any ceiling-mounted fixtures or vents for cobwebs. Guests will naturally be lying on the beds looking at the ceiling, ceiling fan, vents, etc. and will see all those things that you may not regularly look at unless you have a habit of looking upwards.

Themed Rooms

One thing you have an opportunity to do to make bedrooms special is to create themed rooms.

Guests like this—a themed bedroom is something they would never do at their own home, but they like the idea of staying in the "Christmas Room" or the "Jazz Room" when on vacation.

To state the obvious, but if your city is known for one or more things, choose themes based on those. For example, being in New Orleans, I would do a Mardi Gras Room, a Jazz Room, a French Quarter Room, a Storyville Room (it would be decorated like a bordello) and maybe a Pirate Room.

Your Target Market

Making your place as attractive as possible, as we went through in the previous section, is the first step in determining where you fit into your market. You need your rental to be at its best to evaluate what you are working with and to compare it to what else is available in your immediate area.

Read this section with your rental in mind as it will look when you have made any updates or fixes you plan to make (and be honest), as well as any furniture or decor purchases or other improvements.

If your furniture is generally second-hand, older, and a bit beaten up, look for comparable properties that are similar. Be honest with yourself. If you are furnishing your rental with low-cost items from thrift stores, it will be obvious to prospective guests, and even with good pictures, you place will probably look less than exciting (though hopefully it will look tidy, clean, and have a sense of space). Assume your guests will err on the picky side if you are charging a medium to high price for your area, and on the forgiving side if you are offering a bargain.

The Bargain Traveler

If your rental matches up pretty well with what is described in the last paragraph, your target market is the **Bargain Traveler**. They don't care that all your furniture be new, designer, or even stylish (though everybody loves clean), and probably view the STR just as a place to crash and an expense they want to minimize. Their requirement is that the rental meet their basic needs, that it be "good enough."

This does not mean that they have no standards; everyone is put off by bad smells, dampness, mustiness, dust, stained carpets, dirty dishes, flies, and so on. Those things really need to be off the table if you want to rent anything to people for money.

Of course, there's an exception to every rule. If people are willing to pay $18 a night to stay in your damp basement that you never enter, let alone clean, and that amount of income works for you... congratulations, you found the exception. But remember that platforms like Airbnb and Vrbo have minimum hosting standards you need to meet.

Another thing to avoid at all costs, even for the Bargain Traveler: BUGS.

Regardless of whether your place is dank and unappealing, but habitable, if it is infested with vermin, that is generally a dealbreaker. Control for bugs no matter how low you are aiming. I am not big on pesticides, but when I started renting out property, I found that signing up with a regular pest control service that comes by quarterly and sprays was a necessity.

Targeting the Bargain Traveler you will bring in less money, but you may also have lower expenses and less stress. If a guest breaks a chair, you know you can just replace it for ten dollars, or even grab any old chair from your own living quarters or find one in OK condition on the street and wipe it clean.

I don't target the Bargain Traveler at my rentals, though I have been tempted. I could slack more. I could get all four-star reviews and it wouldn't put me out of business, because less-than-perfect reviews are one of the trade-offs the Bargain Traveler makes when he or she zeroes in on price alone.

The economics of serving the Bargain Traveler mean you won't be able to afford to offer lots of extras (and your guests shouldn't expect them, anyway). I would provide the basics like toilet paper, hand soap, towels, hand towels, dish soap, and maybe some condiments.

I *always* recommend that you provide reasonably fast Internet to guests, regardless of your price point, since it has become an absolute necessity for people today. People would rather have high-speed Internet than coffee, there's no contest. And they'd probably rather have it than anything else but toilet paper. You really should have moderately fast Wi-fi and toilet paper. I'll leave it at that.

I would also keep my thermostat under tighter control (minimum temperature 74 in the summer perhaps, maximum of 66 or 68 in the winter?). You will learn that, while it may seem like you are making a lot of money at times, way more than you would from a long-term renter, there will be months when it will slow down, so your average monthly income over the course of a year will be lower than it sometimes seems. And despite the reputation of Millennials for being environmentally conscious, the guest who cares about conserving your utilities might as well be a unicorn. If you are paying, they are wasting.

If you are targeting the Bargain Traveler, there will, of course, also be the work of managing the rental, doing the cleaning, periodically replacing things like sheets and towels (not to mention washing a huge pile of laundry about once a week on average), and, of course, being on call 24 hours a day. But again, you don't need to get 5 stars from everyone. Could you offer bare mattresses without sheets and get away with it? Hmm...gears are starting to turn.

Targeting the lowest-price-point customer means you will have to cut corners and keep a very close eye on your competition's prices. Take honest photos that clearly show your place to be less than luxurious so guests are not misled. A guest who is misled into thinking they are getting an attractive place for a bargain price will leave you a worse review than one who knows they are getting a bargain place for a bargain price, because that is exactly what they want. They are the Bargain Traveler.

There's nothing worse than seeing in a review, "When we arrived, we were disappointed. The place looked nothing like the pictures."

No prospective traveler wants to read that. And someone who is expecting a hostel-like setting with stained mattresses, regardless of what else they may find to complain about (noise from other guests) they can't complain about *that*.

"The Middle"

The majority of travelers, in my experience, fall somewhere in the "mushy middle," in terms of what they are seeking and what they are willing to pay. Everyone wants to save a little money, but what I'm calling The Middle are people who just want a fair price and a decent—but not extravagant—place to stay. They don't squeeze a dime until it screams, and don't want to be walking around carpet that is more stained than not-stained. These people are looking for the STR version of something between the budget chains (Days Inn, Hampton Inn, Motel 6) and the moderately-priced chains (Courtyard by Marriott, Wingate by Wyndham, Four Points by Sheraton, Hilton Garden Inn).

Say you are working with a property like the one we talked about under The Bargain Traveler. If you decide to target The Middle, you could use that property, but would need to do some work and spend some money. Do all the cleaning described, and from there, evaluate your furnishings.

It helps to have some design sense here. If you have none, enlist a friend who does—and is good at stretching a dollar, because there a bunch of things you could potentially spend money on, but you don't want to get carried away and break the bank. Let's go room by room and see what we can make more appealing to target The Middle.

Front Yard

Make your front yard and/or entrance presentable by planting flowers either in the ground or in pots. Flowers are a better choice than other types of plants, because they are cheerful and inviting. They usually require partial or full sun, and are usually annuals, meaning they have to be planted each year. If you can't do flowers, do other attractive plants, or non-plant décor (this has the benefit of not dying and needing to be replaced if you don't water it).

Foyer

As we go inside, we are now seeing the guest's first impression of the interior space. (You may or may not have a "foyer," of course.) What you can do to add welcoming touches to your entry is highly dependent on your individual space, but the key is to show your rental's best face. Ideas:

- ✓ A clean, new rug for the entry. Practical suggestion: put a mat of some kind just inside the door, just to get any remaining dirt off the bottoms of your guests' shoes that may not have come off on the mat you hopefully also have *outside* your door.

- A tall (2-3 feet) vase—not ceramic, something that can be knocked over without breaking—and some tall dried flowers and twigs sticking out of it, like willows or dried cotton branches. You can get a flower and twig mix at Walmart for about $10.

- If you have a big blank wall, put something on it. Large, nicely-framed mirrors can be a good choice for a reasonable price ($30-$70 at home improvement stores). Or find one of those stretched-canvas inspirationals full of words like "DREAMING" and "JOY." You can find these at discount home stores like Marshalls or Home Goods. Art with words photograph well.

Living Room

Your furniture is the main consideration here. It needs to be newer, or at least rehabbed to look newer. Suggestions:

- Find a new-looking couch and comfortable chairs on sale or lightly used. Not thrift store quality, old and clearly from the 70s, but better. A sofa bed may be a good idea so you can sleep more guests.

- Throw pillows. Find them on sale at a home store or Wal-Mart.

- Throws (small blankets). Make sure they look attractive as well as being functional. Again, look to Marshalls, Home Goods, Tuesday Morning, etc. Have one or two folded and hanging over your couch and/or chairs.

- A decent looking coffee table. This is something you can probably do cheaply. If you are a DIY-er, buy one at a thrift store and put a coat of high-gloss spray paint on it.

- Pictures on the walls. Or anything on the walls that looks attractive and makes your walls something other than…blank walls.

- ✓ Lighting. Find a cheap but good-looking lamp or two online. Look to places like IKEA or Wal-Mart and use your design sense to find inexpensive pieces that look like they cost more than they do.

Dining Room

If you have a small kitchen, you can get good deals on very attractive café tables that seat two, or four in a pinch. (I have this kind of setup in the Bywater Bungalow, since the dining area is small). You can get these tables for about $100. You can also get stools fairly cheaply ($50-$100 each, depending on how well you scour the internet or local stores). If you have a breakfast bar, have stools for guests to sit on.

Kitchen

You need to have the essentials. A few things you might want to add if you are aiming for The Middle:

- ✓ A little more décor (but don't crowd your counters!). A cute cookie jar on the counter or a Creuset teapot on the stove are nice touches.

- ✓ Something higher-end for coffee, in addition to the standard coffee pot, like a French press or a Keurig.

- ✓ A more extensive selection of condiments for your coffee, such as (all of these things): sugar, artificial sweeteners (in packets), teas, coffee (ground in a bag in the fridge, AND a few Keurig cups if you have a Keurig), possibly a bottle of Coffee Mate in the refrigerator, various spices (garlic salt, salt and pepper grinders, pre-mixed spices, cinnamon, etc.), a bottle of olive oil or vegetable oil, and condiments in the refrigerator (mustard, ketchup, mayonnaise, Tabasco sauce, Sriracha sauce). I just listed exactly what I offer in my rentals. I have heard from other hosts that the unofficial rule is that you provide 2-3 days of these kinds of supplies to get people started. After that, they are on their own. I provide a supply that lasts much longer than two days, as far as condiments, but guests almost never use much of it, anyway.

- ✓ A welcome basket. It doesn't have to be extravagant, but guests like them. I try to keep mine about $10-$15. I periodically change what I include, trying to base it on what guests seem to be liking or not liking: 4-6 water bottles, a bottle of white wine (the cheapest available from Walmart, $2.86), a medium-sized bag of locally-made potato chips, a postcard, a couple of mini-Moon Pies, and a couple packets of raisins. I used to leave chocolate, but here's a tip: NEVER leave chocolate. All guests will eat it in bed and get it on the sheets. I guarantee this.

Bedrooms

Bedrooms are where you may need to unfortunately spend some money. Bed size is a factor for most guests (though I have found that double beds are not necessarily a deal-breaker). So is bed quality. You do not necessarily need to spend $600-$700 on a mattress; in fact, I don't recommend it. I do recommend spending $250-$300 per mattress, as I talked about previously, or getting quality toppers for your existing mattresses until you can afford new ones. You will also need to have decent beds (as in, frame and headboard).

If all you have are the old-style, minimal, metal frames to hold your box spring and mattress, that doesn't really cut it if you are aiming for The Middle. Those look aged these days and are in Bargain Traveler territory. You should at least have a headboard.

New beds are not as expensive as you might think ($100-$200). You can order them online and put them together. But it's unavoidable—your beds need to be attractive and comfortable in order to please any guests other than Bargain Travelers. A basic box spring and mattress just sitting there, without any kind of frame or headboard, looks "blah."

Things I suggest you have:

- ✓ Pillows, the sleeping kind. Four per bed (except twin beds, which get two).
- ✓ Zippered pillow covers.
- ✓ A *waterproof* mattress encasement. Don't get the crinkly plastic kind, get the softer kind (more expensive at $25-$30). By encasement I mean the kind of cover

that goes around the entire mattress and zips up, keeping out dust mites and bed bugs.
- ✓ A box spring encasement if you have a box spring.
- ✓ Microfiber sheets, white in color.
- ✓ Blankets.
- ✓ A duvet, bedspread, quilt, or coverlet.
- ✓ Decorative pillow (at least one per bed).
- ✓ Luggage racks (the folding kind you see in hotels).

Pillows (the sleeping kind, not the decorative kind), you can buy for literally $4 from Walmart, but those won't last. They will become distorted and mangled fairly quickly. This may be the way to go when you are first getting started, since you need to buy so many up front. Over time, you can upgrade at least two per bed to down-alternative.

Pillow covers: always use them! Otherwise, your pillows will get stained over time. You want your pillows to last as long as possible, even if you are using the cheap kind, and if you don't use pillow covers and the pillows get stained, you will have to throw them out. If you don't, eventually a guest will notice, and their reaction will be... "Ew, gross!"

Get a waterproof mattress cover, but be careful not to get one that feels "plasticky." Guests will be able to feel it under the sheets, particularly if you get the microfiber sheets I recommend. There are waterproof mattress covers that are surprisingly soft and feel like actual fabric, that no one would guess are waterproof. These cost $25-$30 but are worth the expense.

Did I mention microfiber sheets? Yes—buy them. They are not only soft and light, but they *dry really fast!* When you have five loads of laundry to do, it will make your day every time you check a dryer full of sheets after fifteen or twenty minutes and find that yes, they are completely dry.

Blankets: You can generally get decent blankets for $20 at Walmart. Buy enough so you have two per bed. Then put only one on each bed, and have the rest folded neatly in a closet or cabinet. Some guests will need more, and some will need fewer. Do not give your guests more blankets than they need, because some guests will use blankets for non-approved purposes, like to prop their head on while watching TV. If a guest needs something to prop their head while watching TV, well...they can use a throw pillow or a regular pillow. Or their duffel bag or something. But any time a guest uses a blanket, you have to wash it, and that is a real pain because they take a long time to wash and dry. And it's particularly annoying because you know the blankets are probably not actually "dirty," but because people have probably been laying their heads on them, they need to be cleaned before you give them to another group.

Bedspread or quilt: I generally use a medium-heavy white quilt on my beds, over the blanket. It functions as a bedspread in terms of appearance, and also as a second blanket. Plus, because it is white, it can be washed in hot water and bleached.

Decorative pillows: a bed does not look fully made without at least one decorative pillow. But do not put too many, because guests will throw them on the floor.

Extra sheets and pillowcases: you should have at least two sets of all your bedding, including bedspreads. This way you can strip the beds and immediately re-make them, and set your laundry aside to do later. If you have a cleaning person, they will probably charge less if they do not have to do laundry. Drop off a clean set of sheets for the cleaners to put on the beds (or put them on yourself).

Foldable luggage racks: one or two per bedroom, depending on the size of the room and how many people you expect to be sleeping there. Two per bedroom is good if your bedrooms are sizeable. If not, make one available in or near the bedroom somewhere it will fit. Sometimes, other furniture items can take the place of a luggage rack, such as a bench at the end of the bed.

Chairs: having a couple comfortable chairs in the bedroom is a nice touch, if they will fit without crowding. Have a nice throw over one of the chairs.

Full-length mirror: I recommend one. It's likely that your guests are going to be getting dressed to go out at least a couple of times during their trip. They like to see how they look from head to toe. Having a mirror in the bedroom also has another advantage: when one person is done showering, they can finish up their hair or makeup in the bedroom, allowing another person to get into the shower. Particularly if you only have one bathroom, your guests will be less likely to feel your rental has a bathroom shortage.

Specific Products

Other than Nest thermostats and smoke/CO2 detectors, both of which I do use and recommend, I have avoided recommending specific branded products in this book. Richard at the Short Term Rental Hosts YouTube channel has made a video with a bunch of his recommendations, and the reasons for them, that sound good to me. I plan to check some of his ideas out, though his rentals do seem aimed at a higher-end clientele than mine. But many of the suggestions are useful at any price point.

The Upscale Traveler

The Upscale Traveler has money to splash around, but not *wealth*. They cannot afford true luxury, but can afford nice things, what some of us would consider very nice things. Their income is in the top 10-15%, but they also spend too much. Many doctors, C-suite (CEO, COO, CFO, CIO), other successful business travelers, and younger people who have risen fast and want to show off, fit into the category of travelers you would be targeting if you were targeting Upscale.

I am going to exclude whole-house rentals when talking about Upscale rentals because Upscale rentals are mostly—not all—generously sized and appointed apartments at the center of the action, either deep downtown or near the core of the area tourists want to be.

If the Upscale renter weren't staying in an STR, he or she would probably be staying at a fancy boutique hotel ("boutique" hotels run the gamut in terms of quality, but some are very well-appointed, and that is the type at which this traveler would be staying), or at a premium chain like Ritz-Carlton, Four Seasons, or Waldorf-Astoria. Maybe the W. if they are younger and want something less staid.

The economics of the Upscale STR are tricky.

Your STR needs to be in an excellent location (and don't kid yourself that your location is excellent if it isn't), needs to be either fairly new construction or have historic or artistic charm, be in excellent condition from top to bottom, and be furnished with name-brand-quality furnishings—and art as well. Real leather chairs. A sectional that was most definitely not picked up from the Rooms-to-Go Outlet. You can't trick the Upscale traveler too easily, they have an eagle eye for labels and brands, so don't try using a bunch of pieces that look expensive but aren't. (OK, maybe a *couple*.)

When I said art, I meant paintings, not prints.

You don't need to pack every wall with original oils, but Upscale rentals I have seen usually have at least a large oil in the main room and another in the dining room.

In an Upscale rental, each room usually has one or more focal points that say "luxury." The foyer has an impressive chandelier and/or polished marble floors. The living room has a huge picture window with a dramatic view of one of the key attractions of the city where it's located—the Golden Gate Bridge or the Chrysler Building. Or, if not that, something else to make up for it: a painting by a locally-known artist, a baby grand piano, a Bang & Olufsen TV/stereo system. Or, more than one of those.

In other words, things that telegraph that money was spent on them.

The kitchen should have one or more appliances that a middle-class home does not have, like a Viking range, commercial refrigerator, warming oven, wine fridge, drawer microwave, and similar things.

All the bedding needs to be tip-top quality. Down-alternative pillows (actually a better choice than real down, since some guests are allergic to down), high-thread-count brand-name sheets and other features of a bed fit for a would-be aristocrat.

In the bedrooms, and where else there is room, antique furniture (including mid-Century or Sixties if you have a more modern theme, and the pieces are in excellent condition, or newer and highest quality).

All bathrooms should be recently renovated with top-quality fixtures as well. One of those renovations where everything has been done except for the bathrooms doesn't really cut it if you are targeting Upscale. They want shower wands and soaking tubs.

It costs money to make your rental into something that the Upscale traveler is willing to pay a significant premium for over the Middle (probably three to five times the nightly rate), both in terms of owning/renting the real estate itself, and in terms of the sticker-shock furnishings and décor we just talked about. Maybe you can make it work, but I would budget carefully, and make sure your research on what you should be able to charge is careful and thorough.

The Upscale rental is a big bet, and in my experience, the people who do Upscale rentals usually have a pile of cash they could, in theory, afford to lose. Though they certainly don't want to or plan to lose it—they plan to turn it into an even bigger pile of cash—it's not their entire retirement savings, either.

The Upscale rental is very vulnerable to changes in the economy. Your target market is not the truly rich, who can afford pricey accommodations no matter how much the stock market fluctuates. Your target market is the exact kind of people who will take a big haircut at the first sign of a downturn. Overpaid executives who suddenly are not needed when their company goes from flush to belt-tightening mode. Small(ish) business owners who have seen record profits plunge into a sea of red ink. I have seen this happen just in my few years in the STR business (not with my own rentals, which are not Upscale, but in friends' rentals). It is probably magnified since my STRs are in a city that depends heavily on tourism. But business travel and business spending are quickly reduced at this first sign of economic hard times, anywhere.

The Upscale rental is gamble, and I think there is a reason why the people who attempt it are people who can afford to take a hit if it doesn't entirely work out. They have thought through the financials and decided it is worth it.

The Luxury Traveler

The Luxury Traveler wants the finest, and is willing to pay dearly for it. What you need to provide the Luxury Traveler is not merely amenities or nice furnishings, but a true experience.

The Luxury Traveler is more leisure class than the Upscale person, and when traveling, which if they do, they do a lot, they want to be surrounded by accommodations similar to what they have at home. They will prefer a prime location, near shops and sights. But they will also want space, and will not choose a cramped rental. Even if the place is nice, that would be like camping to them. They might have quirky needs that you will have to accommodate if this is your traveler. That's just part of it. If they have an incontinent dog they must travel with, tell them that's OK, but they will need to pay for any cleaning or replacement costs necessary due to the dog's accidents, and some of your things are very expensive (rugs, bedding, etc.).

If they don't say that is perfectly fine, they are not the Luxury Traveler, they are masquerading as the Luxury Traveler, and that is a red flag.

The furnishings, appliances, and accoutrements required for the Luxury Traveler are not that different from those required for the Upscale traveler, but the scale of the rental is larger. The Luxury Traveler usually wants a house or a mansion—again, right in the middle of things. They will probably want off-street and/or covered parking. Fifteen foot ceilings (which require custom curtains). *All* your appliances should be top-end, not just some. Oil paintings in the bedrooms.

I won't belabor it, because I don't think most of the readers of this book will be aiming at the Luxury Traveler, at least not right away. I would venture to say that most people who want to cater to the Luxury Traveler come from that world themselves, and will have an innate understanding of what the Luxury Traveler wants. Such STR hosts probably don't need the money but may want a career in a "hot" industry like STRs and may be looking to build a chain or an empire. If they are funded by family or trust fund money, they can afford to offer this level of quality and service without worrying about cash flow or their balance sheet.

If you really want to target the Luxury Traveler, and cannot tell from what I have already written in this section exactly what you need to do, I recommend that you meet and befriend at least two hosts targeting the Luxury Traveler. Maybe you already have these connections in your social group.

Where to List

If you have a luxury property to offer, you will want to list it on a luxury property site. Much like rich people, expensive properties don't like mingling with commoners. A couple sites where you can list luxury properties are:

Luxury.homeaway.com

Airbnb Luxe.

And word of mouth is always good.

Outdoor Space

I made "Outdoor Space" its own section because it applies to all rentals, from the low end to the high end.

To quote an experienced host, **"Guests love their outdoor spaces!"**

That may sound like a statement so generic it borders on meaningless, but it's a good one to keep in mind. I, for one, tend to spend so much time on interiors of my rentals that it's easy to forget about outdoor spaces (which usually means back yards).

One reason to keep outdoor spaces in mind: having a nice outdoor space can increase your rates, or in a competitive market, can be the factor that makes a guest choose your rental over someone else's.

Think about it: when you browse through 25 listings of 2-bedroom rentals in the $150 to $175 price range, what do you see? Lots of pictures of the interiors of similar apartments. If you're a host, you will even see some of the same furniture from Overstock.com over and over again and even know the prices. Guests may not know the price of the couches, but listings without any standout features will blend into the others.

It's obvious once you think about it, but a really inviting outdoor space is often what sticks in your mind the most when looking at a bunch of different rentals.

If you have an outdoor space, make it inviting. I will go out on a limb and say that most outdoor spaces, rental or otherwise, are not living up to their potential. How many apartments have you seen where the "back yard" is a weed patch full of junk? Probably a lot. How many have you seen where the back yard is a tranquil, landscaped setting, with a couple of Adirondack chairs somewhere near the middle on a circular brick landing with a stone path leading to it? Probably not many, but you can picture it, and it's inviting.

The main reasons that people do not improve their outdoor spaces are money and time. Those are both things that, for most of us, are in short supply.

I'm going to proceed by assuming you are short on both. If you have a lot of money, hire a landscaper to redo your outdoor space so it looks amazing. If you have a lot of time, but not a lot of money, grab some of those "Beautiful Gardens" and "Decks Made Simple" books from the library or Lowes, hit up the scrap yard for inexpensive lumber and things you can make into art (but don't do the plants-in-a-bathtub thing, that is so yuck), and get creative.

Some ideas on the easier and cheaper side:

- ✓ String lights. Cliché level: a solid 10. But compared to a back yard without string lights, at night, your yard will look incomparable.

- ✓ Furniture. Your guests can't use an outdoor space without seating, and preferably a table. You can get a metal table and chair set cheaply online ($99). And people are always selling used outdoor furniture on Craigslist.

- ✓ Plants in pots. This is a cheaper alternative to plants and trees in the ground, because plants and trees in the ground have to be bigger, and bigger plants are way more expensive.

- ✓ Plants and trees in the ground. This is a step up from plants in pots, and much more work in the beginning. The large number of plants you will need, even for a small back yard, will surprise you, as will the cost of plants. But it will look great if you can do it. You may already have trees and plants that can be made to look good with trimming, and maybe then you will only need to buy a few more plants for touches of color or to round out the yard.

- ✓ Clear weeds. If you have a brick patio already, you are lucky. If the bricks are all wonky and messed up, re-lay them, presuming they are not mortared together. If you have a cement patio, clean it and perhaps paint it (not a solid color, which tends to look unattractive, but maybe a grid of colored squares or a herringbone pattern of alternating colors. Get ideas online.)

- ✓ Grass. After pulling out the weeds, put down landscape fabric and then strips of pre-grown turf. You can buy these at many nurseries (you might have to order them). It would be much cheaper to grow grass from seeds. But that can be difficult to get right if you don't have a green thumb, plus you may need to buy soil. Perhaps consult a landscaper for your options.

- ✓ Stone paths. Buy flagstones or cement squares (cheaper) from your local home improvement store to make a path through your yard to a central seating area (so the people can sit in an area surrounded by plants that feels quiet and private).

- ✓ Bamboo "fencing." You can buy rolled-up, 6' high mats of bamboo that you can staple to your regular fence to make it look more exotic.

- ✓ Torches. Be careful that they aren't near anything that can burn. This goes against my own policy of not having anything in the rental that can be used to create fire, like matches and lighters. But if your yard is set up so that you can allow torches that don't burn anything, it's a thought.

- ✓ A bucket full of gravel for guests to put out their cigarettes in, so they don't stomp them out on the ground. Drill a hole or two in the bottom of the bucket so it doesn't collect rainwater.

- ✓ Drip irrigation. This is a DIY project that, once done, takes the hassle out of making sure your plants are watered. It is WELL worth the time and effort. I have done it at both of my rentals and never looked back. Once completed, all you have to do to maintain your tranquil garden oasis is come out periodically and pull weeds, sweep off any patio areas, clean fallen leaves off the chairs, and trim back plants and trees occasionally.

Note that guests or tenants, no matter how long they are staying, will not take care of your plants. They will sit there and watch them die. Keeping your plants alive is all on you.

Income Potential

You may notice that in an earlier chapter called, "So, How Much Will I Make?" I didn't actually answer the question of how much *you* would make, I told you how much *I* was making. It was too early to talk meaningfully about how much you might make, because you still had so much more to think about. But now we can look more closely at what you will make.

A quick refresher: **net income** is your **revenues** minus your **expenses**.

Revenues are all the money coming in from your business.

Expenses are the money you spend operating your business. (Technically, in calculating expenses, you are supposed to exclude expenditures on things have a useful life a more than one year, such as a new roof.[37])

This is a simplification, but for our purposes, it works.

So, how much will you make?

It is important to at least *try* to estimate how much you will make before committing to starting an STR.

This is because an STR inevitably has startup costs, sometimes significant, that are not usually present if you rent out your property long-term (unless we are talking about a broken water heater or lack of a refrigerator).

When you rent out your property long-term, the tenant usually just gets a bare house, apartment, or room, and provides his or her own furnishings, kitchen utensils—sometimes even large appliances. The tenant usually pays the utilities. The landlord pays for insurance and property taxes, and occasionally makes repairs or springs for paint, but otherwise just watches the checks roll in and cashes them. For a landlord, that's pretty appealing.

When you rent out your property short-term, you are going to have to pay for some things up front, most notably furnishing and decorating the property, before you make a single dime. You will have ongoing costs as well, costs much higher than just mortgage, interest, property taxes and insurance, repairs, and maintenance. Short-term tenants are more demanding than long-term tenants, and you can't be lazy and put off fixing things like you can with long-term tenants.

Each guest or group who stays at your STR is brand new, and will be judging your property anew.

If your listing promises two full bathrooms, guests will expect two full bathrooms, fully operational from the moment they walk in until they leave. And this is reasonable. For their vacation, they wanted a place with two bathrooms, which is one of the things that put your STR on their list of options.

Unlike with a long-term tenant, you can't have one of the showers out of commission and put off fixing it for a month or two. (A long-term tenant will not like this, but will probably not move out or stop paying rent over it, either.) A short-term tenant may turn around and walk out, and their money will almost surely be refunded by whatever STR platform they are using. And you will be out many dollars. A long-term tenant would, at worst, call a plumber to repair the shower and deduct $150 from their rent.

First: Calculate Your Expected Revenues

By now you have done lots of searches on the STR platform of your preference (Airbnb, Vrbo, etc.). You have found comps in your area, looked at how fully booked they are (or not), and their rates. Without doing any math, you may already have a gut feeling of what you can charge. Let's say, for the moment, you have a general impression that your comps charge in the range of $85 on weeknights and $115 on Friday and Saturday nights for periods of average demand.

A rule of thumb (gleaned from BeyondPricing.com) is that an STR should have 50% of its nights booked for the upcoming 30 days, and 32% booked for the upcoming 90 days (which includes those first 30 days). The best comps are those with booking percentages in those vicinities. At whatever prices they are charging, they are getting a number of bookings in the target range.

The reason to use these properties as comps is that they suggest a good nightly rate for you to charge in order to get the target number of billings.

If you use comps that are far off from those booking percentages, the owners may either be charging too much or too little.

If seemingly all the comps you can find have lower percentages, and their prices also seem low, it could indicate that your market is saturated, with too much supply (too many properties) and not enough demand. You will have to take this into account when you estimate your revenues.

If you can find comps that are 50% booked for the upcoming 30 days...

...that means your market is probably fairly healthy. Using personal experience, if you are 50% booked for the next 30 days, you will probably ultimately wind up 65% booked for those days.

How does this make sense? Looking at the next 30 days means you are looking at both the coming week and days that are two, three, and four weeks out. That means people still have time to book the days that are vacant. By the time those days arrive, some will probably be booked. So, your final percentage will then be higher than 50%.

To calculate a rough approximation of your revenues, take 65% of 30 days, which is 20 days, and multiply that by $85, then by $115. This gives you two numbers—one lower, one higher—that give you your range of revenues. Using the numbers I just gave you, you wind up with a range of $1700 to $2300.

Now remember that you also get a cleaning fee for each group. Suppose you charge a $60 cleaning fee to each group. (The actual amount you can charge is based on what everyone else is charging, so there's no point in me trying to say what a realistic cleaning fee is. It is very local and, from my observations, not really tied to reality. Look at your comps and charge a similar amount.)

Let's say that, when you are up and running with your business healthy, you will have five groups per month. Now you can add $300 in cleaning fees to both ends of your range of revenues, winding up with a range of $2000 to $2600 per month in revenues.

If you cannot find comps that are 50% booked for the upcoming 30 days...

It probably means, at the risk of repeating myself, that your market is saturated, with too many STRs and not enough guests.

Do the same calculations you did above, but using a lower number of nights booked. Let's say you are finding that the STRs in your area are about 30% booked 30 days out. We will assume that they ultimately end up booking 40% of their nights, on average. That is 12 nights per month. Let's assume for simplicity's sake that your comps still are charging $85 to $115 per night, so using those numbers again, your range for revenue is $1020 to $1380. (In reality, in a saturated market, your comps would probably be charging less than they would in a healthy market, but this is just for illustration.)

Now, the cleaning fees. If you are only booking twelve nights per month, you are probably not getting five groups, you are probably only getting three or four. So, let's say you are getting an average of 3.5 groups per month. Your cleaning fees will amount to an average of $210 per month.

So, your total expected range of revenues is now $1230 to $1590 per month.

If the ranges for revenues you calculated above seem very good to you in comparison to what you would make by renting your place long-term, then proceed. (Remember, this assumes that $85 and $115 per night are what your gut tells you you should be able to charge, based on looking at lots of other properties similar to yours, but without doing any deeper analysis.)

If the range seems similar to what you would make from a long-term tenant, or only a little better, then get a long-term tenant.

Your net income is going to be lower than those numbers, possibly *a lot* lower, because we still need to subtract expenses.

Let's do that now.

Second: Calculate Your Expenses

Here are some common expenses you will incur in short-term renting each month:

1. STR platform's fee: 3% to 8%, approximately.
2. Cleaning supplies and consumables (paper towels, toilet paper): $35
3. Cable TV (basic) and high-speed Internet: $75
4. Electric and Gas: $100
5. Replace linens and towels: $20
6. Replace furniture, broken things: $50 (on average, i.e. $600 per year)
7. House cleaning: $350 to $500.

   TOTAL: $630 to $780 per month, which does not include #1. We will account for that later.

I have estimated the house cleaning cost at $100 per cleaning, and am presuming they are doing all the cleaning as well as the significant amount of laundry (sheets and towels). You will probably need to adjust that cost for your area.

If you are booking 65% of your nights every month, after subtracting expenses, your range of net income is now $970 to $1570 per month.[38]

If you are booking only 40% of your nights every month, after subtracting expenses, your range is now $600 to $960 per month.[39]

And remember, we have not subtracted the STR platform fee yet. We will get to that.

A key factor for most STR hosts with only one or two properties is house cleaning, because it can make the difference between whether short-term renting is worth it or not.

You may be able to reduce your cleaning costs by, after each group leaves, stopping by and stripping the beds and taking home the dirty towels and linens to wash at home yourself, and dropping off clean linens at the rental for your house cleaner to use. (I know I already said this, but it bears repeating.) This way your cleaner will charge you less, because all they need to do is make the beds. Laundry takes house cleaners a long time, and will correspondingly increase what they charge.

Let's say this enables you to knock your cleaning costs down to $65 per visit, saving you $122.50 per month if you have 3.5 cleanings, or $175 if you have five cleanings.

If you do *all* the cleanings yourself, like I do, and save $500, your expenses are only $280 per month. So, your net income (revenues minus expenses) goes back up to:

> 65% of nights booked: $1420 to $2020.

> 40% of nights booked: $950 to $1310.

Keep in mind that you are likely to make in the *middle* of those ranges, because the lower end is calculated as if every night booked was for only $85, and the upper end is calculated as if every night booked was for $115.

The reason I am not simply using a price of $85 for 71% of the nights and $115 for 29% of the nights (since weekdays comprise 71% of the days in a week and weekends comprise 29% of the days in a week), is because weekend nights are more likely to be rented. There's no real way to know what your ratio will be, since it can vary a lot even for one property. I would guesstimate that the breakdown at my properties is in the area of 50/50 weeknights vs. weekend nights. So, whatever number is smack in the middle of each range is the number I would use.

One benefit to doing your own cleaning is that you know your standards will be met. You also know that your rental *will absolutely, positively be cleaned* before your guests arrive.

So, doing your own cleaning makes you more money and can give you more peace of mind. But it's also hard work. Do you really want to have a side job as a house cleaner? Wouldn't it make more sense just to collect checks from a long-term renter and cash them, even if the checks aren't so big? Sometimes, the answer will be yes.

Where to Find Information about Rates Online

Above, I described one way to estimate what you can charge for your rental, and I suspect it is the best method, if you have studied your competition carefully as I recommended you do. By going over all the data yourself, you can make judgments about the desirability of your property versus others, based on details specific to your area.

But there is information available online that can give you other perspectives.

InsideAirbnb.Com

InsideAirbnb.com scrapes Airbnb listings and puts the data they collect into spreadsheets for your perusal. Plus, they give it away for free. Not a bad deal.

Go to InsideAirbnb.com and find your city, then download the file listings.csv.gz. Once downloaded, you will need to unzip the .gz file (it is similar to a Zip file, but uses a different method called Gnu Zip). You may need to download some free software like WinZip to open it.

After installing WinZip, navigate to your listings.csv.gz file and right click on it, then choose "Open Archive." A window will pop up showing all the files that were in the .gz archive, which in this case, will probably just be one file called listings.csv.

Csv files are tab-separated data files that can be opened in Excel. They can also be opened in Notepad or even MS Word, but the data will not be as easy to manipulate.

Double click on listings.csv and it will open in Excel by default. The file will probably contain a huge amount of data. Press CTRL+A to select the entire worksheet, and click "Filter" on the Data tab at the top of your Excel window. In the column "room type", you want to hide any property types that are not like yours. Click the dropdown arrow in the "room type" cell, and un-check any property type that does not match yours (private room, etc.).

Next, do the same thing to filter by "neighborhood," to hide all the listings that are not in your neighborhood. Next, filter by "bedrooms" column (number of bedrooms). By now, the Excel file should be displaying just a few listings.

Now you should filter out listings that are not truly available. Anything with a zero in the "availability_365" column is not actively being rented. Filter it out.

Now look at the Price column, and calculate the average. (Add them all up, then divide by the number of listings.) That gives you the average price being charged for active listings in your neighborhood, of the same property type and with the same number of bedrooms as your rental.

When you calculate the average, if you see that any of the individual prices are extremely low or extremely high compared to the others, leave those out. They will skew your results.

You now have the average price being charged per night for comps in your neighborhood on Airbnb. If it's close to the number you came up with on your own, that's a good sign.

Keep in mind that, though these places are nearby and have the same number of bedrooms, and are the same property *type* as yours, there's nothing in the data about condition or desirability. Those are the unique aspects that it takes human observation to really process.

So, InsideAirbnb.com gives you an imperfect picture, because some of the results may not be similar enough to yours to be considered actual comps. They may be way nicer than yours, or way crummier.

BeyondPricing.Com

BeyondPricing.Com is another tool for STR hosts, but its purpose is more to help hosts price their rentals on a day-by-day basis by calculating demand in the property's particular location.

As an STR owner, you may be sitting in front of your computer at the beginning of summer with no idea how to price your rental for the summer months, except for knowing that Fourth of July weekend is likely to be busy and command a higher price. BeyondPricing takes into account events you may not know about that cause surges in demand, and lets you know that certain dates have limited availability and should therefore be priced higher.

The method they use to calculate their prices is slightly questionable, in my opinion, because what really drives prices is demand, and I'm not sure if they have access to much more demand data than anyone else does. They probably scrape the rental sites, like InsideAirbnb does, but the further out you go from the date being priced, the less data is available about demand, since most people haven't booked yet.

That said, I do use them, since I have basically *no* information about what upcoming days or weekends will be in high demand, except past experience, and I don't have the time or the technology to scrape all the data from Airbnb, Vrbo, and other sites. Questionable information is better than none.

To use BeyondPricing, you will have to set up your listing on Airbnb, Vrbo, or another site compatible with BeyondPricing, then let BeyondPricing access your account and calculate suggested prices for you.

One thing that limits the usefulness of BeyondPricing is that you need to set a "minimum" and a "base" price that BeyondPricing will use as a starting point to determine what your day-to-day prices should be. On days where BeyondPricing predicts high demand, it will bump up prices from your base price, and on days where it predicts low demand, it will knock down your price to either the minimum or something close to it. So essentially, it is only telling you what to charge *relative to what you already think your normal rate should be.*

Nevertheless, it is helpful. You can always take the average price you got from InsideAirbnb.com and plug it into BeyondPricing as your base price, choose a minimum that you are comfortable with, and then let BeyondPricing tell you what to charge. BeyondPricing can actually go into Airbnb, Vrbo, etc. and adjust all the prices on your calendars on the respective sites, too, which is a huge help. Setting prices on the platforms is a large amount of work if you do it yourself, presuming you do not just set base (default) prices for weeknights and weekend nights. I definitely do not recommend you do that, because you will sometimes be overcharging and sometimes be leaving money on the table (for example, if you don't set your prices higher for a holiday weekend).

Airbnb's Price Tips

Of course, if you use Airbnb Price Tips, that's another way to update all your prices in an automated fashion.

The problem is, *DO NOT USE AIRBNB PRICE TIPS!*

Why? They greatly underestimate what you can charge, and you will leave a lot of money on the table.

Why do they do this? I believe it is because Airbnb Price Tips pricing is designed to help Airbnb, but not hosts.

My interpretation is that for Airbnb, any night booked is better for them than a night not booked. They are trying to push you from a 65% booking rate to an 85% booking rate, and they calculate that you reducing your price will benefit them more than if you were to charge a higher price but get fewer bookings.

The benefits to guests of lower rates are obvious, or should be—they save money.

Low prices also benefit Airbnb in that, if prices on the site are low, customers won't be tempted to look elsewhere. Customer acquisition is expensive, and Airbnb doesn't want to lose any if they can help it.

Mark Up to Mark Down

One theory of pricing is "mark up to mark down." Figure out the rate for your place that is competitive for your market, then increase that 30% or 40%. Then mark it down.

Both Airbnb and Vrbo have updated their discounting interfaces so you can finely tune the discounts you offer. On Airbnb, you can choose exactly what discount to offer for exactly how long a stay. You can offer a 20% discount for a one-night stay, a 30% discount for stays from 2-6 nights, a 40% discount for 7 to 29 nights, a 50% discount for 30+ nights, and so on. Airbnb will display your prices, in search, as your regular price with a line through it, followed by the discounted the price the guest will get if they book now (or, really, any time, but they don't know that). It does work. People always want to feel they got a discount.

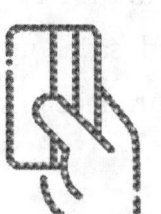

Getting Your First Bookings

I recommend that anyone getting started in the STR business, particularly with a whole-home or whole-apartment rental, have some cash saved up. It's likely you will need some money (or at least credit) on hand in order to get your place in shape to rent, and you may have income ups and downs, particularly at first.

It's a fact of this business that, until your property gets a few good reviews, prospective guests will be leery of booking. There is nothing to reassure them that you are not a scammer or that your place (or you, the host) won't turn out to be awful. Getting bookings when you first get started can be frustrating.

So, in order to get travelers to take a chance on you, you will probably need to set your prices a bit lower, for a while, than the values you spent so much time calculating in your research above. Those calculations were based on you being able to charge market rate for what you are offering. But you can't do that until you have some positive reviews from guests testifying that your place is as good as it seems on paper (or on their smartphone display, as the case may be).

One thing that new hosts often do to reel in guests is to loudly proclaim, "NEW HOST! SPECIAL PRICING THIS MONTH ONLY," or something of that nature, at the top of their listing's description. Letting people know you are a brand new host, and that is why you have no reviews yet and why your prices seem to be low for what you are offering, answers their questions about why you are cheaper than comparable properties and why you have no reviews.

Cash Flow vs. "Cash Flow"

Since we are talking about having cash on hand, this may be a good time to talk about the difference between the term *cash flow* as used in the business world, and "cash flow" in the everyday (i.e. virtually meaningless) sense.

Cash flow as used in business is a critical concept, and cash flow problems can sink a business even when everything seems to be going well.

In simple terms, cash flow refers the amount of money coming in minus the amount of money flowing out. It's like a checking account—very simple. And just like with a checking account, if you should ever go into overdraft, that's a problem. In fact, in your business, it's a much bigger problem than a small overdraft in your checking account.

As one business website puts it:

> Lack of cash is one of the biggest reasons small businesses fail. The Small Business Administration says that "inadequate cash reserves" are a top reason startups don't succeed. It's called "running out of money," and it will shut you down faster than anything else.[1]

Cash flow can become a problem when you have to spend money now but the money you have coming in is not here yet (and may not be here for a while). Having a line of credit or even credit available on credit cards is a huge help to keep you from going under, though obviously, high-interest credit cards can be a trap with their own set of problems.

Both Airbnb and Vrbo issue payments to you only 24 hours *after* a guest checks in, *not* at the time they book. The money doesn't appear in your bank account until somewhere between two and five business days (weekends and holidays not included!) *after* the day the guest checks in.

(Both sites have experimented with paying out funds to hosts immediately upon guests making payment. Airbnb had such a program a few years ago, which I know because I was in it, that they ended abruptly for unknown reasons. Vrbo is getting ready to launch an "invitation only" program where hosts can choose to get early payouts for a fee of 1% or 1.5%. This program, I am not joining.)

In my experience, Airbnb is much faster and more consistent at getting you the money you are owed. On average, in the first half of a recent year, money from Airbnb showed up in my bank account 2.5 business days after a guest checked in. Money from Vrbo showed up an average of 4.2 days after guest check-in.

---

[1] Thebalance.com, Cash Flow – How It Works to Keep Your Business Afloat, https://www.thebalance.com/cash-flow-how-it-works-to-keep-your-business-afloat-398180 (retrieved 9/5/2017).

Regardless of which platform pays faster, it takes time for the bookings on your calendar to manifest as cash in your bank account. This can be a double-whammy if you get off to a slow start. Money flies out but only trickles in.

Because of unexpected expenses, cash flow can be a real problem. Try to save up what you can so you always have a cushion. I bolded that because I know a certain contingent of readers are hearing, "Yeah, yeah, save up some money, I know, I know" in their heads. But this is real. This is business. It's something you *have* to do if you want to operate an STR.

It is also a good idea to map out your expected revenues and expenses a few months ahead; I started doing this shortly after I began short-term renting because the timelines for getting paid can be so long. (For example, people in March are booking dates in May; I have a big expense coming up, and I want to see if I can buy the thing in April, or if I should wait until my May guests have showed up and checked in.)

It can be very sobering to see how low your balance is going to dip (at least, from today's perspective, when you are still waiting for bookings to come in and book all those empty, upcoming dates). You may have $7000 in the bank right now, which feels healthy, but when you look ahead to three months from now, and see that you will run out of money on the 9th of the month unless you get some more bookings between now and then, it has a way of keeping you conscious of not overspending.

If your business is going well, you should, of course, get some bookings between now and that future date, and running out of money probably won't happen. But remember, even with a strict cancellation policy, you can get legitimate cancellations—or even have to cancel on guests yourself if something goes wrong with your rental.

And I know I don't need to remind you what something like Covid-19 can do to your best-laid plans.

Upselling & Add-Ons

Any retailer, restauranteur, hotelier, owner of a car wash, or...well, anyone selling anything, will tell you that upselling and add-on sales are great ways to juice profits. In some industries, they are considered indispensable.

Upselling

Upselling usually involves getting customers in the door by offering something at a cheap price, then trying to get them to buy a more expensive thing instead.

A restaurant may offer a steak dinner for $9.99, but when you get there, you find it's a 5-ounce strip steak. You also see they also have a special that day, an eight-ounce filet mignon topped with crab meat for $19.99. That really sounds a lot better. Sure, you were hoping to get dinner for $9.99, and some people will stick to that, but many won't.

The people who order the filet mignon just got upsold.

Add-On Sales

Add-on sales are similar. When you place your order for that $9.99 strip steak dinner, the waiter will ask if you would like anything to drink. You order a gin & tonic, which, unlike the bargain strip steak, turns out to be $8.00, though it probably cost the restaurant 40 cents. There's a reason why drinks in restaurants (other than soda and wine) rarely have prices next to them. It's a tradition restaurant owners are more than happy to keep alive.

At the end of the dinner, you also order a warm chocolate lava cake topped with crème fraiche for $7.99. Since you are sharing it with your dining companion, it's not really costing you that much, right?

Bam and bam. You just bought two add-ons, and your final bill is now $25.98, not $9.99. But the gin & tonic was pretty strong, and the lava cake was really good, so you don't really care. (If you had also gotten upsold and bought the filet mignon, your bill would have been $35.98—so you did exert some self-control.)

Another common place you see add-ons is at the grocery store, the car parts store, or pretty much any store: all those little items (and they are always *little* items) lining the walls of the checkout line.

Can, and should, you try upselling or add-on sales at your short-term rental?

It depends.

Upsells and Add-Ons for Your STR Business

What would upselling look like in the STR context?

For most hosts, unless they get really creative, there are not too many options. If you have multiple properties near one another, some of which are more expensive than others, and you have a group who has booked a cheaper one but nobody has booked the more expensive one, you can offer your guests the more expensive property for an increased price. Maybe not full price, but you can split the difference.

If they accept the offer, those guests will have gotten upsold.

As for add-ons, I can think of a lot of possibilities:

- ✓ Rent bicycles.
- ✓ Have a mini-bar.
- ✓ Go shopping for your guests (for a fee).
- ✓ Offer airport pickup (for a fee).
- ✓ Offer laundry/dry-cleaning pick-up and drop off (for a fee).
- ✓ Cook meals for guests (for a fee).
- ✓ Offer an "Airbnb Experience" and encourage your guests to attend.

- ✓ Leave tour brochures with your code on them so you get $5 for each person who takes the tour.

The list is endless, and I'm sure you can think of some that are specific to your rental. Price the add-on services at whatever amount you think is fair and that your guests will pay.

The bigger question is, do you *want* to offer add-ons?

The relationship between host and guest is already fundamentally transactional. Airbnb was, originally, very much based on personal relationships between hosts and guests.

Today, the STR industry is more businesslike, with about 35-40% of hosts owning multiple properties and running them like businesses. (The 40% number is from a Fast Company article from 2015,[40] and the 35% number is from my own non-scientific survey, just now, of the first 11 cities listed on InsideAirbnb that were scraped in a recent year. The numbers ranged from 12.6% (Copenhagen) to 57.5% (Barcelona).[41])

Particularly if you are doing a whole-house or whole-apartment rental, and are not staying on the premises with the guests, you too will most likely have a low-touch, more transactional relationship with your guests. But there is still a lingering impression that the Airbnb experience is supposed to be more personal and less money-focused than just renting a hotel room.

For that reason, trying to get your guests to buy add-ons can give the impression that you are just trying to squeeze money out of them rather than *host* them.

I do not do add-ons, though I think the brochure idea is a good one, since just putting your code on a brochure does not really telegraph to the guest that you are trying to "sell" anything. Most guests will probably not even know the code is yours, or that you will be making money if they take the tour.

My reasoning for not doing add-ons comes down to an abundance of caution. In addition to the fear of coming across as money-grubbing, I'm also cautious about doing the add-on I think I would like to do, other than brochures—a mini-bar—is because the opinion of some hosts is that mini-bars are "tacky" and make a bad impression.

I'm not sure I agree. In fact, it might even be appreciated. New Orleans is a bit of a food desert, with a lack of grocery stores in many areas. I have seen Airbnb reviews in my local area where the guests have actually *thanked* the host for offering the convenience of a mini-bar.

And yet, I also know that guests *hate* extra charges. Hate, hate, hate.

But an extra charge that is completely voluntary? Would the guests appreciate having the option, even if they didn't choose to use it? Or would they resent it and think I was a jerk or a price-gouger if I charged any more for the mini-bar items than they would pay at the world's cheapest liquor store?

I am stuck on this topic. Feel free to go ahead and try it yourself, and let me know how it works out (email josh@americanbnb.com).

One additional reason I've never done mini-bars is that I'm not sure it's legal to sell alcohol out of your home. And alcohol is kind of critical to have in a mini-bar.

How to collect the money is also an issue. Would you charge the guest's security deposit, and deal with some of them inevitably saying they didn't take anything out of the mini-bar and shouldn't have been charged?

Some hosts say they have an "honor bucket" where guests are supposed to leave money for things they've taken. My gut feeling is that some of my guests would leave money and some wouldn't, so the whole exercise would be a bunch of work and net out to $0.

Having a mini-bar would also mean you would have to carefully count what was in the mini-bar when your guests arrived and again when they left. And if you were to leave this responsibility to a cleaning person, well, make sure he or she doesn't sneak something from the mini-bar and blame the guest.

So, the conclusion I'm leaning towards seems to be that mini-bars are not practical and are more trouble than they're worth.

Legal (Again)

City and County-Level Regulations

Well before opening your STR for business, you need to look into the regulations in your area on STRs, if any. I hope you followed what I said earlier, and at least found that STRs are legal or in a gray area where you are, and you feel comfortable dealing with that uncertainty.

If your city, county, or state has passed laws regulating STRs, you need to comply with them. The first place to look is on your city's website. Hopefully it has been kept up to date. If you can find nothing addressing STR's on your city's website, look on your county's website.

If you cannot find anything addressing STRs on your city's or county's website, your work is not done. Any website can be out of date or incomplete. Failure by the city or county to have anything on their website addressing STRs does not give you a free pass to operate an STR in an improper or illegal fashion; ignorance is no defense.

When it comes to complying with the law, websites are a starting place that hopefully can help you get your basic questions answered. But no news (i.e., no content) is not good news. It's just a lack of information.

To confirm whether there are local city or county ordinances governing STRs, pay a visit to city hall and find the department of safety and permits or the one that deals with real estate in your municipality. Every city is organized a bit differently, so wherever you go first, if that is not the place, ask where that place is. Don't just quiz the clerk you encounter whose job does not involve short-term rentals and take their word as gospel ("Oh, yeah, I think they're legal now"). Find the office that governs rental properties and confirm with them what the rules are. If the city has a brochure (because something they actually went to the trouble to print is probably more reliable than a statement that comes out of some employee's mouth), it will hopefully also have information about rules at the county level. County rules will probably apply to the city. If they do not have a brochure or a handout, ask what code numbers or ordinances apply to short-term rentals. This is important, and something you should research on your own if you cannot get complete information. Get whatever you can that points you in the right direction. Do a search on MuniCode.org, which is a repository that contains municipal ordinances of many cities and counties throughout the country.

At this point in time, most states have not passed statewide laws regulating STRs, with a couple of exceptions. STRs, from one point of view, really come down to a question of zoning (should they be considered residential? commercial? hotels?) which has historically been determined at the city or county level in the United States.

Because most densely-populated urban areas have relatively high housing costs, and STRs are often thought to make that problem worse, some of our larger cities and counties have already spent years wrangling over whether and how to regulate STRs to best address perceived problems.

Suburban and rural cities and counties, however, have tended to not feel much urgency to regulate STRs, and if your proposed STR is suburban or rural, you may find that short-term rentals lack any specific regulation (though there are probably rules in place where you live governing rental of properties, tenants' rights, and so on. And your city, or its code enforcement department, without any actual written law or ordinance to follow, may choose to interpret STRs as being hotels with all that entails.)

Many cities that are larger and/or see large numbers of tourists have been in the news about their STR fights and subsequent regulations, particularly San Francisco and New York, but also Seattle, Los Angeles, Miami, New Orleans, and many other places. (I just did a Google search, and it's—*many* other places.)

Here's the part where I suggest, in all seriousness, that you consult a lawyer in your area who is knowledgeable about STRs and the laws and regulations that govern them before you begin operating your STR. He or she may keep you from making mistakes which may cost you.

State-Level Regulations

It is likely that if your city or county provided you any kind of brochure or handbook, it addressed any state-level laws. But just to be safe, visit your state's website to confirm that the information you got from the city and/or county is accurate, current, and complete.

State laws will usually apply to, and supersede, any ordinances or regulations at the city or county levels. A lawyer can help clarify these things for you.

Once again, while this book provides general legal information, it is not legal advice tailored to your specific situation. Questions about city, county, and state rules governing STRs are good things to talk to a knowledgeable lawyer in your jurisdiction about.

Do You Need a Lawyer?

I cannot tell you whether you need a lawyer or not, except to say that in my experience, most people who go into the STR business do so without consulting a lawyer.

That said, people who do not discuss their plans with a lawyer knowledgeable about local laws governing STRs run a greater risk of being in violation of those laws, and being cited, fined, or shut down.

They also risk having to go to court, and maybe even to jail. **Yes, jail.** There are municipalities both in the US and around the world that have enacted extraordinarily harsh penalties for operating illegal STRs.

For example, New York City can fine you $1000 for having an illegal STR, with higher penalties ($5000 or $7500) after the first offense.

San Francisco can fine you up to $1000 per day, and hand down a misdemeanor charge punishable by up to six months in jail.

Miami Beach can fine you $20,000 per violation.

New Orleans can fine you up to $500 per day per violation, and also hand down up to a year in jail for your third offense.

Outside of the United States, the penalties can be much, much worse.

In Berlin, if you operate an STR without a permit (and good luck getting a permit), you can be fined up to $616,000 US. Gulp. Those Germans are very strict.

Paris may charge you $56,000 US for violating their rules about STR-ing a second residence. So much for *laissez-faire*.

But Singapore may be the winner for harsh fines (not too surprising, since Singapore has a reputation for harsh laws.[42]). If you rent out a home for less than six months, the fine is 200,000 Singapore dollars ($147,254 US), plus a bonus trip to jail for up to one year.

Long story short, STRs are essentially banned in some cities, strictly controlled in others, and lightly-regulated or unregulated in others.

Talk to a lawyer before starting up an STR.

Homeowner's Insurance

According to the Insurance Information Institute,

> Standard homeowners and renters insurance policies are designed for personal risks, not commercial risks. Some insurers now offer a home-sharing liability insurance policy that can be purchased on a month-to-month basis, but there may be exclusions and limitations, so read the policy carefully. If you plan to rent out all or part of your home on a regular basis, many companies will consider this a business use and you may need to purchase a business policy—specifically either a hotel or a bed-and-breakfast policy.[43]

There are currently a few companies that advertise homeowner's insurance specifically targeted to STR hosts. Two that do are Proper Insurance and CBIZ Insurance. There is also a company called Slice that offers "on-demand" insurance for home-sharing via an app. You purchase insurance for a specific range of dates for a flat rate per day. The amount they quoted me was $6.25 per day, to which they add some fees, making the total more like $7 per day. They count the guest's day of arrival and day of departure as entire days. Still, I looked through the policy and it looks intriguing.

(Just to be clear, I do not endorse any of these insurers or their policies; if you are considering using one of them or another insurer, you need to look carefully at what they offer and how it will work with your existing homeowner's insurance. Make sure to look at exclusions from coverage as well as deductibles, both of which can strongly affect how much an insurance policy is actually worth to you if something bad happens. Check with your insurance agent or a local attorney to make sure your policy covers you for what you need.)

To verify whether your current homeowner's insurance policy covers STR activities, call your agent and explain that you will be operating a short-term rental and need insurance that covers it. See what they say.

Your insurance agent should be able to tell you in detail about your coverage *in regards to short term rentals and short-term rental guests and your and their property*. If the answer is that your current homeowner policy does not cover you for anything related to STRs, the agent should be able to tell you what they offer for your needs. Here are some coverages to ask about (not an exhaustive list):

1. Damage to the building caused by short-term rental guests and any people they invite onto the property, with or without the owner's knowledge.
2. Damage to short-term renters' personal property while staying at the rental.
3. Damage to the owner's personal property (furniture, etc.) while short-term renters are staying at the rental.
4. Personal injuries to short-term rental guests staying at the rental, and any people they invite onto the property, with or without the owner's knowledge.
5. Personal injuries to the owner or the owner's agent that occur on the property while it is being used as a short-term rental.
6. Intentional damage or injury to persons or property caused by short-term renters.
7. Damage to third parties caused by short-term renters or people they invite onto the property.
8. Injuries to short-term renters that occur off the property, while they are staying at the short-term rental (for example, if they injure themselves riding bikes you provided).

Pay attention to whether your agent is unfamiliar with the concept of STRs but tries to gloss over that by saying that anything that covers a long-term renter would also cover a short-term renter. There's a good chance that is not correct, and if they say that, you want to verify it by having them point to something in your policy.

Don't be afraid to go to another insurance company if your agent is not able to reassure you that your STR activities are covered. Going without proper coverage could cost you—greatly. It's not your agent's house on the line, it's yours.

Insurance from the STR Platforms

The major STR platforms have been making a lot of noise lately about their $1 million insurance policies. Airbnb and Vrbo include insurance with every stay, both with $1 million limits.

The two companies' offerings are superficially similar. Just from the dollar amounts they are fond of talking about, it sounds like you should be covered for just about anything, right?

In reality, the companies' policies are not similar at all. Airbnb's "Host Guarantee," in my opinion, is much more reassuring than Vrbo's offering, which is close to useless for the host.

Don't be deceived by the way the $1 million figure is thrown around. What's covered and what's excluded are critical.

Airbnb's "Host Guarantee"

Airbnb offers a "Host Guarantee" which they state is "not insurance," and which comes free with every booking. It has a $1 million limit and covers what they define as "Covered Property":

> "**Covered Property**" means and is limited to the following property located at a Covered Accommodation, or within 1,000 feet thereof, to the extent of your interest in such property, unless such property constitutes Excluded Property...:
>
> - A. Real property, including new buildings and additions under construction located at the site of such Covered Accommodation, in which you have an insurable interest.
> - B. Personal property that is:
>
>   1. owned by you, including your interest as a tenant in improvements and betterments.
>   2. not owned by you, but is in your custody and for which you are under obligation to keep the personal property insured for physical loss or damage.
>   3. not owned by you, but is in your custody and for which you have legal liability for physical loss or damage to the property.[44]

If you read that legalese, you will note that "real property" (as in "real estate") is covered—like your house. That's huge. The Host Guarantee also covers personal property "owned by you," and apparently covers guests' property as well (numbers B(2) and B(3)). I am not 100% certain on these conclusions; to be certain about what is covered, you should discuss it with a lawyer or insurance agent, which you will need to do in regards to your insurance anyway.

You also saw that there was something called "Excluded Property," meaning property that is not covered. That is (as of this writing—it could change at any time, and probably will):

1. Currency, money, precious metal in bullion form, notes or securities.
2. Land, water or any other substance in or on land; except this exclusion does not apply to (i) land improvements consisting of landscape gardening, roadways and pavements, but not including any fill or land beneath such property, or (ii) water that is contained within any enclosed tank, piping system or any other processing equipment.
3. Animals, including, but not limited to, livestock and pets.
4. Standing timber; growing crops.
5. Watercraft (including, but not limited to, boats, yachts, jet skis, and similar craft), aircraft, spacecraft, and satellites. This watercraft exclusion does not apply with respect to any watercraft which is a Covered Accommodation. However, this exclusion does apply to vessels that, at the time of the loss, are in transit, or are moving greater than 10 feet from their usual fixed location and moving faster than one mile per hour.
6. Vehicles (including, but not limited to, automobiles, scooters, vespas, and motorcycles). This exclusion does not apply with respect to any vehicle that is a Covered Accommodation. However, this exclusion does apply to vehicles that, at the time of the loss, are in transit, or are moving greater than 10 feet from their usual fixed location and moving faster than one mile per hour.
7. Underground mines or mine shafts or any property within such mine or shaft.
8. Dams, dikes and levees.
9. Property in transit, except as otherwise provided by these Airbnb Host Guarantee Terms.
10. Transmission and distribution lines beyond 1,000 feet of the Covered Accommodation.
11. Any damage to any property that is not in, at, or on a Covered Accommodation.
12. Real property owned by a party other than you and that you do not control.[45]

The exclusions sound fairly reasonable to me. I don't think I'd expect Airbnb to reimburse me for loss of my timber, my dikes, or my sweet, sweet alpacas (even if I wished they would).

Vrbo's Primary Liability Coverage

Vrbo does offer "$1M Liability Insurance" when guests pay through the platform, but do not assume it offers the same coverages as Airbnb's.

When it comes to insurance coverage, every word matters. On Vrbo's website, a page titled "$1M Liability Insurance" says:

> $1M Liability Insurance provides owners and property managers with **liability protection** for all stays processed online through the HomeAway checkout; giving you $1,000,000 in primary liability coverage — at no additional cost to you.
>
> This means that if you don't already have a liability policy, **this policy responds first if someone makes a claim against you**. If you already have a liability policy for your vacation rental, then consider this to be coverage additional to what you have. It will respond at the same time as your current policy and both policies will contribute if a claim is made against you.[46]

Did you see anything about being covered if a guest starts a fire and burns your house down? Or does something else that unintentionally causes a ton of damage? I didn't.

The website goes on to say:

> **If a traveler is accidentally injured** while staying in your rental property, this program may provide coverage for claims made against you.
>
> If a traveler accidentally damages the property **of a third party (such as a neighbor)** while staying in your rental property that third party may sue you for that damage, this program may provide coverage for these types of claims.[47]

This is not a complete list of what they say the insurance may cover. However, the examples they give of what *is* covered are enlightening because of how limited they seem. Here are two examples of things that are covered, taken from the site itself:

> **Example 1:** A traveler is staying in your property and trips, falls down the stairs and breaks their leg. That traveler sues you for their medical bills and other costs. You would file a claim with the $1M Liability Insurance provider, Generali Global Assistance, and the policy would respond to cover the costs of that claim for up to $1 million dollars per property, per policy year.
>
> **Example 2**: A traveler is staying in your vacation rental and leaves a bathtub running while they cook dinner. **The bathtub overflows and starts to flood the unit below your vacation rental unit. The owner of the unit below you sues you for the cost of the damage to their property.** You could file a claim with the $1M Liability Insurance provider, Generali Global Assistance, and this policy would respond to cover the costs of that claim for up to $1 million dollars per property, per year.[48]

Did you see anything about damage to your *own* floors being covered? Nope. Again, check with your insurance agent and/or a attorney to verify what you are covered for with this policy in place. But to me, this appears to be very spotty insurance for an STR host to rely on. If your homeowner's insurance does not cover your damaged floors because you are renting the property out short-term (and my understanding is that many don't because they consider using your property as an STR to be a commercial purpose), then what?

I think it tells you a lot that Vrbo advises STR operators, separately from their $1M Liability Insurance, to purchase "comprehensive vacation rental insurance," and they recommend Proper Insurance specifically.[49]

Rental Agreements

Airbnb

Do you need your STR guests to sign a rental agreement? After all, they will only be in your rental for a few nights, possibly even just one night. Is a rental agreement—or "lease," if you like—really necessary?

My opinion, and that of many other hosts I know, is that it a good idea to have a signed rental agreement, because it provides you protection in case something bad happens.

Airbnb makes numerous statements on their website and in their Terms and Conditions that legally-binding agreements are formed when a guest books. Airbnb's Terms and Conditions say to hosts, "When you accept or have pre-approved a booking request by a Guest, you are entering into a legally binding agreement with the Guest and are required to provide your Host Service(s) to the Guest as described in your Listing when the booking request is made."[50]

The Terms and Conditions say to guests, "Upon receipt of a booking confirmation from Airbnb, a legally binding agreement is formed between you and your Host, subject to any additional terms and conditions of the Host that apply, including in particular the applicable cancellation policy and any rules and restrictions specified in the Listing."[51]

Airbnb does not prevent hosts from having guests sign an agreement with them directly. Airbnb advises:

> Some hosts require guests to sign contracts or rental agreements. If they do ask you to sign a contract, **they must disclose this requirement and its terms prior to booking**.
>
> If you're not comfortable with the contract, you may want to discuss your concerns with the host or find another place to stay.

> If your host asks you to sign a contract that you weren't notified about before you made the reservation, you can decline to sign the contract and ask your host to cancel your reservation instead.[52]

In summary, make sure to mention the fact that your guests will be asked to sign a separate rental agreement in the House Rules to which guests agree when they book, or somewhere else, such as in your listing description. Airbnb has said it is "easiest" to "include the terms in a message thread with the guest.[53]

They also are clear that they will not assist you in enforcing anything in your contract with the guest.

Third… well, Airbnb kind of evades the question of the guest actually "signing" the rental agreement. Does pasting the agreement into a message thread and having the guest read it, constitute signing? Or does the guest have to affirmatively respond that they agree to all the terms?

Is even *this* enough to create a legally binding agreement? Maybe.

The website for DocuSign offers the following language, and though I cannot vouch for the legal accuracy of this, I know that DocuSign is widely used in real estate purchase and sale transactions in the U.S.:

> Both the United States Electronic Signatures in Global and National Commerce (ESIGN) Act, and the [United States] Uniform Electronic Transactions Act (UETA), have four major requirements for an electronic signature to be recognized as valid under U.S. law. Those requirements are:
>
> **Intent to sign** – Electronic signatures, like traditional wet ink signatures, are valid only if each party intended to sign.
>
> **Consent to do business electronically** – The parties to the transaction must consent to do business electronically. Establishing that a business consented can be done by analyzing the circumstances of the interaction, but consumers require special

considerations. Electronic records may be used in transactions with consumers only when the consumer has:

- Received UETA Consumer Consent Disclosures
- Affirmatively agreed to use electronic records for the transaction
- Has not withdrawn such consent

Association of signature with the record – In order to qualify as an electronic signature under the ESIGN Act and UETA, the system used to capture the transaction must keep an associated record that reflects the process by which the signature was created, or generate a textual or graphic statement (which is added to the signed record) proving that it was executed with an electronic signature.

Record retention – U.S. laws on eSignatures and electronic transactions require that electronic signature records be capable of retention and accurate reproduction for reference by all parties or persons entitled to retain the contract or record.[54]

In their Terms and Conditions, Airbnb *does* say that the legally-binding agreement formed between guest and host when guest books is "subject to any additional terms and conditions of the Host that apply, including ... any rules and restrictions specified in the Listing."

This suggests that, if Airbnb's Terms and Conditions are legally binding on the guest (and you), so are any "rules and restrictions" you specify in the listing. Have you put the text of your rental agreement *in your listing*?

Recommendation (this does not negate the advice to consult a local attorney): cut and paste your entire rental agreement into your listing at the end of your House Rules (which guests must explicitly agree to at the time of booking). Make sure to edit the agreement so that it makes grammatical sense in the context of where you put it. And keep in mind the terminology "rules and restrictions."

Vrbo

Vrbo, by contrast, used to "strongly encourage you to use a rental agreement for each reservation and be sure to include the names of all parties, check-in/checkout dates, rental amounts, payment schedules, and of course, your cancellation and refund policies. We also recommend including house rules and policies around cleaning fees, pets, and smoking."[55]

But that's changed. Vrbo now explicitly states that **"House Rules supersede the rental agreement."**

And yet they hedge their bets, saying that a rental agreement "can help outline your policies and behavior guidelines. If you have uploaded one, travelers receive the rental agreement after booking or inquiring… we also recommend the use of House Rules because potential guests see them before booking or even inquiring about your property."[56]

They no longer post a Sample Rental Agreement[57] online for hosts' use. But they still describe how to upload a rental agreement to your listing:

> **Uploading your rental agreement**
>
> 1. Log in to your account.
> 2. If you have more than one property, click on the appropriate listing. You can repeat this process for each listing you have.
> 3. Click on the Property icon in the left navigation menu.
> 4. Click Rules & policies.
> 5. Click House Rules, Rental Agreement and Cancellation Policy.
> 6. Scroll down to the Rental Agreement section and click Upload Rental Agreement.
> 7. Locate and select the rental agreement on your computer.
> 8. Click Save. Please note your rental agreement must be saved as a PDF file.[58]

Vrbo makes it easy to have your guests agree to the terms of your own rental agreement by including it as an attachment to all bookings (if you want), and having their booking process include a statement that, by booking, the guest agrees to the terms of the attached agreement.

Sample Short-Term Rental Agreement

I have posted the short-term rental agreement that I personally use with guests on my website, at the below URL. Disclaimer: I cannot warrant that it is fit for your purposes, and cannot not be liable if it is not, or for any damages flowing from the use of this document for any purpose. It is an example agreement only; you should consult a lawyer in your jurisdiction for assistance in creating a valid and binding rental agreement for your own use.

http://www.americanbnb.us/sample-rental-agreement.docx

Waivers, Releases of Liability, and Other Contracts

Even if you don't have all your guests sign a rental agreement, there may be situations where you want to have them sign a *waiver of liability*.

Signing such a document means *they* are waiving *their* right to sue *you* for any liability *you* might otherwise incur for their injuries, damages, or other things. So, even though the signer is the one doing the waiving, the liability referred to would be yours.

You may also see this type of document called a *release of liability*, or similarly, it may appear as a *hold harmless clause* as part of a larger contract. Sometimes the shorthand terms "waiver" or "release" will be used.

An example situation where you might want to ask a guest to sign a waiver of liability is if you want to provide bicycles for guests to use while staying at your rental, but you want the guests to specifically absolve you of liability before you give them guests access to them.

(Incidentally, you should have each guest sign a waiver; a person cannot waive liability for another competent adult. A competent person generally *can* sign a waiver for his or her minor children of whom he or she has custody.)

Sample releases or waivers of liability can easily be found online. But because the law of liability (and of waiving it) changes from state to state and jurisdiction to jurisdiction, only an attorney in your jurisdiction can ensure that your waiver is properly drafted to protect you.

If your release is not property drafted, there is a danger that it may not protect you in court.

Taxes

Death and taxes. First, the good news: we don't really need to talk about death. If it happens, the coroner will handle it.

But taxes—*oy!*

If you have not been a small business owner in the past, or if you have not concerned yourself with the tax aspects of your business, well, there is some good news when it comes to taxes: operating a rental property tends to give you numerous opportunities for tax deductions.

The tax rules for rental property do get complicated, and short-term rentals, being fairly new to this world, can be kind of a square peg when you try to fit them into the round hole of IRS rules on tax deductions.

Though tax preparation software has gotten better over the years (I use Turbo Tax, Professional Edition, and I like it), you still may need assistance accurately figuring out what you can deduct and what you can't.

You are operating a short-term rental, as opposed to a long-term rental, which is what tax software has been designed to address when it comes to figuring out rental property tax deductions (at least, as of tax year 2019).

A consultation with a CPA before you start your business will help ensure you get started on the right foot, and that you track all the things you should be tracking in order to get all the deductions to which you are entitled.

A CPA can also advise you on tax-friendly investments and help with things like tax payments you may owe to your city, county, and/or state throughout the year. A CPA can also advise on tax planning approaches, such having your property in an S corporation, that may be able to reduce what you ultimately owe.

Figuring out whether you need to collect and remit taxes, or whether the platform does that for you[59], is another very good reason to consult a CPA.

Now Accepting Reservations!

By now, you have the information you need to actually list your rental on one of the STR and start accepting reservations.

Congratulations, you made it!

This, of course, presumes you have acted on all the important things you need to act on, like reviewing the state of your rental objectively, getting it ready for guests, researching your market and determining what price you should charge, and consulting a lawyer and/or a CPA.

Sync Your Calendars

One thing that can make your life easier as a host is syncing your calendars across different platforms.

Luckily, the platforms mostly allow you to export your calendars, or read your calendars on other sites. (Channel management software can also, of course, sync your calendars.)

So, if you are on Airbnb, you can input the URL of your Vrbo calendar and Airbnb will automatically go grab all your booking information from Vrbo and put it into your Airbnb calendar (not the full information for each listing, but it will block the dates and show the guests' names). And vice-versa.

What Platform Charges the Most?

After you have been operating your STR a while, it will probably get under your skin how much of your money gets drained off by the platforms and taxes. Airbnb is the best deal, in my opinion, charging the host about 3%, though they charge the guest anywhere from 5-15%[60]

(based on the total of the nightly rental plus cleaning amount; for higher totals, they charge a smaller percentage).

Vrbo has two systems for charging hosts: you can either pay 5% of the rental amount each time a guest books ("pay-per-booking"), plus a 3% payment processing fee (i.e. 8% total), or you can pay $499 per year—for each of your listings—and the 3% payment processing fee.

Vrbo also charges the guest 5-12%, based on the total nightly rental plus other fees you charge. My average booking (rental plus cleaning) is around $600, and my average guest gets charged 11% by Vrbo and 12.5% by Airbnb. Neither platform releases a guide to what amount correlates to what guest fee rate. Unless you get a lot of large dollar-amount rentals, assume your guests will end up being charged 11-13% of whatever you are charging them for rent plus fees on their bookings.

You can set up both Airbnb and Vrbo to collect occupancy taxes for you as well. In some locations, such as Portland, San Francisco, and New Orleans, the companies have made agreements to fully or partially collect taxes due and hand them over directly to the government.[61] In New Orleans, for example, Vrbo collects and remits city taxes, but not state taxes.

View this page[62] for further information about what the platform collects, if anything, in location.

Vrbo Example

As you can tell, the charges that guests see add up. All these fees (and taxes), in my opinion, suggest to the guest that you are making a lot more money than you actually are.

Here's the data for a sample reservation on one of my rentals, made through Vrbo for a three night stay. I rounded most of the numbers to keep it simple:

Rental cost for 3 nights:	$361 ($120.33 per night)
Cleaning fee:	$69

Service Fee:	$50 (Vrbo's charge)
Tax:	$54 (to the government)
Damage Deposit:	$200

_____

TOTAL PAID BY GUEST: **$734**

Though the guest will eventually get $200 back, their initial impression is that they paid $734 for three nights, or $246 per night. That is the number that many guests are going to have in their heads. Even if they remember to consider the refundable deposit, they paid $178 per night.

Meanwhile, the host is actually getting only $361 + $69, or $430. This is after having paid $499 for the year to avoid Vrbo's 5% per-booking fee. If you have 60 bookings per year (five per month), that's another $8.32 you can subtract. So now you're down to $421, or $140 per night, not the $178 the guest has paid. If you have decided *not* to pay Vrbo's $499 yearly fee, you can subtract $21.05 (the 5% per-booking fee) from your profit, so now you're only making $133 per night on this stay.

But remember, there is another 3% payment processing fee. Now you're at $129 or $128 per night, depending on if you paid the $499 for the year or are paying 5% per booking. This includes your cleaning charge. (Note that while this example makes pay-per-booking look like a slightly better deal, if you are keeping fairly well booked all year long, it's usually not.)

Though Vrbo has now taken out everything they have decided you owe them, the money-drain isn't over. Remember the $780 per month in expenses we discussed earlier? That chips away at your $128 or $129 per night, too.

Say $129 is your nightly average for the month, and you book 21 nights per month. You gross $2709, minus $780, which equals $1929.

But to a guest, they still have in mind the $246 per night number. Their back-of-the-envelope calculation suggests that, if you rent your place out 30 nights a month (not realistic, but the guest doesn't know that), you are making $7,380 per month! No wonder they keep the A/C at 68 degrees and leave the windows open during the summer. The owner is making a fortune!

Airbnb Example

Here is an example stay booked through Airbnb where the guest was charged almost exactly the same amount as the guest in the Vrbo example for rent + cleaning:

Rental cost for 3 nights:	$390 ($130 per night)
Cleaning fee:	$40
Service fee:	$55 (Airbnb's charge)
Occupancy taxes:	$43 (to the government)

TOTAL PAID BY GUEST: $528

The rental plus cleaning fee comes to $430, just as in the Vrbo example. But the guest pays a total of $528, and that's all they have to pay. Interestingly, this *includes* the $200 security deposit, but that is not shown to the guest, and they do not have to pay it.

Airbnb handles security deposits in a strange way. The owner chooses a security deposit amount, but the guest is not charged for it, and no money stays with Airbnb on deposit. There is no hold on the guest's credit card, either. Airbnb just uses the dollar amount chosen by the host as the maximum the guest can be charged for damages.

If you want to charge any damages to your property against the guest's deposit, you must prove the damage to Airbnb's satisfaction, a process they make lengthy and difficult. If damage is proved, Airbnb charges the guest's card for the damage up to $200. Beyond that, Airbnb will pay for the damage if covered by their "Host Guarantee," which covers some damages up to $1 million.

But back to our analysis. The guest pays $528, so they accurately conclude that their room cost them $176 per night, avoiding the confusion and possible misunderstanding of how much they are paying when going through Vrbo (due to the security deposit).

The host gets $390 + $40 = $430, minus Airbnb's 3% charge, so the host makes $139 per night. That's $10 more per night than the host would have made through Vrbo under their $499-per-year plan (and you never hand to hand over $499 to Airbnb!), or $9 more per night than the host would have made under Vrbo's 5%-per-booking plan.

So, I'm not really seeing any pluses in Vrbo's column, except that with Vrbo, the host gets to hold the guest's security deposit and has discretion over whether to keep any of it.

But don't be deceived that this is a huge advantage: you may be free to withhold money from the guest's security deposit, but do you really want to? Charging someone extra money for something they are likely to claim they either "didn't do" or "it just broke" or "it was broken when we got here" creates a big risk of a bad review.

After a few bad experiences, take it from me, it is better to just eat the cost of broken knick-knacks or a soiled sheet or two rather than go to war with a guest. They will almost never admit to causing damage, and a bad review has a financial cost.

By the way, with Airbnb, the guest's back-of-the-envelope calculation concludes that the host is only making $5,280 per month (30 nights at $176 per night). Still a fantastic amount, but not as much as the guest guesstimates you are making through Vrbo.

No wonder so many people are pouring into the STR business.

Conclusion: Airbnb is a better deal for the host, and gives the consumer the impression they are paying less money. The consumer thinks you are making a fortune either way. With Vrbo, though, if something goes seriously wrong and you do need to charge the guest's security deposit, reviews be damned, it is a frictionless process where you simply decide how much to keep and that's it. You don't need to call Vrbo and convince them you should get to keep money from the guest's security deposit (which Vrbo actually *did* collect from the guest at the time of booking, unlike Airbnb, which sometimes finds it cannot give you money from the guest's security deposit, even if they agree to, because they are unable to charge the guest's card for it). You don't need to call them at all.

Creating Your Listing

Just to make everything crystal clear: your advertisement on one of the STR platforms is called a "listing."

A "listing" is for a single rental of some sort, whether that is a whole house, a whole apartment, a bedroom, a shared bedroom, an igloo, a shed, a tent, or a yurt.

So, if you have two properties available for rent, you will have two "listings."

But could technically have more than that. A "listing" can also be for a combination of rooms or properties that *also* have their own, separate listings.

For example, if you own a three-bedroom house and live in one, you have two other bedrooms you could rent out. You could have listings for:

1. The Entire House (sleeps six)
2. Bedroom A (sleeps two)
3. Bedroom B (sleeps two)
4. Bedrooms A & B (sleeps four).

This route—multiple listings and configurations—will most likely make you somewhat more money than just having one listing and renting the house one way. But you need to be careful not to double-book. If a guest books Bedroom A for one week, you cannot rent the entire house or the "two bedroom" configuration for that period. But you can still rent Bedroom B. You need to be careful to block off everything you can't rent and not get mixed up.

Also, if you are putting these listings on Vrbo, you will need to pay $499 per year for *each*, or pay Vrbo's 5% per-booking fee for any bookings you get for listings for which you did not pay the $499.

I recommend that if you are renting out multiple single rooms to travelers who are not known to each other, you add something like the following to your House Rules: "Many of our guests prefer privacy and quiet. Please confine conversation and socializing to the living room. Please consider the kitchen, hallways and bathrooms to be quiet areas." I'll explain in a moment.

There are more complexities if you choose to have multiple configurations:

1. *Cleaning*. With so many configurations, and people booking different ones all the time, you need to make sure that each day that someone checks out from one of the rooms, or both of the rooms, and you have a same-day check-in coming, you can clean the rental during the window when it is guest-free. This can be source of stress and make you feel like the cleaning schedule is hanging over your head all week long, every day. Keeping the property solely as a whole-home rental will reduce much of this stress, because you will generally know your schedule much further in advance. Groups of six book well in advance, as a general rule.

2. *Guest questions and problems*. Having just one listing for a whole-home rental means you only have one guest or group calling you with questions, issues, or problems. Though I have emphasized elsewhere that, as a host, you need to be on call 24/7, and that is true, most groups who rent whole homes, in my experience, don't have a lot of needs during their stays. My two rentals are whole-house and whole-apartment, and guests on average contact me one or two times during a stay. And it's usually something like, "Where are the garbage bags?"

3. *Common areas*. If you book multiple configurations, you need to somehow keep the common areas clean. Ideally the place should look clean when a new guest arrives, even if it doesn't stay that way throughout their stay. So, before each guest arrives you should clean not just their room, but do a quick cleaning of the kitchen, bathroom, and floors.

4. *Rules*. If you book multiple configurations, you need to inform all guests of the House Rules and ensure they follow them, as you would with any group. But there is an extra twists: some guests will follow the rules, and others inevitably won't. Since these people are not all one big group who know one another, except when it is an entire-house group, the ones who don't follow the rules may create conflicts with other guests. The ones who want to complain about the others will contact you to do it. If your rule is to wash your dishes and wipe down the kitchen counters after cooking/eating, and some guests follow the rules and some don't, naturally the rule-followers will quickly get annoyed at the rule-breakers. You will have to play yard-duty for these grown adults.

5. *Intra-guest conflicts*. Beyond just house rules, guests can have larger conflicts that you will be asked to solve. One common problem is a (usually) female guest getting "creeped

out" by a (usually) male guest. If the male guest has truly crossed a line, like gone into the female guest's room and disturbed her things, you will need to kick him out. You should go through Airbnb for that. But if he is simply "acting creepy," like trying to make conversation with the female guest every time she comes out of her room (and she has started to stay exclusively in her room because she does not want to encounter the male guest), what do you do? Ideas:

➢ Remind the male guest of your rule against conversations and socializing outside of the living room. Put the blame on yourself ("I have to wake up very early which is why I enforce that rule.") If he continues to cross boundaries, kick him out.

➢ Offer the female guest a refund for the remainder of her stay if she would like to stay somewhere else.

➢ Offer the male guest the same. This can get touchy because you should not tell him the reason is because he is bothering the female guest. Tell him you have a sibling coming into town and it would be very helpful if your sibling could stay in his room.

➢ If you have another option, such as a room with its own entrance to the outside, offer to move the female guest there. Consider giving her a partial refund if this means she cannot access the common areas.

Though renting out multiple configurations may bring you more reservations, and possibly more money, expect to keep busy.

Your Listing: The Specifics

Your listing is what sells your property to prospective guests, so it needs to make your place look as appealing as possible, and as perfect for their needs as possible, while also being honest about the areas where it is less-than-perfect.

Among all the skills that are useful to have as a host, a gift for selling, for spinning flax into gold, is possibly the most valuable.

When a guest sends you an inquiry, but does not Instant Book, what you say may make or break the sale. Focus on the positive. Tell them you are sure they will love staying at the rental like so many previous guests have, which is why it has five stars and 54 reviews.

Tell them it's a wonderful time of year to visit your city.

Tell them the location is spectacular and guests love having public transportation just a block away.

And the outdoor space is an oasis of calm lit by beautiful string lights, perfect for having a glass of wine after a long day of sightseeing.

But... don't oversell.

One way to counteract possible overselling is to make sure you are present when your groups arrive, and personally give them a tour of the rental. This gives you a chance to counter any negative impressions they may have with a positive spin.

Here's a real-life example:

Guest says: "The bottom of your tub looks dirty, like it wasn't cleaned." The guest is correct, it *looks* dirty, but it's not dirty, it was stained by a previous guest stupidly dyeing her hair in the tub.

Me: "I'm so sorry, a previous guest dyed her hair in the tub, and the black stain went right into the antique porcelain and won't come out. I've scrubbed it and scrubbed it and let bleach sit on it, but all I've been able to do is lighten the color. I guarantee you, it's very clean, it's just discolored."

Guest: "Oh, I see. That's fine then."

Crisis averted. If I hadn't been there, she would have spent her entire stay thinking I left her with a filthy tub.

Here are some tips for writing a listing that will grab guests' attention and get them to book.

Headline

Your headline is really the only text your guest will see in search results (other than price, number of bedrooms/bathrooms, and maybe square footage), so make it count.

Think about what your property has that is special that not everyone has. Do you have a pool, hot tub, beautiful gardens? 5+ bedrooms? Are you walking distance of one of the most popular destinations in your city? Over time, as you get inquiries and bookings, you will learn what guests value the most, and be able to tailor your headline to fit what you have that the largest number of people are looking for.

But for now, put your best face forward, and grab guests with a couple of your listing's best qualities:

Large garden in-law w/koi pond, quiet, walk to Downtown!

Penthouse views, free breakfast, walk or bike to Qtr!

Historic luxury on Bayou St. John. Water views, location!

You don't necessarily have to use all those exclamation points, but I think they generate excitement. Some reasons why I think these are good headlines:

- Each one contains a visual or paints a picture.
- Each one inspires a mood or feeling.
- Each one mentions why its location is a good choice.

- Each one mentions its proximity to a specific site of interest to travelers.
- Each one mentions something it has that other places may not.

I recommend reading through a bunch of search listings and seeing what grabs you. Write your headline like those. You will also notice how incredibly bad some people are at writing headlines. Avoid writing headlines like theirs.

Don't waste words. Keep in mind that your listing is not being seen in a vacuum, it's one of dozens your guests will scan past in search results before they finally book.

If I'm looking through listings for New Orleans short-term rentals, about 50% of headlines will have the words "New Orleans" or "French Quarter" fully spelled out.

People, you only get 50 characters! "New Orleans" has 11 and "French Quarter" has 13. Those terms use up 22% and 26% of your characters, respectively.

People searching for a place to stay know your rental is in New Orleans, because they searched for rentals in New Orleans. You don't need to waste space saying it in your headline.

Secondly, people who are going to New Orleans probably have heard of the French Quarter and know that it's a key destination. "FQ" or "Qtr" will do. Your guests will likely have seen multiple pages of search results, possibly on multiple sites, before they look at yours in detail. They will have seen "French Quarter" and "Qtr" and 50 times.

Also, don't waste space on generic things guests already know or don't need to see in the headline. The results page states whether the property is a "house", "apartment", "private room", "condominium", etc. Especially if your thumbnail photo makes it clear, those terms probably don't need to be in your headline.

An exception might be if you want to put "garden cottage," "bayou shack," or some other vivid phrase that gets across a key quality or paints a picture. That might be worth the characters.

Photos

Any Airbnb host worth their salt will tell you that good photos, and lots of them, are the most important things to have in your listing.

Guess what? They are right. **Photos are everything.**

You are allowed up to 24 by Airbnb – use them all. And make them good.

Guests want to see multiple photos of every room. If you don't show something, like a part of your kitchen that's just a blank wall, guests will wonder why you are not showing it. Give them enough photos that they can fully picture every room.

So as not to waste one of your photos on a boring blank wall, take one of your kitchen photos that *does* show something important at an angle that includes that blank wall, even if the wall just takes up a sliver at the side.

And don't just take photos of your rooms; take photos of details like close-ups of your pillows and bedding. Not too many of these, but for variety, have some.

Also, make sure your photos are taken at the best time of day to show your rental in its best light. This probably means mid-day on a sunny day. You don't want to have the windows in your photos looking out on a gray, bleak landscape, and you want to show any natural light that your rental happens to get on sunny days.

Taking your photos at night is usually a bad idea, except maybe one of the city skyline or other interesting night view, like fireflies on the giant oak in your back yard. (Fireflies may be dull as dirt to you, but for someone from a place without fireflies, they are exotic.)

Don't neglect photos of your outdoor spaces. Include one or more photos of the exterior of your building, and if it's an apartment, the lobby, the stairway, and any amenities that guests will have access to, like a pool or weight room. (Don't post photos of things guests are not allowed to use, or that you do not *want* guests to use.)

A lot of listings also include photos of nearby attractions, but avoid more than two or three of these. If you only have five pics of your rental but 10 pics of random city attractions, some of which are not even near your rental, that is frustrating to guests. *Why are you showing me the ferry when you didn't even take a photo of your bathroom?* Annoying.

Always make photos of your rental primary. Including neighborhood photos that show nearby conveniences can be good, but put them at the end of your photo gallery after you've shown plenty of photos of the rooms and amenities, including mundane things like your washer-dryer. Even if your listing states that you have a washer-dryer, guests may not have read it closely enough to notice that, or may have gotten confused about which of the last 12 listings they've viewed had the washer-dryer and which didn't. A photo reminds them you do have one.

Who Takes the Photos?

I took all my photos with my iPhone, which has a high enough resolution to capture details sufficient for Airbnb's requirements. Almost any iPhone will take photos at a resolution that more than meets Airbnb's requirements, 1024 by 683 pixels. Airbnb encourages you to have professional photos taken.[63]

Vrbo recommends that photos be 3840 x 2160 pixels, but as of this writing, they will accept 1024 x 683 photos.[64] Photos must be JPG, PNG, or GIF.

If you're not much of a photographer, you can go to Airbnb.com/professional_photography to be referred to some local ones.

Airbnb does not currently allow you to post videos of your rental, but Vrbo does, and in fact encourages it. They even have a tab for it on your Edit Property page, where you can add a link to your property's video on YouTube. Your video on YouTube must have embedding enabled, and may not show contact information (phone number, email address, and/or website).

To Watermark or Not to Watermark?

I have never watermarked my photos, or put any kind of copyright notice on them, but I have heard people recommended that hosts do so because of a certain scam: the scammer grabs all your photos, and possibly even copies your entire property description and details, then takes everything and creates his own (fraudulent) listing, advertising your property as if he owns it. He does not use your phone number or email address, he uses his own, but he will probably give guests your actual property address, so his victims can view it on Google Maps if they want to double-check that a property matching the photos actually exists at that location. Checking your address on Google Maps is something that many guests do.

This scam is terrible, of course, but you may wonder how it involves you, if some Internet thief in Bulgaria chooses to rip off unfortunate people by using your photos.

Well, it involves you because the people being scammed *are going to show up at your property thinking they have a reservation!*

It then becomes your very unpleasant job to explain to them that you have no idea who they are, they do not have a reservation, and please vanish back into the night, unfortunate scam victim.

Watermarking your photos interferes with this scam because no scammer is going to use watermarked photos. If you put your own watermark across the middle of the image, it's basically impossible to remove, and no scammer will use your place as his scam-bait. You've made your listing more trouble than it's worth to use in a scam.

That said, watermarking can be highly distracting, and kind of ruins your carefully taken and curated photos.

The reason I've never done watermarking is that the chances of this scam happening to any given individual seem very remote, and I don't like the idea of my pictures being marred by an ugly watermark. However, I would think the chances of you being a victim of this scam go up exponentially if your property is luxurious and in a desirable location. This way the scammer can charge more and thereby rip people off for more money.

Whether to watermark your photos is up to you.

"About this listing" (Summary)

The first things guests will see if they actually click on your listing on Airbnb are your headline, your nightly rate, the type of space ("Entire home/apt," "Private room," or "Shared room"), the number of guests your place sleeps, the number of bedrooms, and the number of beds. After that follows a Summary of your listing, written by you, of 500 characters or less.

I have always found the Summary a bit irritating, because it is basically a summary of the Description (called "The Space" by Airbnb), which immediately follows the Summary. So, if you aren't careful in how you write your Summary, and it flows into the Description in such a way that your Description immediately repeats some of the things that you said in the Summary, it reads very oddly. So, you have to be careful when writing the Summary that it and the Description flow together in a way that is not too repetitive.

In the Summary, you want to again sell your listing as the best place for your guest, reiterating its key characteristics. To me, the Summary is a bit more challenging to write than the Headline because there's room in the Summary to say more than you can in the Headline, but you can't go into great detail about anything, as you can in the Description.

Here's the Summary I am currently using for the Duplex:

> Spacious 3 bdrm (2 queen beds, 1 double bed, plus a sofa bed), 2 full baths. 50 Mbps Wi-Fi throughout, cable TV in living room and master bedroom, digital antenna in back bedroom. Recently renovated with full, modern kitchen. Located in New Orleans' safest neighborhood, Historic Algiers Point, near the River. Minutes to French Quarter via ferry or car.

I did not realize it until now, but I only used 294 of my 500 characters. But it feels the right length to me. Scrolling through other listings, I notice that many of the other hosts have also used around 300 characters.

This may be because, if your Summary is too long, the guest may feel like they've read enough, and not have the desire to keep reading into the Description, which is where you have an opportunity to list more details about your property and why your rental is a great choice for your prospective guest.

Here's the summary to the Bywater Bungalow; it is only 216 characters. Maybe this one is a little too short, but then the Bywater Bungalow is pretty small.

> Classic Bywater Craftsman, recently renovated with 2 bedrooms, tons of sunlight, personality and history. Full kitchen, central A/C & heat, back and front porches, and large brick patio lit by festive string lights. Enjoy king sized and queen-sized beds.

"The Space" (Description)

The Description section of your listing (which Airbnb calls "The Space," but most people refer to as the Description) allows you to go on a free-form excursion into what you offer, why it's great, and why the person reading it needs to book your place right away.

Unfortunately for most hosts, the Description section is full of pitfalls.

The Description *should* do at least the following:

- ✓ Provide a full inventory of all the things you could have put into your Headline but didn't. Things that make your place special or unique, nearness to sights/shopping/points of interest, convenience to transportation, luxuriousness, nice neighbors, and so on. You can now go into detail. Rather than just saying "2 blocks to Qtr," say, "Just a short walk away from the antique stores and art galleries of Royal Street, the always-open bars and restaurants of Bourbon Street, the festivals and events taking place every week at Armstrong Park, and the upcoming Creole Tomato Festival at the Old Mint." (Make sure to update your Description frequently so it doesn't say "upcoming Creole Tomato Festival" all year long.)

- ✓ Give the guests a feel for YOU. If you are offering a whole-home rental, you may not have a huge amount of interaction with your guests, but at the stage where they are deciding to book your place, they want to know who it is they are transacting with. They want to know that you are nice, considerate, helpful, and dedicated to making their trip as wonderful as possible. If you are doing something interesting with your life, share that. Some people write things like: "As a lifelong resident of New Orleans, I love welcoming visitors to my home, which doubles as my studio where I make jewelry out of sea glass, accompanied by my pet Maltipoo, Joy, and her daughter, Ginger." To me, this is oversharing, but I know I am in the minority. Guests like to feel a sense of "localness" from you, or at least positivity and a sense of welcoming. Not giving them at least some sense of your personality is a missed opportunity.

- ✓ Talk about your neighborhood, including expectations of how the guests should behave. This is a big one, because unless you want your neighbors to hate you, you need to make some effort to keep your guests behaving appropriately for the neighborhood. Describing the kind of environment in which they will be staying helps them decide if it is right for them, or if what they want to do (party around the clock) would make it a bad fit. One ad I read recently said things like, "Nod hello to your neighbors. Miss Julie across the street is always walking her dog, Tom. Tom loves his back scratched. Miss Julie is 84 and proud of it. She won't hesitate to tell you, and even count the years off on her fingers. John and Tami next door have a garden where they grow vegetables for the neighborhood Fresh Vegetable Festival which they put on every year in the park across the street. Make sure to ask them what's coming up, and maybe even make a donation. They would love your used paper bags, or anything they can add to their ever-growing compost heap. And Barney, who lives in a shed behind the house, loves to play his banjo music late into the night. A true Cajun, he is self-taught, and it shows. Feel free to make a request, and toss him a quarter if you can." If you are throwing up a little in your mouth, that's okay, so am I. But guests seem to be drawn to treacly nonsense like this. And it does let undesirable guests know that your rental is not a "get drunk/throw up/repeat" sort of location.

- ✓ Describe the rental and the amenities offered. Remember to let guests know everything you offer (and, when necessary, what you don't). Saying "full kitchen" isn't enough. You're selling yourself short if what you really mean by "full kitchen" is that you provide "everything you need to cook a gourmet meal, including plates, glasses, long-stem wine and champagne glasses, silverware, cooking utensils and implements, a full-size blender, a toaster, a coffee maker and a coffee press, coffee mugs, cloth napkins, a microwave, a 4-burner gas stove, a chef's refrigerator with filtered water and ice dispenser" (etc.). Sell it!

Now, for some things to *not* do in your Description.

First, don't be negative. I frequently see listings written by hosts who radiate the fact that they have been burned in the past. Everyone who has hosted (or guested) for a while has, in fact, been burned in some way or other. Unfortunately, some hosts transcribe their burn scars directly into their listings. Bad strategy.

Often, this takes the form of the host sounding like a strict schoolmarm, with an undertone of all-guests-are-guilty-until-proven-innocent. You can almost picture them holding a switch ready to start whipping you as soon as you violate one of their MANY house rules.

Here is an amalgamation of things I have actually read in listing descriptions, and things I feel like I've read, even if I haven't: "DO NOT make noise late into the night. The couple next door have a young daughter with developmental delays, and it is not fair to them when our guests disrupt their lives. Remember, THIS IS OUR HOME. Please don't slam doors, or show disrespect to our carefully curated Victorian furniture by putting your feet on anything. Many of these pieces are more than 100 years old. And please, USE COASTERS. Water stains wood. All we ask is that you treat the property and its contents WITH RESPECT, and be considerate of the community you would like to be a part of, even if you will only be with us for a few days."

Do you feel like you just got chewed out? Two of those gems are word-for-word from an ad I read earlier today. "THIS IS OUR HOME" is probably the most common, and therefore the worst offender. It manages to sound both furiously resentful and grievously wounded. This is not what you should be going for. I'm sure it does work to scare off people looking to be boisterous, but I wonder how many perfectly nice, would-be guests it scares off as well. *Please back away slowly from the crazy, angry/sad, crying/yelling person*, this ad says to me. I think I'll keep scrolling.

House Rules

The House Rules section is subject to the same pitfalls as the Description in terms of sounding negative and off-putting. In fact, it's worse.

A section called "House Rules" practically *begs* the host to address every possible thing a guest could do wrong, and strictly ban everything that comes anywhere near it.

I myself have been tempted to add another House Rule every time a guest does something stupid or lacking in common sense. (Like…spilling a sugary drink on a wooden table, not wiping it up, and letting it soak into the wood for a week.)

But venting, whether in your House Rules or your Description, works in direct opposition to your overall goal of making your rental seem inviting, welcoming, and like the perfect place for a prospective guest to want to stay.

Avoid having a listing that veers back and forth between obsequious descriptions of how thoughtful you are and how ready you are to meet your guests' every whim, and commands not to wear shoes in the house, eat food anywhere but the kitchen, play the television louder than volume six, and to always greet the neighbors, empty all trash cans before departing, and be utterly silent after 7pm because the owner's toddlers go to sleep at that time.

That said, Airbnb relies heavily on House Rules when mediating any claims or problems between hosts and guests. Violation of House Rules can sometimes allow the host to cancel a reservation, or end it early, without penalty. Or to claim legitimate damages from the security deposit. So, there are things you really need to have in there even if they sound school-marmish.

Both Airbnb and Vrbo have been tinkering with their House Rules sections in recent days. Both now have a number of default rules to which you check "Yes" or "No," or input numbers or short answers.

House Rules on Airbnb

Airbnb first asks you to answer the following questions, yes or no:

- Suitable for children (2-12 years)
- Suitable for infants (under 2 years)
- Pets allowed
- Smoking allowed
- Parties and events allowed

After that is a text box in which you may input "Additional Rules." This is the free-form section where you need to be careful not to go crazy, but also need to put anything about which you may need to someday have Airbnb on your side if a dispute occurs. These are the rules I am currently using, though I do tinker with them, depending on what bad things guests have been doing recently:

- Check-in time: 4pm
- Check-out time: 11am
- Late check-out policy: $50 per hour charge for late checkout.
- No smoking
- No pets
- No parties or events
- The number of people permitted on the property is limited to the number of guests stated at the time of booking
- Quiet Hours are 10am-7pm (noise should not be audible from outside the rental during those times)
- Booking guest must be 25 or older, as confirmed by government-issued photo ID. Guests from the local area must contact the host in advance of booking.
- Please keep exterior doors and windows closed and locked.
- Travelers' insurance and trip cancellation policies are highly recommended; host cannot be liable for injuries, damages, or losses incurred by guests, of any kind. These policies are available from insurers.

- The rental is regularly treated for pests by a professional exterminating company, which includes placing of traps and bait which are harmful to humans and animals if ingested.
- Animals must be licensed and permitted as required by the City of New Orleans, and a copy of any health certificate required under New Orleans Municipal Code Sec. 18-202(b) must be provided to Host at the time of booking.
- The following fees will apply as appropriate: smoking of any kind in the rental, $500 cleaning charge. Cost to replace keys: $50 per key. Extra cleaning charge for cleanings that require more than 4 hours: $75 per hour.
- By booking this rental, guest agrees to be bound by the terms of the Louisiana Short-Term Rental Agreement electronically provided herein.
- (Include the entire text of your Short-Term Rental Agreement here)

The Quiet Hours period I used follows from my local zoning rules. You should look into yours to see if your municipality has regulations about reducing noise levels during certain hours. Having your Quiet Hours backed up by local ordinance can be helpful when asking rowdy guests to keep down the noise.

Make sure to also include any important rules specific to your rental.

Though Airbnb has a Policies section under Booking Settings on the page where you edit your listing which asks for your "check-in window," checkout time, and cancellation policy, I always put the check-in and checkout information at the top of my House Rules so guests have a second chance to see it. Then I put it in my welcome message I send right after they book, and in the message I send them the day before or day of their arrival with check-in information. This is so they will be sure to see it. People who arrive hours early then act indignant and wait around the property until check-in time are not pleasant to deal with.

You are also required to check "yes" or "no" next to each of the following on the House Rules page. For surveillance, you are given a text box to "specify each device's location and whether it will be on or off." If you checked "yes," you'd better do that or they will suspend your listing.

- Must climb stairs
- Potential for noise
- Pet(s) live on property

- No parking on property
- Some spaces are shared
- Amenity limitations
- Surveillance or recording devices on property
- Weapons on property
- Dangerous animals on property.

House Rules for Vrbo

Vrbo has recently tried to simplify their House Rules section so that you are mostly answering questions, and your ability to make up your own rules is severely limited. The saving grace is that, with Vrbo, you *can* attach a rental agreement (or any other attachment you want) that guests will have access to and must agree to *before* booking. This is a major positive for the Vrbo platform.

Here are the standard questions Vrbo asks you to answer:

- Property Cancellation Policy (choose one)
  - Relaxed – if guest cancels 14+ days ahead of arrival they get a 100% refund; 7-14 days ahead, 50% refund.
  - Moderate – cancel 30+ days ahead, 100% refund; 14+ days ahead, 50% refund.
  - Firm – cancel 60+ days ahead, 100% refund); 30+ days ahead, 50% refund.
  - Strict – cancel 60+ days ahead, 100% refund.
  - None -- No refunds.
- Check in after (choose time)
- Check out before (choose time)
- Max. occupancy
  - Total travelers (input number)
  - Max adults (input number)
- Min. age of primary renter (input number)
- Parties/events allowed (yes/no)
- Pets allowed (yes/no)

- Children allowed (yes/no)
- Smoking allowed (yes/no)

After that, you can input three Additional Rules of up to 150 characters each. I have used the 150 characters to actually put multiple rules into each box, as follows:

(Rule 1)

NO SMOKING. NO ALCOHOL OUTDOORS.

NO EVENTS/PARTIES/VISITORS. NO CONGREGATING ON FRONT PORCH/STEPS AFTER DARK. NO PETS. THIS IS NOT A "PARTY HOUSE."

(Rule 2)

MAX. OF EIGHT (8) BOOKED GUESTS MAY BE ON THE PROPERTY AT ANY TIME.

GUESTS/GROUPS WHO VIOLATE HOUSE RULE(S) MAY BE ASKED TO VACATE. KEEP EXT DOORS/WINDOWS CLOSED/LOCKED

(Rule 3)

LATE CHECK-OUT: $50/HR CHARGE.

MIN AGE TO BOOK, 25.

GUESTS AGREE TO TERMS OF RENTAL AGREEMENT PROVIDED.

TRAVELERS INSURANCE IS HIGHLY RECOMMENDED.

Vrbo also has a space for you to write a "Note for Traveler" below your answers to the Parties, Pets, Children, and Smoking questions, in case you want to clarify whether you have any flexibility on those or make any comments. I answered "Yes" for "children allowed," and added the note "Home is not child-proofed."

(Dis)Allowing Children & Infants

Disallowing children and/or infants in your rental without a valid reason could violate the federal Fair Housing Act, and possibly other federal and state laws, so it is best to consider carefully whether you want to do that. Here we will talk about the federal Fair Housing Act, but keep in mind that your state may have additional rules and you need to abide by them.

You are generally exempt from the Fair Housing Act, according to Nolo.com[65], when you rent out units in a building with four or fewer apartments where *you actually live in one of them.* (But keep reading—even if you are exempt, there are things you *cannot* do, so you need to be careful.)

You are also exempt if you rent out a single-family home without a broker. But is Airbnb a broker? Not clear.

The Fair Housing Act states, in part:

> [I]t shall be unlawful--
>
> (a) To refuse to sell or rent after the making of a bona fide offer, or to refuse to negotiate for the sale or rental of, or otherwise make unavailable or deny, a dwelling to any person because of race, color, religion, sex, **familial status**, or national origin.
>
> (b) To discriminate against any person in the terms, conditions, or privileges of sale or rental of a dwelling, or in the provision of services or facilities in connection therewith, because of race, color, religion, sex, **familial status**, or national origin.
>
> (c) To make, print, or publish, or cause to be made, printed, or published any notice, statement, or advertisement, with respect to the sale or rental of a dwelling that indicates any preference, limitation, or discrimination based on race, color, religion, sex, handicap, **familial status**, or national origin, or an intention to make any such preference, limitation, or discrimination.

> (d) To represent to any person because of race, color, religion, sex, handicap, **familial status**, or national origin that any dwelling is not available for inspection, sale, or rental when such dwelling is in fact so available.[66]

Discriminating against someone based on "familial status" includes discriminating because they have children under the age of 18, or are pregnant.

But there's another wrench in the works: even if you are exempt from the Fair Housing Act's requirements, *you may not include discriminatory statements in your advertising*.

In other words, even if you are exempt from Fair Housing Act rules regarding discrimination based on familial status, you can't advertise in a way that discriminates based on familial status.

Would that include answering "No" to the "Children allowed" or "Infants allowed" questions in your listing(s) on Airbnb or Vrbo? Maybe or maybe not.

There have been a [number of court cases](#)[67] that have found that the FHA applies to "dwellings," and STRs are not dwellings, so the ban on discrimination based on familial status does not cover STRs. However, to my knowledge, none of these cases have been at an appellate court level and therefore have not created any binding precedents. Meaning, none of this is settled law.

My thinking is that, to be on the safe side, hosts in the USA should *not* choose "no" to "Children allowed" or "Infants allowed," because if you were to answer "no," you would be making a statement in your listing (an advertisement) that you do not allow guests under the age of 18. This is just my opinion, and is not intended to be legal advice regarding your own situation. Consult a local lawyer.

Why would STR platforms even offer you the option to answer "yes" or "no" to these questions, if it were not legal to discriminate based on familial status? It could be because they think the word "suitable" protects them. That's just a guess. Another reason could be that the platforms have listings that are worldwide, and laws vary from country to country. Hosts should, naturally, not choose answers that would put them in violation any of their countries' laws.

Pets

You may notice I put "no pets" in my House Rules. Whether to accept pets or not is a decision you must make and then stick to it. You can't go back and forth. If you do accept pets, even some of the time, you MUST inform prospective guests that pets are sometimes present in the rental.

(For purposes of this section, assume we are talking only about *pets*, not "service animals" or "assistance animals" as defined by various laws or by Airbnb. We will address those animals in the next chapter.)

This is important for several different reasons:

Allergies. Some guests are allergic, and cannot tolerate pet dander, hair, or other allergens. Even if the previous guest's pet has gone, they may have left behind allergens which your current guest cannot tolerate.

Indoor Pest Control. If you live in an area like I do (New Orleans), pest control is a major concern. Most New Orleans landlords take a multi-pronged approach to roaches and Palmetto bugs, the two main bugs that infest dwellings in the area, which includes spraying, traps and roach-killing gel. (I know, gross, but it's important.) **The bait is poisonous to pets, and often there is no practical way for you to locate and remove all of it.** A dog's sense of smell is 100 times better than a human's, so if you miss one Roach Motel, you can be sure a dog will find it.

Outdoor Pest Control. Similarly, snail- and slug bait is highly attractive, and *highly* toxic, to pets. Dogs tend to ingest it more often than cats, but it is deadly to both.[68] If you have any outdoor plants that pets have a chance of encountering, and are in the habit of spreading snail and slug bait, this could put guests' pets at risk. Particularly if the bait gets rained on, or if you are tossing it into bushes or tangled plants, your chances of being able to remove it all before guests arrive with pets are nil.

The above is, of course, not an exhaustive list of possible dangers to pets.

If you are going to allow pets, you need to make very clear to guests that pets may have been present in the rental as little as a few hours before their arrival, and you need to come up with pest-control measures that will not put pets at risk.

Personally, because of the climate I live in, I have to choose either allowing roaches or allowing pets. It's not a hard decision.

In addition to safety, there are the smell and mess issues. Even if most pets are well-behaved, some won't be.

Another issue for STR hosts that you might not think about right out of the gate is that, when you allow something and you are in the minority, you won't just get a couple of guests, periodically, who are seeking that feature. You will find that *almost all* of your guests are seeking that feature.

If you are one of a comparatively few rentals that accept pets, an unusually large percentage of your guests *will* have pets. That's just how it works. If you sleep six, you will get lots of parties with five or six. You will not get parties of one. If you accept pets, and most STRs in your area do not, you won't get a guest with a pet once in a blue moon. You'll get guests with pets almost every time.

But then again, if your rental is one that can handle the extra wear and tear, and you don't mind a bit of extra cleaning, and you've figured out a magical way to mostly get rid of pet odors, accepting pets could be a good angle for increasing your bookings.

In a market with too much supply and not enough demand, allowing pets may be something that allows you to thrive where others cannot.

Pot Smoking

As of this writing, many states have legalized marijuana for recreational or medical purposes. However, many states have not. Additionally, marijuana is illegal at the federal level and classified as a Schedule I drug, meaning it has a high potential for abuse, has no currently accepted medical use, and is not accepted as safe for use under medical supervision. Federal law supersedes state law, so it is misleading to discuss marijuana as "legal" anywhere in the United States.

Regardless, host opinions tend to cluster around highly against or highly tolerant of pot use on their premises. The best thing you can probably do as a host is to extend your rule "no smoking" to "no smoking or vaping of any substances." Because it is becoming so ingrained in US thinking that pot use is either legal or should be legal, lecturing guests about the legality of weed in your area is probably not a road you want to go down. Instead, if you do not want pot used on your premises, treat it like smoking and make your House Rules on the subject clear.

Service Animals, Emotional Support Animals, Therapy Animals

The Americans with Disabilities Act (ADA), the Fair Housing Act (FHA), and the Rehabilitation Act of 1973 are federal laws that require housing providers to allow, under certain circumstances, people with disabilities to bring service animals and "assistance animals" (we will get into the difference shortly) with them while staying at rental property, even if the provider does not otherwise allow animals.

These laws disallow any extra charges or deposits for these working animals, even if such charges and/or deposits are applied to other tenants with pets.

Housing providers *are* permitted to charge tenants for damage caused by their working animals beyond normal wear and tear, but only if it is the property owner's normal practice to charge tenants for damage.[69]

Your state may have its own laws with further rules on this subject. To go into every state's laws is beyond the scope of this book, but you do need to be sure you are in compliance with them. To find out the laws of your state, start at the Regional ADA Center for your area. And talk to a local attorney.

There are significant restrictions on your ability to say "no" to working animals.

ADA

ADA uses the term "service animal" to describe animals that meet its criteria. I will refer to animals that meet these criteria as "ADA-defined service animals."

ADA law gets complex, but know these key points:

1. **Service animals are defined as dogs that are individually trained to do work or perform tasks for people with disabilities**.
2. The work or task(s) **must be directly related** to the person's disability.
3. Generally, [government and businesses] must allow service animals to accompany people with disabilities in all areas of the facility where the public is allowed to go.[70]

To repeat, an ADA-defined service animal must be a **dog**, and it must be **trained to do work or perform tasks directly related to the person's disability.**

ADA gives the following examples of qualifying work and tasks:

- Guiding people who are blind
- Alerting people who are deaf
- Pulling a wheelchair
- Alerting and protecting a person who is having a seizure
- Reminding a person with mental illness to take prescribed medications
- Calming a person with Post Traumatic Stress Disorder (PTSD) during an anxiety attack, or
- Performing other duties.[71]

Dogs "whose sole function is to provide comfort or emotional support do not qualify as service animals under the ADA."[72] Note the word "sole." If an animal provides comfort *and* is individually trained to perform a task directly related to the person's disability, it *can* be an ADA-defined service animal.

You can only ask two questions about a person's service animal, and only when it is "not obvious" that a service animal is required because of a disability and what work it performs. (A good example of "obvious" is a guide dog for a person you know, or can tell, is blind):

(1) is the dog a service animal required because of a disability?

(2) what work or task has the dog been trained to perform?

> [You] cannot ask about the person's disability, require medical documentation, require a special identification card or training documentation for the dog, or ask that the dog demonstrate its ability to perform the work or task.[73]

Just to make that perfectly clear, in regards to ADA-defined service animals, *all you are allowed to ask is*:

1. **"Is the dog a service animal required because of a disability?"** and
2. **"What work or task has the dog been trained to perform?"**

If a person answers the second question by saying that the dog has not been trained to perform anything, then it is *not* an ADA-defined service animal. ®

Some more things you cannot do beyond asking the two questions above:

➢ Ask about the person's disability
➢ Require medical documentation
➢ Require a special identification card or training documentation for the dog, or
➢ Ask that the dog demonstrate its ability to perform the work or task.[74]

You can only ask that a legitimate service animal be removed from the premises if the dog is out of control and the handler does not take effective action to control it, or the dog is not housebroken.

This is important, and often misunderstood, since—you would think—a person with a service animal would receive *some* kind of certificate or card from the government identifying the dog and its purpose. They don't.

Adding to the confusion, there are many official-sounding organizations online that will happily sell *literally anyone* a certificate or card saying an animal is a service animal, emotional support animal, or therapy animal.

For example, if you Google "register service animal," one of the first results you will probably see leads to an official-looking page with a government-style badge at the top, and it has a

".org" domain name. The site is doing everything it can to look "official," governmental, and/or nonprofit (for example, by using a ".org" domain name, which does not actually indicate nonprofit status; anyone can register one and use it for any purpose).

On the site's home page, you can select whether your dog is a service animal, emotional support animal, or therapy animal, and order a kit that includes "lifetime registration," a certificate and ID card (both of which will include your name and the name and a photo of the dog, which you will be prompted to upload) and a service dog tag. You will also be offered the chance to buy add-ons like a "service dog collar," "service dog leash," "service dog pouch," card holder and lanyard (to "wear around [your] neck for easy identification"), and a service dog vest.

You won't need to provide any documentation of any kind. Just your credit card and a couple hundred bucks.

Adding still more to the confusion, an animal's owner may be led to believe, by the fact that they have been permitted to purchase all these official-seeming items, that their animal *has now been officially registered with the government and does in fact have official status as a service animal.*

It can be difficult and awkward to tell a guest who presents you with a card stating that their animal is a registered service/emotional support/therapy animal that the card means nothing.

I wish I could give you a one-size-fits-all instruction on what to do. I highly recommend reading the ADA's document on Service Animals at ada.gov/service_animals_2010.pdf (it's only three pages). Because the confusion around service animals is so great, and the rules are complicated, it's good to have a firm grip on the rules for when these situations come up. Talk to a local attorney if you have questions about the subject.

FHA and Section 104

But wait, there's more.

The FHA and Section 504 of the Rehabilitation Act of 1973 both address "housing providers' obligations...to provide reasonable accommodations to persons with disabilities."[75]

Both laws require housing providers to accommodate not only ADA-defined service animals, but also what FHA and Section 504 refer to as "assistance animals," which are "other animals that do work, perform tasks, provide assistance, and/or provide therapeutic emotional support for individuals with disabilities (referred to in this guidance as a 'support animal.'"[76][77]

Unlike the ADA, neither FHA nor Section 104 require that assistance animals be individually trained, or that they be dogs.[78]

The U.S Department of Housing and Urban Development ("HUD") published a notice on January 28, 2020, "[Assessing a Person's Request to Have an Animal as a Reasonable Accommodation under the Fair Housing Act](#)."[79]

The linked document is something I recommend you take a look at, and if it is too complicated for you, consult a lawyer to help you understand it. HUD tried to make it straightforward, but any time you are required to use a 5-part, 8-step process to determine whether you must allow an assistance animal for a given person, it can get confusing.

But there is reason for optimism: FHA rules apply to "dwellings," and a number of courts have been finding that the FHA's definition of "dwelling" does not apply to short-term rentals.

This appears to be a genuine trend. The 11th Circuit Court of Appeals (governing Alabama, Georgia and Florida) wrote: "the more occupants treat a building like their home [and] the longer the typical occupant lives in a building, the more likely it is that the building is a 'dwelling.'" While the interpretation is only binding on the states listed, any federal circuit court opinion is usually highly influential on other courts.

But then, the 11th Circuit (along with the 5th Circuit) is considered one of the most conservative, so another Circuit Court may not be persuaded by them, and reach the exact opposite conclusion.

My sense, so far, is that courts are concluding that the FHA rules on assistance animals were written with long-term renters in mind. But I still encourage you to read the "Assessing" document and consult a lawyer about any questions.

A Word of Warning

I hate saying this, but when it comes to Airbnb and assistance animals, you have one or two hands tied behind your back if you don't want to host them or their owners.

Though Airbnb does *not* have the power to take away your rights to request documentation for assistance animals as allowed under FHA and Section 104, it *does* have the power to take your listing off Airbnb if you do not operate in accordance with Airbnb's policies.

(Vrbo does not have its own animal-accommodation rules, which means that you only have to follow the ADA, FHA, and Section 504 rules already described, as well as any state or local rules, or other federal rules I may have missed.)

"Assistance animal," as defined by Airbnb, includes ADA-defined service animals, *and also* "emotional support animals," "comfort animals" and "therapy animals."

Airbnb's website is unclear on what you are allowed to ask guests about "assistance animals." Their webpage on the subject switches to using the word "service animal" when discussing what you may ask guests, and simply restates the two questions that the ADA allows you to ask guests with disabilities about their service animals.

In other words, they are unclear on the question of whether you have greater leeway to ask for documentation about assistance animals than about ADA-defined service animals.

However, in my experience, they operate as if you *are not* permitted to ask for documentation for *any* service- or assistance animal.

Here is the heart of Airbnb's policy:

> **Are hosts required to accept assistance animals?**
>
> Generally, yes, unless there is a threat to health or safety ... At Airbnb, we acknowledge that assistance animals are not the same as

pets and serve a crucial function for their owner. As stated in our Nondiscrimination Policy, hosts are expected to reasonably accommodate reservations where an assistance animal may be present, even if their listing/house rules state "no pets".[80] ...

Is it okay to request documentation for an assistance animal?

Airbnb does not require documentation when traveling with an assistance animal.[81]

While the language "Airbnb does not require documentation" does not clearly state that *hosts* cannot ask guests for documentation, in my experience, it has been applied to mean that: **hosts may not ask guests for any documentation regarding assistance animals, period.**

(When I say "in my experience," I mean in my own personal experience, this past month, being told by an Airbnb rep that I could not ask a guest for any documentation about her assistance animal. I had already determined that the animal was not an ADA-defined service animal, by asking the guest whether the dog was trained to assist her in any work or task, and the guest gave a clear "no." Airbnb might well argue that the rep was wrong and that is not their policy, but if that is the case, they should clarify their help pages to provide better guidance to both hosts and guests.)

Hosts of shared spaces will be relieved to hear that Airbnb's rules are not as restrictive for them.

> [I]f your listing includes a shared space and an assistance animal would create a health or safety hazard to you or others (e.g. allergies and pets who are unable to share space with other animals due to a safety concern), we will not require you to host the guests with the assistance animal.[82]

Miniature Horses

I won't spend a lot of time on this, because it is extremely uncommon, but miniature horses have recently become eligible to serve as ADA-defined service animals. The rules are much like those for dogs—the miniature horse must have been "individually trained to do work or perform tasks for people with disabilities."[83] Housing providers must accommodate miniature horses much as they must accommodate service dogs, "where reasonable." The factors in assessing reasonableness are:

> (1) whether the miniature horse is housebroken;

> (2) whether the miniature horse is under the owner's control;

> (3) whether the facility can accommodate the miniature horse's type, size, and weight; and

> (4) whether the miniature horse's presence will not compromise legitimate safety requirements necessary for safe operation of the facility.[84]

I suspect that miniature horses will not catch on as dogs have, so it's not something I would spend too much time worrying about for now.

It May Get Worse Before It Gets Worse

I think Airbnb's assistance animal policy, because it does not allow the host to ask for *any documentation at all*, has a great potential for abuse.

I have noticed, just in the past couple of months, an increase in people sending me inquiries on Airbnb before booking and saying that they have a therapy/support/comfort animal of some kind (never the ADA- defined service animal kind) and asking if it will be a problem.

As we have learned, if you want to follow Airbnb's policy, you cannot just respond, "The listing says, 'no pets,' that means NO PETS!"

I suspect it has begun to spread among travelers that hosts are essentially not allowed to say no.

So, what can you do?

Local Rules and Regulations about Animals

Well, one thing to note is that federal law *does not* exempt service animals from local rules on registration and permitting of animals. Airbnb certainly does not have the power to do that, either.

In fact, according to its own website, "Airbnb recognizes that some jurisdictions may require prohibitions on all animals, including assistance animals, and **we do not require hosts to violate local laws or take actions that may subject them to legal liability**."[85]

One thing about travelers staying at your STR is that they tend to come from outside your city. Does your city have licensing requirements for animals? Mine does. Cat and dog owners must comply with New Orleans Municipal Code, Sec. 18-202(b), which I read as being very helpful to STR hosts:

> Any cat or dog **brought into Orleans Parish from outside the State of Louisiana** must have a health certificate from a licensed veterinarian in the state from which they came, issued no more than 30 days prior to arrival in Louisiana, certifying that the animal is free from contagious diseases. Certification shall be filed with the [city/parish] within ten days of arrival in the City of New Orleans.
>
> (1) For dogs, this means the dog has been vaccinated for rabies, distemper, hepatitis, parvo virus, parainfluenza, and bordatella."[86]

Notice that the bolded words do not say the rule only applies to cats and dogs that have been brought into Orleans Parish to reside indefinitely. It says "brought into," period.

Also notice, on the negative side, that the law does not say that an out-of-state pet owner must prove to an STR host (or anyone) that the animal has been certified free of contagious diseases.

However, I do not think it is out of bounds for you to ask your guest whether all laws regarding licensing and health (vaccinations) have been followed, and to inform guests of those laws. This is something I have done via message thread when a guest has informed me, pre-booking, that they will be traveling with some kind of assistance animal.

My reasoning is that a landlord has a legitimate interest in ensuring that there is not a threat to public health, to himself, to other guests, or to workers or others who may need to be on the property occasionally, and that all local laws regarding animals are being followed.

To be clear, you cannot use pretextual reasons to discriminate against people whom the law protects on the basis of disability. But the same law (ADA) also says that it *does not* override local requirements about licensing and vaccination.

The only way I can see to reconcile these two things is that you *are* allowed to ask:

1. whether the animal that will be staying on your property has been properly licensed and permitted, and
2. whether the owner of an out-of-state animal has obtained the required health certificate from a veterinarian (if your city has a rule to that effect, like New Orleans does).

Because one of the world's most feared and most lethal[87] diseases—rabies—is spread to humans almost entirely by dogs (99% of the time[88]), the vaccination status of a dog that will be staying at your rental seems like information it is reasonable for the property to inquire about before renting. This bears no relation to whether a guest may be disabled or an animal brought onto the premises may be an assistance animal.

I recently put the following notification in my House Rules (in my Rental Agreement in the case of Vrbo):

> Animals must be licensed and permitted as required by the City of New Orleans, and a copy of any health certificate required under New Orleans Municipal Code Sec.18-202(b) must be provided to Host at the time of booking.

I can't guarantee that Airbnb will not object to that language, perhaps by deciding it violates their "no documentation" policy. Of course, that would require that they admit that they have a "no documentation" policy.

Wait and see, I guess.

Accepting Reservations & Screening Guests

These two topics go together hand in glove, so I'm addressing them together.

The STR landscape is constantly changing, because the STR platforms are constantly tinkering with their sites, algorithms, and pretty much anything else they can tinker with.

This includes the booking process, insurance (who provides it, what it covers, what the requirements are to file a claim, and how to do it—for both hosts and guests), and expectations of hosts and guests.

Changes to the platform can be difficult and confusing for you as a host, because what you ideally want in the platform is stability and predictability. Good luck. Learning the systems of all the different STR sites you use, perfecting your listings and tailoring them to each site, perfecting your house rules, and the all-important how you interact with guests, all take time to learn.

But you have little choice but to modify everything and follow along every time Airbnb decides to tinker. This is compounded by the fact that, because Airbnb is the real innovator, other sites will usually follow Airbnb's lead, *eventually*, and implement the same changes, but not *always* (they let Airbnb experiment then cherry-pick the best ideas). So, different platforms, realistically, will always require slightly different approaches, or, at minimum, yield you groups of guests who all are governed by different rules.

The Booking Process

It used to be that an agreement to rent an STR always started with the guest sending an "inquiry" or "request to book" to the host, almost always with a brief explanation of who they were, why they were coming to town, and (sometimes just by implication) why you should allow them to rent. *They* had to sell *you*, in addition to the reverse.

Guests would commonly write things like, "3 middle-aged women coming to town to celebrate our friend's 60th birthday." The implication was, "We are sedate people who won't destroy your house, steal your belongings, or scare your neighbors. Let us rent your place!"

This was not a bad thing for hosts.

The prospective guest's message to the host would either be followed by the host asking a couple of follow-up questions, calling the guest on the phone to get a feel for them, or by simply sending an acceptance or an offer to rent. Because I hate talking on the phone and don't want to grill people too much who want to give me money, I usually fell into the latter camp. I always responded to inquiries, and sometimes asked a question or two if I felt the need, but I usually just sent an acceptance at the same time as my response.

An agreement would be formed, and the guest would pay, pretty much the same way they do now, often through the platform. In the past, Vrbo did not much care whether the booking and payment were made through their platform, or if you and the guest just made your own arrangements. But they have moved completely to an Airbnb-like model. Personally, I have always thought it was a good idea to keep all transactions on-platform, in part to ensure that the guest's stay will be covered by any insurance offered for on-platform transactions, and in part just to have a large company as a legal buffer between the guest and me. I also try to communicate with guests almost entirely through platform messaging, and I recommend you do, too. (Guests will often begin texting you instead of messaging you through the platform as soon as they have your phone number; I usually answer their texts through the platform.)

But that was then, this is now. We have entered the era of... *Instant Book*.

Instant Book

Today, most hosts have enabled Instant Book (introduced in 2016). If the host enables it, it mostly cuts out the back-and-forth between guest and host. If you have Instant Book enabled on your listing, a guest, provided they meet Airbnb's requirements (confirmed phone number, email address, payment information, and agreement to your House Rules), acknowledge that "Airbnb homes can be different from hotels," and either have submitted or agree to submit a government-issued ID, if you require that, just has to click "Book It!" and make payment in order to book your rental. The guest is also required to answer any questions you ask them in response to their booking.

There are several options for limiting who can Instant Book. You can limit Instant Book to guests who (1) have a photo in their Airbnb profile, (2) have at least one recommendation from another host.

Like most hosts, I have mixed feelings about Instant Book. I see why Airbnb did it, and I see that it removes a lot of friction between the guest thinking about booking and actually booking, which is good for both Airbnb and for hosts. But it also removes the opportunity to exchange even a little bit of information with your prospective guest before you commit to having them rent your property. It removes the opportunity for those gut feelings to occur that help you decide whether the guest is a good fit.

You do have a limited escape hatch from Instant Bookings. Up to three times per year, you can cancel an Instant Booking if you are "uncomfortable" with the guest for a reason that does not violate Airbnb's non-discrimination policy. Some examples (from Airbnb's website) include:

- The guest has several unfavorable reviews that concern the host
- The guest hasn't responded to questions the host needs to know about their trip
- The guest makes it clear they'll likely break one of the host's house rules, like bringing a pet or smoking.[2]

Though you can choose Instant Book options to require that the guest provide a government-issued photo ID to Airbnb before their date of arrival, have at least one recommendation from another host, have a profile picture, and send you a message saying something about themselves and their trip...enabling any of the above can reduce the number of people who see your listing.

---

[2] Airbnb.com, How do penalty-free cancellations work for Instant Book hosts?, https://www.airbnb.com/help/article/2022/how-do-penaltyfree-cancellations-work-for-instant-book-hosts (accessed Nov. 2, 2019).

A traveler who is not logged in will not be shown your listing as offering Instant Book, because Airbnb does not know if that guest meets your requirements to Instant Book. (Example: because they don't know if the person searching even has an account, they don't know if that person has a profile picture.) And if the person decides to search "Instant Book only" listings, yours won't show up. This is understandable, because if the guest does happen to not have a profile picture, or a recommendation from another host, or whatever else you require, your rental is one that they cannot Instant Book.

The basic thing to remember is that if you put up any hurdles, your listing will appear in fewer search results. Add to that, Airbnb penalizes you in search results if you do not have Instant Book enabled.

A significant majority of Airbnb hosts have Instant Book enabled. I recommend you do too, even though it can be frustrating to be pressured to accept guests about whom you know next to nothing.

Other Ways to Screen Guests

On Airbnb, if a guest has numerous positive reviews from previous hosts and no negative ones, and has a verified photo ID, and has had an account for 3+ years, that is pretty much the Holy Grail of verifying that they are going to be a good guest.

Even a couple of positive reviews is greatly reassuring. As is an account that was created sometime before the month in which the booking was made. As is a guest with two or more "verifications."

"Verifications" are different than Verified ID, which is the gold standard. Verifications are more like the nickel standard (because they are very easy to get), but they are better than nothing. A guest who has numerous verifications has shown commitment to the platform; they are less likely to be trouble than someone who has not. Verifications result from doing things like linking your Airbnb account to a valid Facebook or Google+ account, verifying the email address you gave and/or your cell phone number, etc.

The opposite of the Holy Grail would be a guest with no profile pic or last name. Airbnb says on their site that a profile pic is required to book, but they do not show you, the host, the photo until after the guest has booked.

Airbnb's rule that guests who have booked your property do not have to reveal their full names to you is quite puzzling. I don't think wanting to know the actual name of the guest who has rented my property unreasonably intrudes on that person's privacy. But Airbnb says guests are allowed to withhold their real names.

If you have the guest's full name, because they have actually put it on their profile, or maybe because their email address shows it, you can Google them. You often have their city and state, but not always; guests are not required to include their city of residence in their profiles, and even if they were, they could lie. I believe that Airbnb does show the guest's country of residence ("USA") even if the guest chooses not to show their city and state.

Regardless, it's surprising how often a full name, even an unusual name, brings up too many results on Google for you to really be sure of anything.

Should I Accept A Guest with No Reviews?

One of the biggest questions new hosts have is whether to accept a guest with no reviews. It's easy to see why they are asking the question. Reviews, if they are good, are reassuring. At least *someone* has given a personal opinion on the guest. All the other booking factors are impersonal data points.

But, chances are, if you only accept guests with reviews, you will probably not have enough guests, especially if you are using Vrbo and the rest of its family of sites. Many people booking through Vrbo and family will not have previously stayed at a short-term rental and will not have any reviews.

Should I Accept Local Guests?

The short answer is no. Locals are much more likely to be renting your place for a party or illicit activities. I have heard hosts speak of one or more prostitutes renting their place for a night or two in which to see a large number of clients; people renting a place to go on a drug binge; people renting a place from which to sell drugs; or people renting a place for what they suspect is an illegal transaction so neither has to give away their actual residence. Sometimes guests (not necessarily local guests) will ask if they can have packages sent to the listing address. No!

One way to deter locals is to have a two-night minimum (or more). Also, put in your House Rules, "Local guests: please message the host before booking." This way you can ask them what brings them to town and let them explain why they are renting your place. If it sounds fishy, don't let them book.

The biggest problem is parties, as already discussed in an earlier chapter. Why get one's own house messy when I can just rent out an Airbnb, invite my 100 best friends over, and just pay a cleaning fee so someone else can clean up the mess? (And who cares if the listing says "no parties," really?)

Read the Guest's Profile

Beyond reading the guest's past reviews, if any, there are other ways to read between the lines of a guest's profile.

A large number of hosts state that they will not rent to a guest without a fully filled-out profile that includes a photo of the guest. I think that is going a little too far. It would very likely reduce my bookings if I screened those people out.

Despite my mixed feelings about the system as it currently stands, I understand that the idea of staying at a short-term rental is still new to many people, and many have not yet done it. They may be browsing Airbnb or Vrbo out of curiosity, and see a listing that makes them decide they want to take a chance and book it, instead of the hotel they would probably otherwise stay at.

That means, as on many websites, the guest needs to "register" first. The guest will be asked to provide all the usual information, like their name, address, phone number, email address, and credit card information, and the site will then strongly suggest that they complete "verifications" and/or a "verified ID."

As the prospective guest navigates the maze that we have all encountered so many times when we have had to register with a website that wants a lot of information, it's understandable that a guest may choose to avoid filling out fields that aren't mandatory. The guest is, after all, trying to book a property, not trying to date the owner. Why, the guest might wonder, does it matter if I have a profile pic?

So, filling out a profile telling everyone their backstory and finding a nice head shot and uploading it may not be at the top of a guest's mind when they first register with Airbnb and shoot you an Instant Book. Over time, if they become repeat users of one or more of the platforms, they may realize that hosts like to know more about guests, and may find the time to flesh out their profiles.

Long story long, this is why I don't auto-reject guests without a profile photo.

That said, if a guest *has* posted some information about themselves, you can probably gather something about them from it. If they are snarling at the camera surrounded by empty bottles of Jack Daniels in their photo and pointing a Glock at the camera, and their entire "About Me" section consists of "LIVIN THA THUG LIFE," they may not be the right person with whom to entrust your house.

Talk to Your Guests

An additional way to screen, either pre- or post-booking, is just to converse with your guests, whether it is through the platform messaging (always use the platform messaging as opposed to regular text messaging. Don't get in the habit of exchanging text messages with guests) or by phone. Phone is better if you want to get a sense of the person.

Popular questions to ask are:

What brings you to town?

One answer you don't want to hear is, "Oh, I live in town. I just need a place for this weekend."

Whatever they say after that, the chances are much, much higher than average that they will be doing something you don't want. Try to wiggle out of hosting these guests (call Airbnb and tell them you are "uncomfortable" based on your phone conversation).

How many people will be staying at the rental?

The booking guest will have input a number when they booked, but you want to see if they will say the same thing when asked. In my experience, the answer is often not as clear-cut as "5," or whatever they input. It's often more like, "Well, we originally had 5, but another couple might be joining us, and one friend might have to drop out, so I don't really know." This is a good time to remind them of the maximum number of guests who can stay at the rental. You don't need to justify yourself, since they are the ones who stated the number, not you, and they didn't feel the need to reach out to clarify anything, they only admitted a different number when asked.

But if the guest gives you a number that is going to be over your limit and you do not want to allow that, you can blame it on consideration for neighbors, city ordinance (if true), size of the rental, or something else, and call Airbnb and have the booking canceled since the guest has told you they intend to violate your house rules.

Speaking of Number of Guests

How do you determine the maximum number of guests you should allow?

Greed.

Kidding not kidding.

Single Rooms. If you are renting a single room in your apartment, could the room accommodate two guests?

Do you want to limit how much your guests use shared space in the apartment, or are you laid-back about that?

If you allow two guests, they are more likely to spread out into the rest of the apartment, whereas a single guest is more likely to stay much of the time in their own room, except for occasional trips to the kitchen and bathroom. There are exceptions, and some single guests can be fairly obnoxious about making themselves overly at home, commandeering the best seat in your living room and parking in front of the TV for their entire stay. (Don't ask me why some people go on vacation then stay in the rental the entire time, but they do. I don't rent out single rooms or live in my rental, but I can assure you that these are some of hosts' least favorite guests.)

While a lot of hosts do allow two people to share a single room, some prefer to allow only one. I would be in the latter camp. But, if you allow two guests in a single room, you can charge more. You will probably also be booked more if you allow the option of either one or two. But don't be surprised if you have two much of the time, unless your extra charge for a second guest is high enough to keep it at some kind of equilibrium between one and two.

But never mind two in a bedroom. How about six?

Sometimes a host will jam as many beds in a room as will fit. There is a listing near me where one large bedroom is jammed with three queen beds. I can't even remember what the other rooms are like, probably equally horrible.

This setup might be appealing to large groups of people with little money, but few others.

If you have a 3-bedroom rental that contains 13 beds, cots, airbeds, sofa beds, futons, and/or bales of hay, keep in mind that groups of six, who would normally see a three-bedroom as a good option, will very likely not book yours. They will prefer a three-bedroom that has one bed per bedroom, rather than a place where the bedrooms are jammed with extra beds they won't need.

Needless to say, larger groups almost always generate more problems and neighbor complaints. The number of complaints you will get if you allow 12 guests, rather than the 4-6 people your two-bedroom rental can comfortably accommodate, will skyrocket. So will the amount of damage and wear and tear. It's well-known that responsibility is diffused when there are a large number of people, so everyone will be on worse behavior and they will leave a bigger mess.

And, speaking of mess: Cleaning. It's hard to overstate how much work cleaning becomes as an STR host, at least if you are renting out an entire house or apartment.

12 people? Ugh.

And don't assume that people will always share beds to maximum efficiency. In fact, they will do the opposite. If you have 13 beds or sofa beds, a group of 13 may very well use all of them. That is a heck of a lot of linens to wash. And towels. And even blankets. People who sleep on a sofa bed generally do not make it up fully with the sheets you provide; instead, they just grab a blanket and sleep on the bare couch. Hopefully yours is imitation leather or vinyl, so any drool stains can be more easily wiped away.

If you allow too many guests, you will also find yourself having to do things fairly often that normally you might only have to do once a year, like steam-cleaning carpets. Invest in one of those mini-steam cleaners to remove the spots that will be appearing with greater frequency. Or heck, just buy a carpet steamer. Or a carpet steamer franchise.

Also: Expenses. You will definitely have more if you allow big groups. Your house cleaner will charge more money. Your utility bills will be higher. You will go through more toilet paper, coffee, condiments, spices, and everything else you choose to supply your guests. Guests will break more things. More sheets and towels will wear out or become stained and need to be replaced.

Even your doorways will get beaten up. Even not having large groups, I have had to replace broken doorknobs four times in the past couple of years. Breaking doorknobs is just something guests do. I have no idea why; I have never broken one in my own day-to-day life.

The above is not an exhaustive list of the problems that overly-large groups can cause. But I am tired of thinking about it. If your dream has always been to be a fraternity den-father or sorority house-mother, by all means, go for it.

Recommendation

I am actually glad that New Orleans passed a firm limit of two guests per bedroom, because that is all I really want in my rentals.

Pre-regulation, I allowed two guests per bedroom plus two in the shared space on a sofa bed. Doing so will probably increase your number of bookings, since larger groups can stay at your rental. But it will definitely increase wear-and-tear, amount of cleaning required, burden on your neighbors, and the obviousness that you are using the house or apartment as an STR.

And just to reiterate, whatever your guest limit is, the groups who reserve your place will gravitate toward that maximum size. This is because the number of available listings on the STR platforms decreases dramatically as the number of guests a place can accommodate goes up. There are WAY more places that sleep two than four. And WAY more places that sleep four than six. And WAY more places that sleep six than eight.

Tip: if your municipality does not have a number-of-guests limit, and if you have the patience, you could open up your calendar for only 60 or 90 days in advance, and initially set your guest limit higher until the period was *partially* filled up (and charge more for those larger groups), then reduce your guest limit, so that all further groups in the open period would be smaller. This would give you a better mix of larger and smaller groups.

You will learn over time how far in advance your guests tend to book. For mine, for the first couple of years, it was generally 1-2 months in advance. Now that I have been in operation a while, I still get the majority of reservations 1-2 months in advance, but a larger percentage (25%?) of people have started booking further out for key weekends and events. For example, I started getting quite a few reservations for October (the month in New Orleans with arguably the best weather, not to mention Halloween, which is a lot of fun in a town where everyone loves dressing up in costumes) in the spring.

Should I Charge More for More Guests?

You may be considering charging more for any guests beyond a number that you choose. The platforms make this very easy to do. If you have a two-bedroom that you would really like to keep to four people, but it could sleep six, you might charge an extra amount per night for any guests above four.

Lots of hosts choose to do this, but I do not recommend it.

It is confusing to guests and increases the need for you to answer their questions about what they are being charged. (One of my least favorite questions: "Can you please break down all the charges?") The charges are already spelled out as clearly as they are going to get on Airbnb, with little question marks the guest can click on for even further explanation. What they really want, I think, is to have you tell them why you think they should get charged an extra $60 due to having 6 guests instead of 4.

One reason this "surprise" extra charge may confuse a guest is that, if they initially searched using the default number of guests (one), they will see the price jump when they go to actually book and put in an accurate number of guests.

When you have any kind of per-guest charge, guests being surprised that the price was higher than they expected happens, a lot. The tone of their messages asking you to explain also tend to be unpleasant. The guest is wondering, *Why are you hitting me with extra charges at checkout?* Everybody hates that.

In hosts' defense, it is definitely more work the more guests you have staying in your place, and results in more wear and tear. Guests either don't have the imagination to understand why this is, or choose not to. They may figure that, much as with a rental car, it's the same car, so why should the person renting it out care how many people the renters cram into it?

But the reason I don't recommend doing this is simple: it's one of the biggest sources of complaining among hosts. Simply having a per-guest pricing strategy, in itself, creates stress.

Even if the guest books without incident and you aren't asked to explain yourself, during every group's stay, you will find yourself being on alert to determine whether the group has more guests than the number stated on the reservation. You will stress yourself out trying to count guests, either through security cameras or some other way.

And if you do actually determine a group has 5 guests, not 3 like they stated in the reservation, you have to wrestle with what to do about it. And inevitably you will wrestle. Because guests *hate* extra charges, we know that. If the group is still there, you can ask them to modify their reservation to include the correct number of guests. Or you can modify the reservation and send a request to them to accept the changes, which will result in a higher charge, of course. People are on vacation are always thrilled to get a request for extra money out of the blue.

Adding to that, the guests may not know why they are being charged. They made the reservation months ago. They don't remember the details of the process. Sure, at that time, they probably noticed that the reservation said 1 guest, and changed the number to 5, then saw the price jump up, thought for a moment, and reduced the number back down to 3, splitting the difference. Much more affordable. Then they paid, and immediately forgot all about it.

Now, you want to dredge that up and create conflict over money. Downer!

I recommend that you charge based on the number of guests your place can accommodate, and assume that many will be staying. If your place sleeps 4, price it as if there will be 4 there. If it sleeps 6, price it as if there will be 6 there.

This way, if you happen to notice that they have 10 people there—which they should be well aware is against the rules, if you have followed my advice and made it known multiple times that the maximum number of guests is 6 and no visitors are allowed—contact them and tell them they need to reduce the guest count to 6.

In all likelihood, they will get rid of the extra 4 people. (If they don't, contact Airbnb about it, but in my experience, you will rarely need to.) Don't fret over where the 4 extra people will go. The group took a chance by bringing 10 to a place that accommodates 6, and it didn't work out for them.

Cancelling

Your Policy

Choosing what cancellation policy to use is a fairly important decision.

The platforms are pushing hosts to offer more flexible cancellation policies, even putting properties higher in the search rankings if they have flexible policies. This puts hosts, especially of properties that sleep more than 4, in a tough situation.

Groups of more than 4 tend to book well in advance, not last-minute. Which means that places that sleep more than 4 tend not to be booked last-minute.

Which means that, if a group of 6 cancels close to their date of arrival, the place they booked is unlikely to be booked by someone else (because groups of 4 are not looking for places that sleep 6; they just don't, though there is of course a chance they will book one if the options that sleep 4 don't look appealing).

The more flexible the host's cancellation policy, the more likely they will get nothing for the period that had been booked by those guests, and this goes double for places that host larger groups.

There has been a lot of tinkering going on with cancellation policies, particularly Airbnb's. They have added, very recently, "or non-refundable" options to all their cancellation types, and I wouldn't be surprised if they removed or changed them and continued tinkering.

Airbnb Policies

Airbnb has [nine basic cancellation policies](#)[89]: Flexible, Flexible or Non-refundable, Moderate, Moderate or Non-refundable, Strict, and Strict or Non-refundable, Long-Term and two that are invite-only, Super Strict 30 Days and Super Strict 60 Days.[90]

In all cases, guests have 48 hours to cancel for a full refund, as long as they are cancelling at least 14 days before check-in (or 3:00 PM local time if a check-in time is not specified). This includes Airbnb's service fee. Any other time guests are refunded, Airbnb's service fee is kept by the company.

Flexible

If the guest cancels at least 24 hours before the listing's stated check-in time (or, if not stated, 3:00PM local time), they get a full refund.

Flexible or Non-refundable

Same as Flexible, but guests may choose a non-refundable option and receive a 10% discount, in which case they will not receive a refund no matter when they cancel.

Moderate

If the guest cancels at least 5 days prior to the listing's stated check-in time (or, if not stated, 3:00PM local time), they get a full refund. If they cancel less than 5 days before arrival, the first night is non-refundable, and 50% of all subsequent nights of their booking is refunded.

Moderate or Non-refundable

Same as Moderate, but guests may choose a non-refundable option and receive a 10% discount, in which case they will not receive a refund no matter when they cancel.

Strict

If the guest cancels at least 7 days prior to arrival, they get a 50% refund. If not, they get no refund.

Strict or Non-refundable

Same as Strict, but guests may choose a non-refundable option and receive a 10% discount, in which case they will not receive a refund no matter when they cancel.

Long-Term

This policy automatically applies to all stays of 28 nights or more. Under Long-Term, if the guest cancels at least 28 days before check-in time on the first day of their booking (or 3:00 PM local time if not specified), they get a full refund. If they cancel less than 28 days ahead, they forfeit the first 30 day's rent.

Super Strict 30 Days and Super Strict 60 Days

Super Strict 30 Days and Super Strict 60 Days are invite-only. Guests can cancel at least 30 (or 60) days before check-in and get a 50% and cleaning fee.

Vrbo Policies

Vrbo has [five basic cancellation policies][91] that have not changed much over the years:

Relaxed

Bookings cancelled at least 14 days before the start of stay will receive 100% refund. Bookings cancelled at least 7 days before the start of stay will receive a 50% refund.

Moderate ("recommended")

Bookings cancelled at least 30 days before the start of stay will receive 100% refund. Bookings cancelled at least 14 days before the start of stay will receive a 50% refund.

Firm

Bookings cancelled at least 60 days before the start of stay will receive 100% refund. Bookings cancelled at least 30 days before the start of stay will receive a 50% refund.

Strict

Bookings cancelled at least 60 days before the start of stay will receive 100% refund. Otherwise, there are no refunds.

No Refund

No refund is offered for any reason or timeframe. [92]

Vrbo uses the cutoff time of 11:59 PM in the property's time zone to determine how many days in advance a cancellation was made (as opposed to Airbnb, which uses either the property's local check-in time , or 3:00 PM local time if a check-in time is not specified).

Vrbo also specifies that the cancellation policy chosen in your property listing overrides any cancellation policy specified in your rental agreement.

What You Need to Consider

Many hosts recommend Strict cancellation, including me. I have always used it and never had any problems. My reasoning is that STRs are not hotels; we cannot absorb the losses resulting from people cancelling at the last minute.

At my rentals, I know that if I have a weekend one or two weeks from now that isn't booked yet, there's a good chance it is not going to be.

I personally feel that, the looser your cancellation policy, the less money you will make in comparison to a stricter policy. People who are most concerned with the cancellation policy are the most likely to actually cancel, so you will get more bookings from these people, more of whom will cancel, and you will not make up those amounts from last-minute bookings.

However, as Airbnb keeps pushing hosts to be more flexible, if a large segment of the market does become more flexible, it may happen that being strict may make you an outlier in a negative way, in which case you may begin to lose bookings if you have strict cancellation. I don't think we are there yet.

Everybody Has an Excuse

Whatever your policy is, you will get some guests who want to cancel. It is very rare that any of them will simply forfeit the 50% or 100% that cancellation would cost them, if they are outside the full-refund period.

Real-life example: you receive a message from the booking guest saying that, due to a member of their group needing heart surgery, they unfortunately need to cancel. They don't ask straight out for a refund, and they don't *actually* just go ahead and cancel the reservation, either, because they know they will only get, let's say, 50% of their money back. So, they decide to engage you in a delicate dance where they try to feel out whether you will give them a 100% refund due to their unfortunate situation.

Is your heart going to bleed for them, and are you going to offer them a refund if they cancel now? No.

Why? Isn't heart surgery a good enough reason for a refund? Yes—if someone actually needed heart surgery. But they don't.

Needing to cancel for a medical reason is the default excuse that, over time, you will hear over and over and over, because people are not that creative. The other obvious "good excuse" for cancelling, claiming that someone close to one of the guests has died, doesn't sit well with a lot of people. Telling a lie like that just feels wrong. So they will make it medical, not death.

But back to the heart surgery story. One problem with it is that heart surgery causing a group of friends to cancel a vacation doesn't make sense.

Here's the story you are hearing, as you try to piece it together from what the booking guest has told you: a person has discovered they need heart surgery, but it's not an emergency (otherwise they would have gone to the ER, been admitted to the hospital, and had the surgery already). So, that means some kind of serious problem must have just come up just in the last couple of days where surgery is required in the next week or two, but not immediately. And, the whole group of friends now cannot go to New Orleans, even though they have already told you they live in different parts of the country and are meeting up in New Orleans. Why can't the other friends go? Apparently because they all need to be at their sick friend's bedside as he or she goes through this traumatic, non-emergency surgical procedure.

Are you buying that?

I might sound cynical, and I am on this issue. This is because, almost every time I have denied a refund, a miracle recovery has occurred.

The heart surgery example is real, as I said. When the guest contacted me with the story, I was nice about it, but I did not offer a refund. I eventually had to tell her, as nicely as possible, that I was very sorry, but I can't give refunds for bookings only a short time away.

Miraculously, *none* of my guests who have tried the serious medical issue excuse have canceled, and all have shown up for their trips. I have not even noticed any of the groups having one fewer person than they stated when they made the booking. That includes a group of women of whom one, herself, allegedly needed heart surgery. I didn't inquire about the surgery when I talked to them, and it was never brought up again.

Extenuating Circumstances

You might think I am just being heartless. Well, not really. If a guest *truly* has a death happen or a major medical problem, they don't need to bother trying to work it out with you, and they probably won't. Under certain conditions, Airbnb will just give guests a full refund regardless of the timing.

These include a death in the family, disaster, major weather issues, and serious illness. Guests who want to cancel on you and get their money back figure this all out right after looking at their reservation and seeing the cancellation policy is "strict," after which they immediately Google "Airbnb strict cancellation refund" and come across Airbnb's Extenuating Circumstances policy.

If a guest has a genuine serious medial issue or a family death, the way you will find out is via message from Airbnb saying that the guest has canceled for Extenuating Circumstances and they have received a full refund. You won't be hearing from that guest again because they don't need anything from you.

The only time you will hear from a guest about cancelling for a medical reason is when they actually *don't* have a valid medical reason. They didn't have any proof they could show Airbnb, so Airbnb told them they could always talk to the host about a refund. Now, if they still want to try for a refund, they have to bargain with you and try to appeal to your sense of kindness or fairness.

Super-Predators

A number guests have begun to use photos of bedbugs, often from the Internet, and other methods to try to both stay at your rental *and* get a refund. They will tell outright lies about the host and/or the accommodations, and some are very creative. They bolster their argument by saying that the incident(s) did not happen until after they have stayed a number of days. That way the usual policy of the guest being required to notify Airbnb of any problems within 24 hours of their arrival can be gotten around.

These guests can be very dangerous to your business, because their lies may not always work to get them a refund, but they can still hurt you as a host, or even get you banned from the platform.

The best thing you can do about these guests is to already be doing the things you should be doing. Greet each guest and form a personal connection with them. People have a harder time ripping someone off if they "know" them. Do little things that show you care (like have a gift basket waiting for them). Let them know more than once that if there is anything wrong with the rental, to call you anytime and you will fix it.

In short, kill them with kindness. Sure, some people are psychopathic enough to ignore all these things and *still* screw you over, but not as many.

Trip/Travelers Insurance

Another reason I prefer to be fairly strict about refunds outside the already-reasonable refund periods offered by the platforms: all guests have the opportunity to purchase travel insurance.

There are many varieties, including traveler medical insurance (covers medical only), named perils insurance (costs 7% to 9% of your trip costs and excludes some things—such as pandemics), and "cancel for any reason" insurance (costs from 10% to 12% of your trip cost).[93] more comprehensive types of travel insurance, covering things like los baggage, emergency evacuations, rental car coverage, and even

On Vrbo, trip insurance is offered during the booking process, and is again offered in the booking confirmation email. Airbnb does not offer trip insurance directly, but a plethora of are available online.

In my experience, even on Vrbo, most guests affirmatively choose not to purchase travel insurance, preferring to take their chances.

In other words, they actively choose to take a gamble that they will not need to cancel their trip.

You are not responsible for your guest's gambling problem.

Cancellation by the Host

There is another cancellation policy you need to keep in mind in the STR business: the policy of the STR platform as it relates to *you* cancelling on a guest.

Let's just say, the platforms discourage it. To put it mildly.

Certainty that guests will have a room, apartment, or house waiting for them when they arrive is critical to guests and therefore to the STR platforms.

Guests have all heard horror stories about scams, last-minute cancellations, properties not being what they claimed to be, and so on.

Unlike a booking at the Hilton or the Marriott, guests are dealing with you, Some Guy or Girl, who claims to own Some House. It's normal for them to freak out a little bit about it, particularly if it is their first time using an STR.

One of the very worst things you can do is confirm your guest's worst fears by cancelling on them, particularly at the last minute or close to it. If their trip is not far off, they may find that there is very little available, maybe nothing, at least anywhere near the price they paid for your place. Airbnb will give them a voucher for $100 or $150, but after that, they are essentially on their own. They may well be screwed, and their vacation may be ruined.

This, understandably, causes huge headaches for the STR platforms. If even a tiny fraction of hosts cancel a tiny fraction of reservations, the platforms will experience that as a deluge of frantic, irate, sleep-deprived travelers calling them in desperate need of assistance in finding alternate accommodations.

Nobody wants that, so the platforms **really** don't want hosts to cancel on guests. Particularly last minute.

On Airbnb, if you cancel on one guest, you will not be eligible for Superhost status for an entire year. That sucks, because Superhost status is a reassurance to guests that you, well, won't do things like cancel on them. The dates of the cancelled stay will also be blocked off on your calendar so that you cannot rent the place to anyone else for that time period (through Airbnb).

You will also have an automated review posted in your Reviews section saying that you canceled on someone. It stays there permanently. This is if you cancel before the start date of the guest's reservation. If you cancel *on* the start date, the guest can leave a review, and I guarantee you, it won't be pretty. Rather than just saying that you cancelled last minute, the guest will go into detail about how your cancelling essentially was so disappointing it caused their grandmother's early death.

If you cancel a second time within six months, on Airbnb at least, you will be charged either $50 or $100, depending on whether you canceled more than seven days or less than seven days ahead. The days you canceled will also be blocked off on your calendar so Airbnb users cannot book them.

And, if you cancel three reservations in a year, Airbnb may suspend your account.

On Vrbo, the policy is not as clear-cut, but cancellation is equally discouraged. One of Vrbo's "Marketplace Standards" that hosts must follow is, "You cannot cancel a material number of confirmed reservations."

In a way, this is even scarier, because they uncertainty allows your imagination to run away with itself. My brain basically translates this as, "There is only one punishment for cancelling, and that is death."

There's no way to know for certain how many times you can cancel reservations on Vrbo before your account is deactivated. You may even be suspended after one cancellation.

That said, Vrbo does not block days off your calendar that you have cancelled, or make you ineligible for Premier Partner status (their version of Superhost status). Their website says[94], "owner-initiated cancellations can affect your ranking metrics."

It doesn't say they *do,* or by how much. I would avoid cancelling.

Search Rankings

This is probably as good a time as any to talk about search rankings on the platforms. This refers to searching properties on Airbnb.com, Vrbo.com, or another platform, *not* Google. Google is separate.

The platforms offer a lot of information about what things can affect your ranking in search results, but it's hard to tell what is actually key at any given time. Vrbo gave boosts to people who fully refunded guests for Covid-19 cancellations, and reverse-boosts for those who didn't.

Airbnb states that number of clicks your property gets, and the percentage of those clicks that become bookings, are important.[95] I am pretty certain that value plays a part as well; that is, where are you in comparison to similar properties in terms of price. Properties in the sweet spot, where the platform could make the most money out of a particular traveler without leaving any on the table, would thereby be ranked well.

Tip: it seems to be that when a platform rolls out a change that is key to their business strategy, they crank the importance of that factor WAY up to encourage adoption by hosts. After enough hosts have converted, ranking goes back to whatever makes the platforms the most money.

Airbnb

Airbnb says, "the exact list of features we consider is confidential, but here are the basic categories":

> ➤ Guest needs – "factors related to the guest, including where they're searching from, their previous trips, which listings they've added to their Wish List or clicked on, and more."

- Listing details – "number of five-star reviews, price, location of the listing, if Instant Book is turned on, how quickly the host of the listing responds to requests, and many other factors."
- Trip details – "how many guests will be traveling, how long the trip will be, how far in the future the trip is, if they have set a minimum or a maximum price, and a variety of other factors."[96]

They consider:

- Clicks on your listing, and percentage of those clicks that convert to a booking.
- Good reviews.
- Price – "set a competitive price within your market."
- New listings "show up well in search rankings."
- Response rate (whether you respond to guest queries at all).
- Response time (how fast you respond to them).
- Rejections (don't reject too many people).
- Instant Book (if you have it enabled, you "get a boost in the algorithm").
- Location.
- Number of nights the guest is looking to book (if you have a 2-night minimum, guests seeking a 1-night stay will not see your listing).

Of note:

- There will be a 6-24 hour delay between making a new listing "live" on Airbnb and it being visible in search.
- Being a Superhost "doesn't boost [your] listing."
- In order to host long-term travelers (over 28 days), you *must* have a monthly discount set.

It would not be a waste of your time to review Airbnb's entire webpage on this subject here.[97]

Vrbo

Vrbo has updated their search ranking information in the last year or two. They used to have a system called <u>Best Match</u> (and maybe they still do, because there is still information about it on the Vrbo website[98]). But the following seems to be newer:

> Vrbo uses machine learning to understand what travelers want for an upcoming trip. Our ranking system looks at all the properties in the area, comparing amenities, number of bedrooms, location, reviews, and other criteria. Then, it ranks all properties—including yours—based on how well it fits the traveler's needs.
>
> This ranking is combined with an individual traveler's preferences (including stay dates, search filters, and other personalization factors) to determine where your property shows up in their search results.[99]

To "stand out in search results," they say to:

- ➢ Create quality content. "First impressions are critical! How travelers respond to your headline, photos, amenities, and descriptions affect your rank." They say to look at win/loss posts in your marketplace feed for "valuable insight" on how to do this.
- ➢ Set competitive rates. "Set prices appropriate for your property, area, and goals. Tools like MarketMaker can help!"
- ➢ Accept and honor bookings. Responding promptly to inquiries and booking requests, accepting most bookings, enabling Instant Booking, and not cancelling reservations all "help boost your market rank."
- ➢ Earn great reviews. "Four- and five-star reviews show you're committed to your guests and can influence your rank."[100]

Vrbo says that you can improve your search ranking "by focusing on the following key metrics located in the Ranking Metrics page of your account:

- ➢ Cancellation rate (keep it low).
- ➢ Bookings (accept "most booking requests").
- ➢ Acceptance rate (accept "most booking requests." Isn't that kind of the same thing as "Bookings"? Looks like it).
- ➢ Reviews – "encourage travelers to submit feedback after their stay."

Be warned: the above appears the be the *newest information* on their website, which is why I have emphasized it. Vrbo does not do a good job of deleting legacy pages from their help section, so consequently they have old pages that talk about Ranking Metrics and their Best Match system, both of which I think are either gone or have been absorbed by their new "AI" system.

A Couple More Tips

The way Airbnb and Vrbo show properties in search results are probably a good guideline for other platforms you may use. It all really comes down to matching a traveler with what they want that will get the maximum amount of money out of them they are willing to spend.

From what I have seen and heard over the years, a few more things that the platforms don't openly talk about seem to be factors as well:

1. How much money you bring in for the platform (you have multiple listings, high-profit listings, or both).
2. Complaints or claims against you.
3. Claims made by you in relation to your rental(s).
4. How often you update or "touch" your listing. The consensus seems to be that this is particularly important with Airbnb. Log in and tinker with your listing frequently.

When Guests Arrive

Guest arrival is no doubt the most critical time of their stay, and there are many things that can go wrong, or right, depending mostly on the host's efforts and actions.

The primary thing I try to keep in mind on a guest's arrival date is that they are traveling.

Traveling is something that can consume someone's entire focus. So, while your arriving guest may have been highly responsive and communicative in the days leading up to their arrival, on their actual arrival date, they may go radio-silent.

It's pretty common for guests to be uncommunicative on the day of travel. You have to cut them some slack. Keep in mind that they may have gotten up at some ungodly hour, like 1:30AM their time, and may be so frazzled they can't think about anything but sleep. Or maybe their dog-sitter didn't arrive when they were supposed to, so they were calling people at 5AM to arrange a replacement, making them almost miss their plane. During travel, something always goes wrong, even if it's just something taking longer than it should.

One way to avoid stress on arrival day: get pertinent information from guests, such as their expected time of arrival and airline and flight number, and any special needs they may have, *during the week leading up to their arrival*. Don't wait until their arrival date.

Also, send them the information they will need about the rental, such as the door code or entry process, the day before arrival. Some hosts say they do not give guests information such as the door code or gate code until right before check-in time, because they don't want guests arriving way too early and checking themselves in. This can indeed be a problem, especially if the cleaners are still working, or haven't even arrived yet.

Here is word-for-word what I send my guests in advance of their arrival (I've changed the codes and passwords):

> Hi _____, here is some information you will want about the rental for your upcoming trip to New Orleans. Please let me

know if you have any questions about anything. Welcome to Nola!!
Josh

FRONT DOOR CODE: 5291.

To enter, input code into keypad, then turn deadbolt to the left. To lock deadbolt upon leaving, press the "Schlage" button, and turn deadbolt to the right. you may need to try a couple of times, this lock has been giving me a bit of trouble.

ADDRESS: 555 Apple St., New Orleans, LA 70114

WIFI NETWORK: Guest 555

WIFI PASSWORD (case sensitive): Wireless555

JOSH CELL #: 504-XXX-XXXX

PARKING

—Parking is on the street. You can park in front of the building if there is space available, otherwise there are spots available on the block. Do not park too close to the fire hydrant (150' down the street). It is painted bright red so it's easy to see.)

—Two-hour parking, should you see any signs, is not enforced in this neighborhood.

—It is illegal to park within 15' of a street corner anywhere in New Orleans, including this neighborhood.

LINENS

—Extra blankets are on the shelves near the laundry in the rear bathroom. In case you plan on using the sofa bed/futon, there are sheets and a memory foam pad in the hall closet.

A/C

—As a reminder, the A/C system has a minimum setting of 72F during warmer months. Thank you for understanding.

BACK BEDROOOM

—The back bedroom has its own A/C (window) unit with remote. Please leave remote near the A/C unit when you depart.

—The back bedroom has a plug-in radiator. To use it, place it away from walls, furniture and objects, and plug it in. Adjust the temp using the buttons. It does not have a fan and makes little or no noise. That is normal. The radiator only reaches a temperature of 85 degrees, so it is not dangerous. Please ask me if you have questions about it.

TVs

—Living Room: Cable channels can be watched on Sling, and movies and TV series on Disney Plus. To watch Sling, click "Sources" on the remote, then navigate to the Sling icon and click it. Do the same for the Disney Plus app.

—Other TVs in the rental get local channels, via digital HD antennas; use each TV's remote to operate.

KITCHEN

—If there is an appliance or utensil you need and don't see, feel free to text me, I may have one.

—The exhaust fan above the stove is currently under repair.

I could probably put more things in there, but then it's possibly already too long. People don't read.

Point of emphasis: always put the door code, address, and Wi-fi network and password at the top. You will <u>always</u> get an immediate call if guests are doing self-check-in and they do not have these pieces of information.

Also, don't rely on guests calling you well before they arrive in order to meet them to hand over the key or something else critically important. They may call you but you may not hear your phone for some reason. If you are waiting until that phone call to give them the door code, and you do not hear when they call (and often they call when they are at the front door rather than in the taxi or when their plane lands) they are now sitting on your porch with their suitcases, going crazy. Not a good way to start out a visit.

Greeting Your Guests

I recommend being present and personally checking your guests in, but you can't always. I highly recommend a keypad deadbolt lock for your front door, so you and your guests do not have to mess with keys (either hiding the key somewhere, or doing a handoff at both arrival and departure). It's easy to change the codes on a keypad lock at any time, even remotely if the lock is Wi-Fi enabled.

Be Ready on Time

One thing you must be very disciplined about is having your place ready for guests' arrival ON TIME.

If your normal check-in time is 4pm, and you and your guests have not discussed otherwise, assume they will arrive at 4pm on the dot. Do not gamble that they might be late.

In fact, they might show up 30 or 60 minutes early. This is not what you agreed on, but people do it. They are tired, their flight got in at 2:30, and they figured they would just drive over and see if the place was ready.

This is not your fault, and if you are still cleaning, don't feel bad about telling them the place is not ready yet and they have to come back at check-in time, particularly if they are hours early.

But if the check-in time you agreed upon has arrived and your place is not ready, guests are *not* going to be understanding. This has only happened to be a couple of times, and the guests were...*not* understanding.

The Hazards of Self-Check-In

Here are some drawbacks of not being present when your guests arrive, and letting them check themselves into your rental (such as by having a keypad door lock and giving them the code).

You don't get a chance to tell them about the little quirks

You can write it all down in the informational message you send them a few days before arrival, or in the binder I recommend you put out for your guests full of information and suggestions for things to do (more on that in a moment). But you can't assume they will read anything, even the very basic day-of-arrival information with the door code, address, etc.

Some will. But a far better option is to walk through the rental with your guests and point out the little things.

Like: the electrical outlet near the sofa doesn't work, that's why there is an extension cord leading to a power strip nearby.

One of the light switches in the hallway controls the attic light, so please leave that switched off.

The kitchen garbage can is inside a cabinet and it rolls out. Trash cans for emptying the garbage are on the side of the house. There is a recycle bin, but recycling only comes once a week (and in New Orleans, that's really more aspirational) so you will take care of that.

You don't get a chance to create a personal bond

Bonding with your guests is very helpful to you as a host. It creates good feelings right out of the gate, and, if you are friendly and welcoming enough, gives your guests a person they know they can call if they have any problems or questions. They have now met and had a conversation with a native of this new city rather than simply checking into their rental while still not having met a soul except maybe their Uber driver, who has already filled them with bitter stories and told them the neighborhood is bad and they'll probably be robbed at gunpoint their first night. You want to defuse that.

Another key reason for letting your guests put a face to your name is that they will be more forgiving of faults and problems. Knowing that you are a real, live person (a friendly one who is really trying!) leads them to have a better experience and leave a better review.

If they have never met you or seen you, a slow-draining bathtub is a gross inconvenience while multiple guests try to get ready, annoying everyone, and making your rental seem to be in a poor state of repair. But if they have met you and you have made them feel comfortable enough to call or text you about it, and not feel like they are being a pest, they can send you a text and you can apologize profusely, and even if you can't fix it right away, it doesn't feel like as much of a negative to them. They know you, and know you would want to know about the bathtub, and will probably even fix it. Maybe tomorrow.

You don't get to size them up

Most of my guests are no trouble, but it's always good for *you* to put faces to names as well. You may get a gut feeling that something isn't right with your guests. It's a horrible feeling, because there is nothing you can do about it but keep your eyes and ears pealed for the duration of their stay. Particularly if you are renting out an entire house or apartment. You can drive by your rental and look at your security cameras more often. You can even stop by unannounced for a made-up reason to check if your guests are up to no good. I rarely do this, but if I felt *really* concerned, I might.

You miss out on a chance to fix major errors

Sometimes, when you are showing your guests around the rental, there will be a major problem that you didn't know about that needs to be fixed immediately. Embarrassing! This can happen even if you were just at the rental this morning and everything was fine. If this happens, you will thank your deity of choice that you were there when your guests arrived. Now they do not have to deal with the issue themselves, or try to get ahold of you or arrange to solve the problem. Because that's not a fun way to start off a vacation.

Gift Baskets

I recommend having a gift basket waiting for your guests when they arrive. It is a personal touch that they always appreciate. Include a few local items you know they will like. One thing my guests always appreciate is water bottles. Bonus: if bought in a large value pack, they are really cheap!

I recommend not including any alcohol in a gift basket, unless you know your guests will appreciate it. Some guests are recovering alcoholics (I know plenty) and would not appreciate having alcohol around.

Your Welcome Binder

We already went over House Rules at great length, but guests who have arrived at your place are probably not going to be looking at that again. I have a binder I leave on the coffee table right inside the front door of each of my rentals, titled, "House Rules and Things to Know."

The first page reiterates all the information I sent the guests before their arrival (door code, Wi-Fi network and password, my phone number, etc.). I also include the following:

- ✓ Maps of the local area that show bus routes and *nearby* destinations (restaurants, stores, tourist attractions). Things they can walk to, to buy a gallon of milk, a coffee, or someplace casual to eat.

- ✓ A map of the city, also showing bus routes and pointing out key destinations, citywide.

- ✓ A short history of the "historic" house, and copies of some documents I have unearthed about it.

- ✓ A history of New Orleans that I wrote myself (mainly just the movie-worthy stuff).

- ✓ Recommendations for restaurants, bars, and things to do, citywide. This list is fairly lengthy, like 40-50 restaurants, bars, sites, and other things. Guests often want to do things that locals do, rather than touristy things. I hate to tell them that in New Orleans, the locals often do the same things as the tourists, like go to the French Quarter and drink, go out to one of our famous restaurants (even the 150-year-old ones you would assume would be clichéd tourist traps). But I created a list of restaurants all over the city that the average tourist may or may not have heard about. I included all price ranges, and places from the very informal to the very formal, and my favorite places for all different types of food.

- ✓ Expectations for guest check-out.

When Guests Check Out

Guest check-out is generally a non-event, except that you should tell guests where they need to leave the key(s), if you use keys. They also need to be told to lock the door upon leaving. A surprising number of people don't.

I have a section called "Guest Check-Out" in my guest binder. The section is mainly to encourage guests to not leave the place a complete disgusting mess. But you have to walk a fine line, so that normal guests do not feel indignant that you are asking them to clean before they leave but also charging them a cleaning fee.

Here is what I am using:

GUEST CHECK OUT

Upon checking out, we would appreciate your help in doing the following.

Place all trash in the garbage bags provided, and empty garbage bags into the garbage can outside (left of the front door). Replacement bags can be found under the kitchen sink.

Clear all contents out of the refrigerator, except for the condiments provided.

Wipe up any spills that have happened during your stay.

Make sure there are no dishes, glasses, or cutlery outside of the kitchen.

Rinse off dishes, glasses, and cutlery and put them in the dishwasher.

Empty coffee grounds and rinse out coffee pot.

Wipe down microwave, especially if there have been any "explosions."

Thank you for making life easier for our hard-working cleaners!

Safety & Security

This section is not about guest safety, which is important, but about *your* safety, both of your person and your property.

My key advice on this topic: **an ounce of prevention is worth a pound of cure.**

Do as much as you can to *prevent* a safety or security problem before it happens.

The major areas of concern:

1. Damage to the rental or its contents
2. Theft of rental contents
3. Physical harm to owner or guest
4. Identity theft of the owner
5. Scams.

There are other risks involved in STR-ing, of course, like guests inviting extra people over or throwing a party and disturbing the peace. Or guests breaking something and refusing to pay for the damage. We've already talked about those. This section is more about keeping you and your property safe from other types of damage or injury that are less frequent but often more serious and costly.

Pre-Arrival

Concerns about identity theft and scams start before your guests arrive. In fact, they start at the moment you activate your listing. Your appetite for risk—and, I hate to say it, but your greed and gullibility—are the main factors here.

Your Appetite for Risk

When you post your property on an STR website, you have to post pretty much everything about it except the exact address. Even if you decline to post the actual address (which guests *would like* to see when they make their decision, but it's a trade-off), your general location in about a ¼ mile radius will be shown. The platform, of course, *will* have your exact address, that's not optional, from which they can generate this ¼-mile approximation.

In this age of Google Street View, it is not hard for a person to locate your home within this area, if they want to, and therefore your exact address. Once they have your address, there is a good chance they can find your full name (if you have not already posted it in your listing, which I personally do not; I post my first name and first initial of my last name, though I share my full name after guests have actually booked. At that time, they have paid the full price of rental along with any security deposit, fees, and costs of insurance they have chosen to buy, so you have a bit more security that they are not out to scam you.)

If you want to be *really* paranoid, you can consider that the guest used a stolen card. But they probably didn't. Booking a rental in advance is not really a good way for a criminal to use a stolen credit card to quickly cash in on it before it gets canceled by the owner. The chance goes up greatly for same-day arrivals.

Point of Clarification

Throughout this book, I often emphasize that all financial transactions, and even all communications, to the extent possible, should be done through the platform. The fact that this also benefits the platforms (via fees) is coincidental. I have no vested interest in the platforms collecting fees. In fact, I am hoping that as time goes on, competition increases and fees go way down.

But, financially, it benefits you to have whatever leverage is to be gained from processing transactions between you and your guests through these big firms when something bad happens.

They have a worldwide reach, whereas you can't do much at all, except maybe sue a guest who you feel owes you money for some reason. This is usually not a realistic option. If you are hosting travelers, they are almost always from out of town or out of state, or even country.

Keep in mind that your name, address, phone number and email address are not a whole lot for an identity thief to work with, unless he or she is very determined. You should consider your risk in terms of, objectively, would someone target *you personally* for identity theft? Why?

People with the most luxurious properties have an obvious answer: "Because I'm rich." Or, to an identity thief, appear to be rich, ergo, their identity is worth stealing. True, you may have a luxury property that is mortgaged to the hilt, and in addition to that, you have student loans, and your credit cards are maxed out, because you committed to your STR being at the luxury end of the market because you know the payoff is high, and perhaps because you think a high-end property will appreciate faster.

Most landlords know that we are almost always less wealthy than we seem from outside. We may have a nice house or apartment building—or two or three—but also significant debt. And almost all properties have issues that are ticking time bombs and could eventually result in large costs, such as having to replace the roof, the HVAC, appliances, etc.

Unfortunately, an identity thief cannot tell from the limited information they can gather about you that you are closer to "bankrupt" than "rich."

How Identity Thieves Make Their Living

Thieves can find out more about you if you reveal things in conversation. Regardless, targeting an individual Airbnb host for identity theft is a labor-intensive process that is not really worth an identity thief's time, for the most part. (Just to be safe, apply the same rules when messaging with guests that you would apply when emailing with Nigerian multi-millionaire princes. If there are lots of misspellings and grammatical errors, and the other person needs some personal information you don't really think he should need, and no other guests seem to ever need—it's a scam. Also, if a guest ever tells you they need to pay by check, because that's the only way their company will pay—IT'S A SCAM.)

I say that identity theft on an individual level has become too labor-intensive because, in these days where large corporations with massive amounts of information on millions of individuals are being almost continually hacked, personal information about a given individual is worth about 10 cents.

When a major company suffers a major hack, the information goes up for sale, or often, just gets posted publicly by the hackers on the Dark Web, so they can show off their work.

So, why would an identity thief spend a bunch of time targeting you and social engineering you to try to steal your identity, when they can find out ten times as much information on you and a hundred and fifty million other people just by spending an hour or two on the Dark Web?

I do not worry that my identity is going to be stolen by any particular individual because of my advertising on a short-term rental website. Of course, I don't give away unnecessarily sensitive personal information to prospective guests, either. I *do* give my full name and cell phone number. In New Orleans, and probably other places, property records are public, so once you know someone's address, you can go on a website and find out the owner's name and his or her mailing address anyway, which is often the address where he or she lives.

Even if the property is registered to an LLC or other corporation, if you know the name of the corporation, in my state you can go to the Secretary of State's website and see the full names of all the owners/partners/board members of the company and the registered agent (the in-state person who can receive service of process). I don't think all states are quite as open with this information as Louisiana, but the information is mostly obtainable, either on the Internet or by physically going to the local land records office or the Secretary of State's office, or perhaps by telephoning.

So, if you own the property you are going to be renting out, don't waste a lot of time thinking you can keep your last name secret from someone who cares enough to find it out.

Scams

Though the average person probably worries more about identity theft than they do about being scammed, being scammed is WAY more likely than having your identity stolen through an STR platform.

Here are three of the most common scams, and they are by no means limited to the short-term rental business. These scams can and do occur to anyone with an email address or phone number.

Check-Refund Scam

The Check-Refund Scam is the number one reason to do all your monetary transactions through the STR platform.

Taking payment by check outside the STR platform may seem tempting, since you can avoid the platform's fees. The Check-Refund Scam is a good reason not to do it. Here is an example of how it commonly works:

Someone contacts you and wants to rent your place. They want to stay for six months, and want to pay in advance. They tell you their company is paying for the rental, and it's easier for them to pay for the entire stay with one check. You agree on a price, say, $9000.

$9000...all at once...wow, that would really get me out of a lot of jams! you think.

Plus, you will save a large amount in fees, and so will the guest.

Win-win, right?

Is greed blinding you a little bit? It's blinding me. I feel like I need a pair of Ray Bans for my Ray Bans. *I want the whole $9000*. More money = fewer jams.

After corresponding with your prospective guest, you wonder if the whole thing will actually happen, or if someone is just messing with you. You hope it's for real.

A couple days later, you receive a Fed Ex package... with a $9400 cashier's check in it!

He paid with a cashier's check! Now you can stop worrying. This guy must be on the up-and-up, since cashier's checks are official and aren't fake. Right?

He also overpaid by $400. That's weird. Well, you decide to deposit it anyway. He can ask for the $400 back if he wants. Maybe the $400 was for something you and he discussed that you don't remember, like the water bill.

A couple days later, he does contact you about the $400, saying he's sorry about the extra work, but there was a mix-up with the check amount. His accounting department, which issued the check, told him it would be easier if he just reimbursed the company the $400, rather than having them put a stop payment on the check and reissue another one. The guy asks if it would be okay if you just sent him back $400 and kept the $9000 you agreed on.

Of course! you say happily. You just got $9400 in your bank account. Giving back $400 is no problem.

You wire him $400 and await his arrival in a month. And, of course, you start spending that $9000.

But then, a week or so later, there's a slight problem.

Your bank has yanked $9400 out of your account, overdrawing you catastrophically.

The cashier's check was fraudulent, and you are on the hook for it.

Yes, cashier's checks can be fake. And generally *do not* eat the cost of fake checks deposited with them.

That's the Check-Refund Scam.

What does the thief get out of it? $400.

Only $400? It doesn't seem to make sense that a thief would do all this for $400 when there was $9000 on the line. Then it dawns on you: that was part of the scam. The big numbers were never real.

To get $400 from you, the thief just had to blind you with greed. He did. $400 goes a long way in Nigeria.

Stolen-Listing Scam

I'm calling this the Stolen-Listing Scam since I'm not sure it has an actual name. It's very devious, and we discussed it earlier in the section on watermarking.

To recap, the scammer steals your entire listing—text, photos, whatever. He uses his own contact information (email and phone), but uses your actual street address, so the guest can look up the property on Google Street View and check that it is "legit."

Guests book "your" property with the scammer (usually not through Airbnb or Vrbo, but through Craigslist, or another site where the guest can mail the scammer their payment well in advance of their arrival). The scammer gets paid, and you aren't aware of the scammer's "guests" until they *show up at your door*.

The scammer may even tell them that the last group lost the house key, and because he is out of town, they should call a locksmith and get the lock changed so they can get in. (I've heard, anecdotally, of this happening, but I suspect it is not common. By the time the thief's "guests" arrive at your door, he has long since gotten his money, and has nothing to gain by continuing to interact with these people or concerning himself with whether or not they can get in.)

This scam is particularly violating and awful, since you now have strangers either at your front door or, worse, *in your house*, and may have *real* guests arriving soon, if you don't have them already!

Hopefully you find out about the situation quickly so the burden of dealing with this is on you, and not on your legitimate guests.

And dealing with it will, of course, be horrible.

The best way to deal with this scam? Make sure it never happens.

Watermark your photos!

Phishing Scam

This is a more general scam that you should always be on the lookout for as a user of the Internet. It involves you getting an email that appears to be from Airbnb or another platform you use, but is fraudulent. The email may look *very, very* legitimate. You can mouse over the links and they look like legitimate links. But this can be faked. In particular, be on the lookout for emails that seem like they, in any way, want to get your login and password, or other personal information. Even ones that have a hyperlink or button that looks like it goes to Airbnb.com, which you click on and then wind up at a site that *looks just like* Airbnb.com.

The best thing to do if you get an email from Airbnb asking you to contact them is to not click on anything in the email. Open up a web browser, Airbnb.com in the address bar, go to the site and log in, and see if there is a message waiting for you, or something on your Dashboard indicating the issue that was mentioned in the email. If you don't see anything but are still concerned, click on Help and contact Airbnb on the phone about it. If nothing comes up, the email may very well have been a phishing scam.

These are three major scams. Because this is not a book about Internet security, and because scammers are creative and are constantly coming up with new gambits, I recommend you periodically read up on the latest scams by Googling phrases such as "Airbnb scam."

And, keep up with STR message boards to see what other suspicious things are happening to other hosts in your community. Some scams are local.

Physical Security

The other category of things people worry about is security of physical things—their property, its contents, and their person.

Security Cameras

Security cameras on your property are a very good idea. They not only record crimes that have occurred (break-ins, trespassing) so you can provide evidence to the police to catch the perpetrators, they have an even more important function: **deterrence**.

Most crimes are crimes of opportunity. The typical robbery does not fit the old-timey idea of a crook in a black mask "casing" a house, then coming back another day to break in through a window with a crowbar.

Instead, it's more common for potential thieves, if they think you are not home, to simply knock on your front door or ring the bell. If you do not answer after a few rings, they can be pretty sure you are not home, so they try the door. It might even be unlocked.

If it's not, since they know you aren't home and they see no cameras or signs of a security system, they may go around the back, if it's not too hard to access, and try the doors and look for a key. Just like lots of people use "password" or "123456" for their computer password, a lot of people put a spare key on the ledge above their door, under the mat, in the flower pot next to the door, or someplace equally obvious.

But if a thief sees a camera near your front door, he goes elsewhere. He is seeking a low-friction, low-effort property to rob, that he thinks contains some easily-sellable loot he can go in and grab. Most burglars spend only a few minutes in the place they are burglarizing.[101] They are not inspecting your vases for their value as antiques, or Googling the names of the artists on your paintings.

Install security cameras conspicuously at the front of your house, and outside all entrances.

Recently, and to what should be the great happiness of STR landlords who do not live on site, security cameras have undergone a burst of evolution.

The newest ones have two-way audio communication, meaning you can both see and hear the thieves, *and* talk to them via a speaker on the camera!

Video resolution has also gotten amazingly better, and cameras can send alerts to your phone. Some can recognize humans, and even track them as they move about the room.

Almost all outdoor cameras today can also see in infrared when it's dark (a feature many have had for years, but it's still cool).

In short: get cameras. They are an ounce of prevention.

Alarm System

A security/alarm system may be a good idea, but they can get expensive. A smart-home system would probably be a great way to keep track of your property if you don't live there.

The one thing you have to be careful about is not have anything that makes your guests feel you are invading their privacy. Definitely no indoor cameras. And motion detectors might be concerning to some guests; many guests won't know what they are, and be suspicious that they are some kind of camera or listening device.

If you have cameras, motion detectors, or other devices whose purpose is not clear, expect to get the occasional guest or group who arrive, see the indoor surveillance equipment, and cancel the booking and leave, unless you are there to smooth it over and talk them off the ledge. If they do leave, they are likely to get a full refund because of legitimate privacy concerns. I, personally, would not want to risk that.

I have security cameras on my rentals but I do not have alarm systems. I think they do provide an extra layer of protection and safety, no question, but you have to weigh that with the practicalities of employing them in an STR situation.

Having to explain to every group of guests how the alarm systems work (and some guests are certain to be technologically illiterate) will be a chore. And if the guest has to set the alarm every time they leave and then rush in and enter a code within 30 seconds every time they come home, it's inevitable you will have lots of false alarms at weird hours and, of course, panicking guests when sirens start to go off and the cops come.

To me, it is not worth the hassle. I would have an alarm system if I had a high-value property and sophisticated guests, though.

Motion-Sensitive Floodlights

This is a common-sense feature that most homeowners have. Have motion-sensitive floodlights in exterior spaces like side yards and in the back yard. You can even put one on your front porch, if appropriate. This helps your legitimate guests find their way around and avoid tripping and breaking something, and scares non-guests away.

Personal Safety

Personal security is going to be a highly individualized matter taking into account you, your property, and your customer base. If your rental is very high-end and in a good neighborhood, your customers are probably not going to mug you, and are probably not going to get mugged themselves. Visible, outdoor cameras reduce the chances even more.

Though I have yet to hear of anyone I know being physically assaulted by a guest, it could happen. I can only recommend the same precautions you might take in any situation where you are meeting an unknown person or group by yourself. If you are a single female host, bring a buddy, or carry any defensive devices that will help you feel safe (personal alarm, mace, etc.). Tell someone in advance that you are going to meet arriving guests, and to call you at a certain time. If you haven't answered in a reasonable time, have them call the police to check on you. Better safe than sorry.

If your property is in a not-so-safe area, make sure you are not followed in by someone who may be looking to commit a crime of opportunity. And make sure your rental is *always* securely locked up between guests. I lock the door of the rental behind me even if I have to run out to my car. This way someone cannot sneak in while I'm distracted.

Paranoid? Yes. Being paranoid is a good way to avoid being robbed or attacked.

Lights on Timers

Sometimes low-tech ideas don't go out of style, because they work. In addition to high-tech security cameras and two-way video Wi-Fi doorbells, it doesn't hurt to put a couple of lights on timers (maybe one in the front room and one in a bedroom). Even put a television on a timer. Nothing signals to a potential burglar "someone's home" better than the flickering light of a TV set.

Minimum Standards

Though some guests assume that all "Airbnbs" are a standardized product, you know by now that they are anything but.

Each platform does have some requirements that you *must* abide by in order to list your property, however.

"Hosting on Airbnb"

A couple of years ago, Airbnb had something called both "Hosting Standards" and "Hospitality Standards," depending on where on their website you looked. Apparently it was too important a subject to give just one name[102]. If you learned the standards, congratulations, it means you are good at learning. Now you can learn the expectations for "Hosting on Airbnb"[103]

Many of them hearken back to the things you already read about that help you appear high in Airbnb's search rankings. For the sake of brevity, assume all those things are necessary, plus the following.

Cleanliness:

- Clean every room guests can access, especially bedrooms, bathrooms, and the kitchen
- Check that there's no hair, dust, or mold on surfaces and floors
- Perform turnover between each stay:
    - Provide fresh linens/sheets and towels for guests
    - Clear trash, food, and leftover items from previous guest

Essential Amenities:

- Toilet paper
- Soap
- Linens/sheets
- At least one towel per booked guest
- At least one pillow per booked guest

Accurate Listing Details:

- Accurate and up-to-date address (this will be shared only after guest has booked)
- Bedroom and bathroom privacy details are accurate
- Listing photos fairly represent the condition and layout of the space
- Amenities are as advertised, present and functional

Amenities: List all the ones you offer and "make sure each one is available and operational."

Nightly Price: "Make sure your space matches the price you set. A very high price may lead travelers to assume your listing is extra luxurious."

Easy Check-In: "A clear and simple check-in process." The following "tips" are offered:

- Create a check-in guide for your listing–we'll share it with your guests 24 hours before check-in so they have everything they need to arrive smoothly
- If you plan to meet guests in person, make sure to coordinate a check-in time in advance
- If you offer self check-in, add those details in the Guest resources section of your listing
- Make sure your guests know how to contact you if they have a travel delay or last-minute question

> Provide your guests with detailed directions for getting to your place—you can save time by putting it all in your house manual

Supporting guests during their stay: Be available throughout the guests' stay and use "clear and consistent" communication. "Tips":

> Be proactive in your communication so guests know you're available. Reach out early to coordinate arrival plans. If you won't be greeting your guests when they arrive, you can send them a message at their check-in time to make sure everything went smoothly.
>
> If you confirm a reservation and something about your listing changes, tell your guest in advance.
>
> Download the Airbnb app so you can respond to messages anywhere.
>
> If you won't be in the area during their stay, you can give your guests a local point of contact.[104]

Guests will be asked to rate you on many of the above things, so make sure you pay attention to all of them.

Airbnb additionally has guidelines for Responsible Hosting in the United States,[105] most of which can also be applied to non-US properties.

Key subjects addressed are: Health and Cleanliness, Safety, Neighbors, Permissions, General Regulations, Local Regulations (Airbnb has a list of cities for which they provide STR hosting information).[106]

Airbnb also offers advice on General Info about Local Regulations.[107]

Professional Hospitality Businesses

Airbnb has separate standards for hotels and other hospitality businesses[108] (formerly called Standards for Professionally-Managed Properties), which include:

- Boutique hotel
- Hotel
- Bed & breakfast
- Serviced apartment
- Aparthotel
- Casa particular
- Condohotel
- Heritage hotel
- Hostel
- Minsu
- Nature lodge
- Pension
- Pousada
- Resort
- Ryokan

These businesses, **in addition to meeting the basic requirements for hosts**, must have "appropriate business licenses" and they "are legally responsible for property management and authorized to sell rooms within the property…directly to the public."[109]

The properties "should have a unique, independent environment and style," particularly:

- Vibrant common gathering spaces and/or events
- Guest rooms with personal touches that are individually unique and/or local in design
- High-quality photos on the listing page that showcase the design of the property and what guests can expect
- Accessibility features that are helpful to guests with limited mobility.[110]

HomeAway Marketplace Standards

Vrbo has something called "Homeaway Marketplace Standards,"[111] (remember, Vrbo is part of HomeAway, which is part of Expedia, and Vrbo's website uses the HomeAway term frequently) whose purposes is to "provide you the most bookings possible," which means "provid[ing] travelers security in their booking experience."

The Marketplace Standards are:

> ➤ **All bookings from HomeAway travelers must be processed through HomeAway checkout or reported through an integrated software.** Content around avoiding the HomeAway service fee or any other request on your listing that attempts to direct travelers to another website or to book outside of HomeAway checkout is not permitted. This includes but is not limited to language, URLs, phone numbers, email addresses, and physical addresses.
>
> ➤ **You must accept a material number of booking requests.** While we understand that not all booking requests are desirable for your property, you should accept a material number of the requests.
>
> ➤ **You must accommodate travelers with service animals.** All property owners and managers with properties located in the United States and U.S. Territories are required to accommodate travelers who require the use of a service animal
>
> ➤ **You cannot cancel a material number of confirmed reservations.** Canceling a confirmed reservation is a huge disappointment and can result in lost time, money, and a bad overall experience for travelers.
>
> ➤ **You must maintain an accurate calendar.** Your calendar should be kept accurate at all times. This will save potential travelers from spending time submitting booking requests for unavailable dates and you time in having to respond about availability.
>
> ➤ **You cannot use one listing to drive bookings for multiple unlisted properties.**[112]

If you violate any of these, "your listing is subject to less visibility to travelers, penalties that include but are not limited to removing or disabling your ability to receive inquiries, demotion or removal from search results, or removal from the listing site all together without any refund." The refund they are referring to is probably the $499 you pay per year for the subscription plan.

You also must follow [HomeAway's Terms and Conditions](#).

One thing to note is that "material number" (of acceptances and cancellations) is not defined.

I would assume they decide whether you are violating those policies on a case-by-case basis.

My Two Cents

Here are the common themes I would follow that I believe will keep you on the right side of almost any STR platform's requirements:

- ➢ DON'T CANCEL ON GUESTS. Keep your calendars synced so you don't double-book.
- ➢ CLEANLINESS.
- ➢ COMMUNICATION. Respond to guests promptly before and during their stay. Proactively provide them information they need to access the rental and other important info they will need for their arrival and stay (like Wi-Fi network and password).
- ➢ ASSISTANCE. Be available to guests at all times during their stay, responding to their texts and calls promptly so you can help them out of any jams.
- ➢ SMOOTH CHECK-IN PROCESS. Be available, have everything ready and in place at the agreed check-in time, no hiccups.
- ➢ ACCURACY. Be honest about your listing and don't oversell. Have all the amenities stated in your listing, working and available, or inform guests as far in advance as possible if a key amenity will be out of service. Make sure your guests are okay with that.
- ➢ PRICING. Keep it in line with what you are offering and what similar properties with those qualities are charging in your area.

Hiring a Property Manager

Does operating an STR sound like WAY more work and stress than finding a long-term tenant and just collecting checks every month?

If so, then I have done my job. Are you ready for all that work and worry, *just* to make substantially more money on your rental property?

We've already talked about how one way to ease the pain is to pay someone to do the cleaning of your STR(s).

A way to almost entirely take away the pain is to find a good property manager who specializes in STRs.

Hiring a property manager is probably only a good choice if you have a large property that can bring in substantial income, enough income so that the property manager can use his or her contacts and network to get you clients and get them to pay healthy rates, and thereby mostly pay for him- or herself.

This is easier said than done. It's a bit like saying, "All you need to do is find a leprechaun and follow him to the end of the rainbow, take his pot of gold, and boom, you're rich!"

Luckily, since I wrote the first edition of this book, firms specializing in STR property management have proliferated.

But also, STR hosts in your area often will also manage other properties. If I were looking for a property manager, this is the route I would go. Find someone in the local area to manage your property, preferably someone who is already managing a property for another host you know, and who recommends them.

Whether someone is recommended to you are not, make sure to interview them, asking questions that will help you decide whether you should give them a chance. They will probably charge a fee of up to 20% of your income, so you need to make sure they are skilled and experienced. The nature of STRs is that a few screw-up (and subsequent bad ratings) can permanently damage you. You need to minimize the risk that your property manager will mess up the business you have so carefully gotten off the ground.

"What services do you provide?"

Let *them* explain their offering. If they sound momentarily stumped, or respond by asking what services you *want* them to offer, that's a bad sign. It means they are winging it.

"How many properties do you manage?"

They should be able to give you a number and break it down. "I have a building on Claiborne Avenue with four 1-bedroom apartments, a large property in the French Quarter that sleeps 10," etc. If they say "about 5," or any other number preceded by "about," that's not good. They don't know how many properties they manage? That person is not detail-oriented. Or maybe they don't manage any properties, other than their own, and you will be their guinea pig for the property management business they hope to get off the ground.

"Do you have any references I can call?"
The references should be owners of properties they manage, not former bosses at unrelated businesses.

"What do you do when a house cleaner calls in sick?"

They should have a plan. Turnovers are critical, and managing them is one of the key things you want a property manager to do flawlessly. You don't want to get any emergency calls asking you to help solve a problem that you hired them to take off your plate entirely.

During the conversation about house cleaners, listen for them to say that they always double-check the work of their cleaners. Don't ask unless it's clear they are not going to say it. Their not saying they do that is a bad sign, it means they probably don't. But do ask the question if they have not said anything about it of their own volition, because quality control is critical.

"How do you manage calendars?"
Managing calendars for multiple properties is complicated, and a prospective property manager should be able to give you a detailed answer to this question. They should mention that the property owner needs to make them a co-host or other platform-specific role that allows them access to the calendar and other information. If they can't tell you the ins-and-

outs, it's difficult to see how they could be managing other peoples' properties, and they probably aren't. Again, you would be the guinea pig.

"How does it work when you go on vacation?"

They should have some kind of answer and not stumble over the question.

Other than that, trust your gut.

Consider Reviews at Every Stage

It's time to discuss that awkward, painful, exciting, excruciating subject that every STR host loves to hate: reviews.

Reviews are critical to your income, and even your survival, as an STR host.

I put that in bold and made it its own paragraph because it really needs to sink in.

Reviews are so important, you need to be thinking ahead to the review at every stage of the process of operating your rental—even before opening.

Creating your Listing

When you create your listing, as I've said several times before, you need to *sell* the customer on why your place is the best choice for them. But, of course, you need to be honest. And your pictures need to be honest. Yes, you've read about this earlier in this book, but I'm going to repeat some things here in case your mind wandered. It's important.

Just as those of us who have used Match.com don't like it when someone uses pictures from 20 years and 20 pounds ago, STR guests don't like to be bait-and-switched, especially if they will be stuck in your place for a week.

You may protest: *but, really, why? The guest has already paid! It's too late or too inconvenient for them to do anything if the rental isn't quite as nice as my listing made it look. I've got their money already. Who cares?*

My answer to that: *the review!*

Most properties that show up higher in search rankings on the platforms have been rated between 4.8 and five stars over the course of many stays.

To get 4.8 stars, it means that for every six times a customer has had their property reviewed, they have received five 5-star reviews, and one 4-star review. In other words, five out of six customers need to give you the top rating, and the sixth customer also needs to give you the next-to-top rating. And nobody needs to have given you anything lower.

If one person gives you three stars, you need *seven* five-star ratings to bring your average up to 4.8 stars.

So, though this may be counterintuitive to most people, 4.8 stars means *seven perfect stays and one average stay*. Unfortunately, the tendency for guests (and I think myself) would be to view a 4.8 star rating as meaning that every stay was a little less than perfect (i.e., everyone gave the place 4.8 stars). That can't be the case, since guests can only give integer ratings.

Such is math.

What you need to do is <u>always aim for five stars</u>, which means a pretty perfect trip with no hiccups.

You will surely miss the mark on a couple things from time to time, due to simply not being aware of something, a guest being overly picky about something, or something happening that was out of your control but is still a legitimate reason for your guest to rate your place as less than perfect.

Such as: your heat or A/C went out for 24 hours, even though you did work your butt off to get a repair person out there who fixed the problem ASAP. Does that stay deserve a perfect rating? A lot of people would say no, despite your efforts.

Some guests will be impressed by your responsiveness and communication during this process and will give you a five despite the problem. When a problem occurs, always make sure you communicate you are working hard and keep them updated. They will appreciate it.

Your guests should come away from their stay at your rental with only a minor quibble or two, no major complaints. (Especially not *multiple* major complaints.) Losing heat or cooling for 24 hours, unless the weather during that period happens to be ultra-pleasant (and even then, what is ultra-pleasant for a lot of people may not be ultra-pleasant for these guests) is probably considered major.

Tip: guests just *seeing you* make a serious effort to solve the problem will arouse their sympathies and help to defuse anger they might otherwise be feeling. If the A/C goes out and you spend a couple of hours jumping through hoops to bring a couple of window units out of storage and install them in the windows of the rental, simply so the guests can keep cool during the one night before the HVAC person arrives, may melt their hearts and get you the five stars you are craving.

Sure, in your mind, you are probably thinking, *This is sooo unnecessary, any normal person would just tolerate the 78-degree "heat" and turn on a ceiling fan and they'd be fine.*

But remember, what you're doing is part service and part theater. The fact that you expended energy, because you care so much about their comfort, is what counts. So always keep them updating, even if they never see you and all you are doing is making calls and keeping on top of the HVAC company so they are out there first thing in the morning.

Another problem that falls in the "major" category: guests feeling disappointment when they walk through the door for the first time. When this happens, you have slipped into four-star territory, if not lower. Your guests are not happy; as they put their luggage down, they look around and experience a feeling of "meh." And dissatisfied guests will be on alert for every problem or deficit that they can find, consciously or not.

It's called confirmation bias—confirmation that you, the host, are a lying liar and your place was made to look amazing in the photos and sound amazing in the description to deceive people and take their money.

This is a good time keep in mind that a guest's feeling of disappointment is directly related to what they were expecting. If you're advertising a hostel and it's $25 per night, and your guests walk in and everything looks "meh," they will not be disappointed. They were *expecting* "meh." They *paid for* "meh"—and were happy to do so, because they are on a tight budget, and everything else available was $110 per night. These guests want a place to crash and that's it. If the place is tolerably clean and the plumbing works, they will sleep the dead cockroaches off the bare mattress and be happy.

But if your prices are on the high end and your pics overpromise…expect disappointment.

Taking Reservations and Booking Guests

During the booking process, be honest and forthright. Before (or after) they book, guests may have questions. Be *very* honest about any negatives guests are trying to tease out of you. You will be able to tell when they are doing that.

In fact, when I can tell a guest is prying me about something that they consider important, I go out of my way to tell them the honest truth they do not want to hear. If what they want—which I don't have to offer—is important, I don't want their booking. Example: just today, a guest asked whether the ferry from my rental to the French Quarter. No, it is a pedestrian ferry. I don't go into a long discourse on how easy it is to drive to the French Quarter, which makes it totally redundant for the ferry to be a car ferry. That might confuse their memory, months later, to make them think I said there was a car ferry. I didn't. No car ferry for you!

But that's just me.

If a guest is inquiring about your place, and something is clearly key to them that you know is one of your property's weaknesses, just accept that you may not get the booking. Your place is not what they are looking for. People won't hold a negative against you if they were firmly told in advance that your rental definitely does not offer the thing they want. Usually. (This does not mean that if the disclosure that you do not offer something is buried somewhere in your listing that they won't hold it against you, of course they will. But that's another thing.)

Another example because this is another one hosts tend to put a positive shine on--distances: a guest asks you how far the bus stop is from the rental. You know it is six blocks, uphill, and a bit of a hike. Don't pretend not to know, and tell the guest, "Oh, three or four blocks. It's right there."

The fact that they are asking about public transportation means they probably intend to rely on it. They will probably be riding that bus every day, and will remember you said "three blocks" when they find themselves walking six blocks, uphill each way.

And yes, I know you said "three or four blocks," but they are going to remember the "three," not the "four."

I once had a guest complain in a review because the bus stop was one block further down the street than I said in my welcome binder. She was right, but it was because *the city had temporarily shut down the regular bus stop and moved it one block down because the street was torn up!*

I can only imagine her dissatisfaction if she thought I had intentionally lied.

Who knows, maybe she did.

Guest Arrival and Check-in

I've already discussed that guest check-in is probably the most critical time of a guest's stay, so I won't belabor it. I'll just remind you that it's a good time to point out quirks in the rental, explain them, and apologize for them if necessary. All this cushions the blow when something doesn't work, or the guest can't get it to work, and helps prevent the problem from winding up as a gripe in the review and a reduced star-rating.

During the Guest's Stay

Answering guests' phone calls or, more likely, text messages, immediately, or as close to it as possible, is critical. (If a guest texts you, answer them through the platform, as I've said before.) Often guests will only contact you about things that are important and time-sensitive, so glance at your phone whenever it buzzes with a new message.

When it comes to phones, I am one of those unfortunate Luddites who often puts my phone down on my desk at work and then pretty much ignores it all day ("If the call is important, they'll leave a message!"). I have tried to get better about reacting to it. You really should, particularly when your guests are arriving that day.

Pre-arrival (except on the date of travel), an immediate response to a guest's message is not completely critical, though it is appreciated by the guest, and "communication" is something on which you will be rated. Guests can get antsy if they have what they feel is an important question, even pre-stay. A quick answer is preferred.

Guest Departure & Asking for Reviews

The morning a guest checks out or early afternoon that day is a good time to send the guest a message saying you hope they had a good time and to have a safe trip home.

There are many little things you can add to that. Some hosts recommend saying something like, "If you enjoyed your stay, remember to give us a 5-star review!"

I would recommend watching some YouTube videos for hosts' thoughts on asking for reviews of your STR.

I don't generally ask for reviews, the whole subject is too fraught for me. But some hosts pepper the guest throughout their stay with nudges to give them a 5-star review.

On the first page of the house manual, or welcome letter, they put something like, "Our goal is to do whatever it takes to earn your five-star review! Please let us know if we have fallen short in any way, so we can fix it and earn your five-star review!"

I suppose I'm uncomfortable with it because the guest is *paying me* for a place to stay during *their* vacation; they are not paying me so that *I* can get something out of *them* in addition to the money they have already paid.

That said, the tactic appears to often work, by the way people online brag about it along with how all their reviews have been five-star. I guess the pessimist in me fears there will be that one person (and actually, there are a lot of them) who resents being told how to rate something, and then gives you 3 stars or even one star, just because.

Cautionary tale: once, when I was just starting out, I had hosted about 5 stays, and decided to be more proactive about asking for reviews, since nobody was reviewing me. It backfired.

I decided to send messages to three recent guests who I thought would give me good reviews, since everything had gone well with their stays. Two of them ignored me and one left a mediocre review with several complaints and an overall rating of four stars.

As is customary with the Internet, the person with the complaint is the most likely to actually leave a review.

Watch the videos and make your own decision. I hope it works out better for you than my little experiment did.

Post-Departure

If you've ever studied game theory, post-departure is the time you get to apply it to a real-life situation.

Reviews, of guests by hosts and of hosts by guests, in the early days of Airbnb, were just a simple, no-brainer way for hosts and guests to evaluate each other, much like buyers and sellers review each other on EBay.

But reviews on STR platforms are not quite the same as reviews of items purchased from an online seller. Because, when you review an STR or a group of guests, you are reviewing... people. Not solely in their roles as buyer or seller, just... *as people*.

Sure, the host is selling a service (a place to stay) and the guest is buying a service (a place to stay).

But, in an STR review, the person tends to become one of the primary subjects of the review, if not *the* primary subject, particularly if the guest really liked them...or really didn't.

And reviewing other people, *as people*, is kind of weird.

Reviews are critical for both hosts and guests. Hosts usually have a lot more reviews than guests, since you can host 52 groups a year if you are booked every weekend. Even if only half of your guests reviews you, that's 26 in a year. Reviews add up a lot more quickly for hosts than guests.

Guests only get reviewed if they take a trip. So maybe they have four or five opportunities a year, at most, to pile up some reviews. Since one bad review can be a huge red flag, guests don't want bad reviews any more than hosts do. It's not a matter of income to them, but each review counts for a whole lot more for them in the scheme of things.

I should point out that reviews on both Airbnb and Vrbo are "blind," meaning you don't see theirs and they don't see yours until both are written and submitted. Once both are submitted, neither can be changed, except that the review writer *may* be able to have his or her review taken down, and will not be allowed to write another. The platforms may also make other exceptions in some circumstances. I would not rely on it, though.

Reviews are pretty much stress-free when you've spent time communicating with the guests during their stay, know you have resolved any problems (all of which have been minor), and they have told you they love the rental, are having a great time, and would love to come back and stay again.

You then both give each other great reviews, and that's that. Sometimes guests will surprise you with a couple of minor jabs, or even a harsh review that seems to have come out of nowhere. Some people just have a habit of always keeping charm at volume 10 when dealing with others face-to-face, and only pull the knife out once their back is turned.

Airbnb asks all guests to give the host between one and five stars on each of the following: Overall Experience, Cleanliness, Accuracy, Value, Communication, Arrival, and Location.

Note that the first one is Overall *Experience*.

Overall Rating

And yet, your "Overall Rating" is an average of all your star ratings given in *all* the categories, including Overall Experience. It is not an average of all your ratings for Overall Experience. Shouldn't it be, if Overall Experience is the guest's summary of their well, overall experience? Apparently not.

Airbnb explains Overall Rating as, "an aggregate of the primary scores guests have given for that listing. At the bottom of a listing page there's an aggregate for each category rating."[113]

Though the meaning of "primary scores" is not clear, I have looked at my reviews, calculated the average of the reviews I have gotten for all seven categories for each of my properties, and found that my Overall Rating for each property exactly equals the average of my ratings for all seven categories on which guests rate hosts (Overall Experience, Cleanliness, etc.).

So, Overall Experience counts for 1/7th of your Overall Rating. This might seem like double-counting, and maybe it is. It could be that Airbnb *wants* to double-count it, to give it more weight, but not so much weight that the other six categories are not weighted.

Just some cocktail party chatter in case you wind up talking to an Airbnb ratings nerd.

Game Theory and Reviewing

Where game theory comes into it is when a guest's stay has been rocky at times…or just downright terrible. Tough times make for difficult reviews.

Suppose you make a major mistake, like, you forgot to change the sheets on the bed in the master bedroom. And they were visibly dirty. And full of hairs and stuff. I've never done that, but it would qualify.

The guests discover this as they are getting into bed at midnight. They notice the hairs, or even a stain on the bedsheet that looks like a bodily fluid. They decide that the best thing to do is strip off the sheets and pillowcases, and sleep on the bare mattress covered by a blanket from the hall closet. This is reasonable. This example is about *you* making a major mistake, not them.

The next morning they message you at 11am to tell you what happened, and say that they didn't want to call you late at night since they figured you would be in bed. That was considerate.

You are, of course, mortified. It is a weekday, and you are at work, so you have little choice but to wait until your lunch hour (or after work) and race around and get over to the rental as soon as you can. When you arrive, the guests are out, so you enter as agreed and put clean sheets on the bed, and confiscate the unclean sheets and blanket and take them home to wash.

You go out to your car, still mortified. What is the protocol in a situation like this? There isn't one. But here are some damage control ideas.

At the very least, you should notify the guests immediately after you have changed the sheets and apologize again, which you hopefully also did when they contacted you earlier. I would recommend a phone call, so you can truly express how sorry you are that this mistake happened. They might not answer, because people are talking less on the phone nowadays, but you can at least leave a voicemail. You should also send a message via the platform's messaging system, explaining the problem and what you did to fix it, so that there is a record of what happened. Apologize profusely there also. Apologize, apologize, apologize. Then at least they know you recognize just how disgusting and unacceptable the error was.

But beyond fixing the problem, apologizing profusely, and making sure everything was worked into a message(s) though the platform so it's on record that you fixed the problem and took responsibility? Like, should you give them some kind of refund?

Many hosts jump immediately to the idea of giving some kind of refund. A partial refund, a 50% refund, a refund of one night's stay, even a FULL refund.

No, no, no!

Though it sounds strange, I have found that guests rarely seem appreciative when you give any kind of refund, even though it is a proportionally large cost for you to bear. To this day, I have not figured out why that is. Are they embarrassed to acknowledge the refund because they feel it is too much, and they weren't expecting you to do that? Or, were they hoping their entire stay would be comped, and think you are being stingy by refunding only one night?

An experienced host I know says a better solution is to give a gift certificate ($25 or $50) to a restaurant you think the guests will enjoy. This both costs you less than one night's stay, and is a more fun "gift," showing that you put some thought into it. This is my new policy. While I think it is appropriate to refund one night if a problem made one of guests' nights truly awful. But as a rule, I don't do it in other cases.

Now, let's add that the guests from the dirty-sheets example seem a little bit chilly about the bedsheet problem even after your apologies and after you have given them a $50 gift certificate, but you can't really tell what's going on in their heads. You fear it's not good. Even after you apologized and gave them a gift, they seemed like they might still be mad. They certainly didn't make clear to you that they were *not* mad, that it was *no problem* and *we understand, these things happen.*

Review-wise, this is a bad situation.

At this point, the most likely scenario seems to be that if they do write a review, the dirty sheets will figure prominently. This may well seem unreasonable, after all your work and running around and apologies. But there you go.

Now you are in game theory territory. Soon the guests' date of departure comes, and they depart without a word. This makes you paranoid for a few moments, but then you realize most guests depart without a word. They are focused on the travel ahead—the flights, the car ride, Dramamine, and so on.

Right now, you should be hoping they do not leave you a review at all. That would be ideal. Because any review they leave, even if balanced, is going to be less than five stars, and half the review is going to be about them finding the previous guests' dirty bedsheets on the bed. And how they didn't discover it until right before bed, so there was nothing they could do about it.

Can't you just feel the disgust creeping over your skin? I can.

They will make a couple brief generalizations about the good things ("nice place, looks like the photos") but go into excruciating detail about bodily fluids on the sheets, finding the hairs, and so on. That's just how it works. A dirty sheet with hairs on it imprints a much more vivid picture on the guest's brain than a clean countertop or a gleaming kitchen sink.

Playing the game, your best move is to not leave them a review, so that's what you should do.

Why? You in no way want to trigger them to think about leaving you a review. Maybe as soon as they left your place, they forgot all about it. Maybe they don't use Airbnb (or email) very much, so they will ignore Airbnb's emails suggesting they leave a review.

But around 8pm on the evening the guests check out, you get a notification that they have left a review.

Sh*t.

Game theory on.

When a guest leaves a review almost immediately upon leaving (like, from their smartphone, in the car), or as soon as they get home and get situated, it's more often than not because something peeved them and they want to complain. (That is, unless you and the guest have engaged in a mutual love-fest like I was talking about earlier.) A good trip where everything went smoothly usually does not inspire a sense of urgency about reviewing. But a person who's annoyed because they feel they've gotten jilted—they want the world to know.

And yet, human unpredictability being what it is, you *still* never quite know what's going through a person's head. You don't know their playbook in this game, so to speak. Are they that irrational person on Yelp who goes to bargain-priced restaurants with a Groupon and trashes them because they aren't Nobu?

Or are they a balanced person who can clearly see the good while even-handedly pointing out the bad as well? The latter is disappointing (you wish they were totally blind to the bad, and you wish they would have not left any review at all if it was going to contain anything negative whatsoever), but fair is fair.

You pray that they are not that person from Yelp. You pray that they do not want...revenge. I have had the guest who does. I have also had people who I was almost sure would be that guest, but ended up being the cool and balanced type.

What is your best move *now*?

Airbnb

Your best move is still to do nothing, for the moment.

Put off writing a review for the maximum length of time possible. On Airbnb, you have 14 days the guest checks to write a review.[114] *Don't write anything until the last possible day.* Spend that time thinking about what to write, or whether to write anything at all.

First, taking some time to think before you act (or publish), if you have the option, is good general practice. Maybe your mind has gone too far down the rabbit hole into paranoia about what a terrible review the former guest is probably going to give you, and how evil and vindictive they are going to be, and how they surely want to destroy your carefully curated business and all your hard work and put you out on the street (or, worse, force you go back to long-term renting).

Second, delaying your review by 13 days means *theirs* doesn't post for 13 days. So, at least you have 13 more days to take reservations without a steaming pile of crud sitting at the top of your reviews page that prospective guests will be able to see, scaring them off.

But after 13 days, you do have to decide whether to write the default "Great guest, five stars!" review, or something else.

(Many hosts ask what is the last possible minute to leave a review and I have to say, I don't know. I do know that if a guest leaves a review on a Tuesday at 10:04am, according to the host's notifications, can successfully submit a review two weeks later, on Tuesday at 10:02am. So, it looks like it is probably 14 days from the exact minute the guest submitted their review. But this cannot be the final word, since we don't know *for sure* whether the host could have submitted their review, say, up until 11:59pm the night of that Tuesday.)

And really, why shouldn't you just give them five stars and be done with it? They didn't cause any problems or have any complaints, except the very legitimate one about dirty sheets. And that was *your* mistake, not theirs.

But here's the problem. Suppose they were so upset about those sheets that they left an awful review way out of proportion to the crime committed. Because, after the sheets incident, they had their eye out for other problems, and found them. Dust under the bed and on top of the bookcase. A spider's web under the kitchen sink. A dirty coffee cup in the dishwasher!

You will have the opportunity to post a response to the awful review, which you really have no choice but to do. It is your only way to even attempt to salvage the situation.

That's the worst case scenario, of course, but it's also, I would say, inevitable. You will get that person at some point.

So, what do you post? (Not in your response to the guest's review, but in your initial, "blind" review of the guest.) I have painted a tough picture here, where the host is the only one at fault.

The guests didn't do anything bad. Except...well...they were not that friendly. You might even say they were kind of frosty. You did run around and fix their problem, which after all was just human error, albeit a gross one. You did go out and buy them a $50 gift certificate, which they hardly acknowledged. And part of the reason you have no idea what they are thinking is that they were uncommunicative.

I only leave honest comments in reviews, but if I decided to do so, it would be fair to say: "I was happy to host the Robertsons. We had only one major hiccup which was cleared up quickly. I hope they enjoyed their time in New Orleans." I might also leave them less than five stars where it was legitimate, like for Communication.

That may not sound like a bad review to the unpracticed ear or eye. But in the STR world, it is fairly poor. Peoples' eyes are pealed to read between lines. And, those lines I've written tell a story that readers can easily fill in with bad things.

But why do that? By leaving a review that, when someone reads between the lines, shouts "Meh!" from the rooftops, are you just being incredibly petty?

No.

The difficulty lies in the fact that if a guest tosses logic aside and leaves you an unreasonably terrible, clearly vindictive review, in which he or she seems to be settling scores you had no idea existed—and, I am sorry to say, this *will* happen—you at least have the right to post a response to it.

But, if you have given that guest a review that says, "Five stars, great guests, welcome back any time!" it would be dishonest for you to then complain, in your response to their review, that the guests were ungrateful and uncommunicative and, well, you really *wouldn't* have them back, ever.

Both your review of them and your response to their review can't be true at once.

So, you have to consider what review they are probably going to leave before you leave them a review, so if they leave you a complaining one, you can leave a response that does not directly conflict with the review you left them.

In the prisoner's dilemma, the ur-example of game theory, two criminals are caught and separated. If neither confesses, the cops have nothing, and both prisoners go free. This is the best possible result for both.

If one prisoner talks and the other doesn't, the one who talks gets a short sentence and the other gets a long sentence. So, talking is the second best option, right?

It could be, but maybe not, because if *both* talk, *both* get long sentences.

Nobody talking is really the only good option. That's why the fundamental rule of criminality is, "Snitches get stitches."

Without lying, you can leave an okay review of a group of guests, since reviews are largely a matter of opinion. This way you are covered whatever they do. They may put you in a position where they punch low, and you need to be able to punch back

Vrbo

On Vrbo, the situation is a little different. The focus is more on guests reviewing rentals than on hosts reviewing guests.

Plus, the parties have a *whole year* to submit a review. Or, more accurately, one of the parties must submit a review within one year, or nobody can.

Once someone does submit a review, the other party has 14 days in which to submit their own review. After both are submitted, the reviews go public. Until that point, the reviews are blind. Once they are public, they can't be changed. However, Vrbo is explicit[115] that a review can be removed at the request of the party who submitted it, but they cannot then post a new or revised review. They are done at that point.

One very important point is that on Vrbo, guest and host reviews are not the same. While guest reviews are similar to those on Airbnb—guests can leave free-form text about their experience, along with star ratings on four criteria (overall experience, cleanliness, communication, and adherence to house rules[116])—hosts *only* get to give star ratings on the four criteria. Hosts cannot write any free-form text.

After a guest submits their review, the review is checked by a HomeAway employee to make sure it meets their "content guidelines."[117] If it does not, it is rejected, and the guest is informed they have to modify the review and remove any offending content before resubmitting. I am not totally clear whether the guest must complete the submit/reject/submit process and get an acceptable review in to Vrbo within the 14 day period that started from their (or my) initial submission, or if the process can be dragged out longer than 14 days until an acceptable review is submitted.

Because the host cannot write any text, only give stars, the game theory aspect of reviewing is mostly absent from Vrbo. Usually with Vrbo reviews, I don't think much about what the guest is going to say, I just give them five stars across the board, unless there was a particular problem in one of the areas, in which case I give fewer for that one.

Then there is the fact that so much time can pass between the stay and the review. It's quite possible you won't remember a thing about the guest unless you write notes about such things, or just happen to remember. But be aware that guests *do* leave reviews months after they've left. And more often than not, these long-delayed reviews are mediocre. Maybe jotting down a few notes on your travelers might be a good idea.

Once the guest's review is posted, the host has the option to write a response to it, in which the host *is* allowed to post free-form text.

Host responses to guest reviews appear on the (host's) property listing page, not on any page of the guest's. So, there is no page you can go to see specific things hosts have said about guests, unless you can find a property where a guest has stayed, *and* the guest left a review, *and* the host left a response to that review.

Otherwise, all hosts can see about guests is their overall star rating.

Responding to Reviews

Some hosts say that it's good to write a brief response to every review. I agree.

Most reviews are positive, so that means writing something like, "Thank you, Linda and Terry, I am so glad you enjoyed staying at the Bywater Bungalow and that you had a great time in New Orleans! I loved receiving your recipe for chocolate oatmeal cookies and I will be making them tonight. Wish you could be here to enjoy some, come back soon!"

Take a Deep Breath...and a Few Days

Responses to negative reviews are harder.

If you get a new review from a guest and it is negative, though you have an option to respond to it immediately, *I strongly advise that you take a day or two to cool down before writing a response.*

Keep it Brief

My second piece of advice in responding to a negative review is...*keep it brief.*

It's *very* tempting to leave a long-winded explanation in defense of your actions or inactions when you receive a bad review.

This is a turnoff to future guests. It makes you seem like you are refusing to admit wrongdoing and creating all kinds of elaborate rationalizations about why nothing was your fault.

Another reason to keep it brief: if you write a long block of text, nobody will read it. Nobody really cares about the owner's response, they want to see what the *guest* wrote. They want the dirt.

Even without reading it, a user of an STR site knows that if the guest left a bad review (and maybe they did read *that*), a 1000-word response from the owner is just going to be a bunch of justifications, rationalizations, complaints about the guest, tedious clarifications, and bile.

So, with just a glance, if they see a giant block of text in response to a review, they get turned off of renting from you.

Keep it brief.

Keep It Positive

My third piece of advice when responding to a negative (or positive) review is...*keep it positive*.

Take the high road in all cases. Apologize for things you did wrong, but don't belabor details. "I want to thank Linda and Terry for visiting, I had a great time talking with them about Philadelphia. And I apologize about the bedsheets problem, that was something I am deeply sorry about. I am glad Linda and Terry enjoyed New Orleans, and am particularly glad they were able to have a meal at one of my favorite restaurants, Commander's Palace!"

Now, while I did just recommend that you briefly mention that you promptly addressed the guest's problem and remedied it, if they list multiple problems, don't go through them all. Just address the worst one and ignore the rest. A laundry list (no pun intended) of all the fixing you did just makes you look like you're making excuses. Focus on not having so many problems next time

It takes a lot to grit your teeth and write something nice when someone has written bad things about you and your business, after all your hard work and all the money you have put into making your rental as nice and hospitable as possible.

But it's part of the game, and it's how you make your business successful and keep it that way.

Final Thoughts

I hope you have enjoyed learning how to start up and host your short-term rental and learned a lot. I know I have. The number of things I had to look up and/or verify in order to write this was astronomical.

I think if you follow the advice I've laid down here, you will do well in the STR business.

Or, you may be wise enough to realize that, based on any number of factors particular to you, your geographic location, and what you have to offer, the STR business may not be for you. Either way, your eyes will be wide open.

Thank you for reading. And remember, if you enjoyed this book… leave me five stars on Amazon!

Kidding-not-kidding! Actually, if you made it this far, you do not have to leave a review, you deserve a medal.

Do visit my website at AmericanBNB.com to read my answers to questions people have asked me, and for video tips about how to get the most out of your STR. And feel free to contact me via email at Josh@AmericanBNB.com.

Also visit my YouTube channel, AmericanBNB.

Until then,

XOXO,

Jeffrey S. Malfatti, Esq.

Notes

1 Sandford, Alisdair, euronews., "Coronavirus: Half of humanity now on lockdown as 90 countries call for confinement," 3 March 2020, https://www.euronews.com/2020/04/02/coronavirus-in-europe-spain-s-death-toll-hits-10-000-after-record-950-new-deaths-in-24-hou (accessed 6/7/20).

2 Vrbo.com, "Guidelines for owners and property managers for enhanced cleaning and disinfection of vacation rentals," https://www.vrbo.com/discoveryhub/tips-and-resources/improve-performance/clean-disinfect-guidelines (accessed 6/13/20).

3 Dain Evans, "Airbnb's future is uncertain as it continues to struggle through its Covid-19 response," May 6, 2020, https://www.cnbc.com/2020/05/06/can-airbnb-survive-the-coronavirus-pandemic.html (accessed 6/7/20).

4 Council for Economic Education, NY, Focus: Middle School World History, Activity 15.1, The Economic Impact of the Black Death of 1347–1352, p. 241, https://msh.councilforeconed.org/documents/978-1-56183-758-8-activity-lesson-15.pdf (accessed 5/31/20).

5 Nature Microbiology, Consensus Statement, "The species Severe acute respiratory syndrome-related coronavirus: classifying 2019-nCoV and naming it SARS-CoV-2," 3/2/20, https://www.nature.com/articles/s41564-020-0695-z?fbclid=IwAR3v3d3IIzJlj81M_zA_kh7LqGsUcXNU0cG5YdGuI2ftarTKWsQ4IqHWMzE (accessed 6/7/20).

6 Blum, Sam. "This Beautiful Treehouse is the Most Popular Listing on Airbnb." Thrillist.com, 20 July 2017, https://www.thrillist.com/news/nation/airbnbs-most-popular-listing-is-a-beautiful-treehouse (accessed 6/13/20).

7 Morrissey, Pauline. "The top 10 most popular Airbnb listings in the world." Domain.com.au, 20 Jan. 2016, https://www.domain.com.au/news/the-top-10-most-popular-airbnb-listings-in-the-world-20160119-gm8rfk/ (accessed 6/13/20).

8 Luisa Beck, "Berlin had some of the world's most restrictive rules for Airbnb rentals. Now it's loosening up." Washington Post, March 28, 2020, https://www.washingtonpost.com/world/europe/berlin-had-some-of-the-worlds-most-restrictive-rules-for-airbnb-rentals-now-its-loosening-up/2018/03/27/e3acda90-2603-11e8-a227-fd2b009466bc_story.html (accessed 6/7/20).

9 Keycafe Team, "Understanding Short-Term Rental Regulations in Paris," May 31, 2019, https://medium.com/keycafe/understanding-short-term-rental-regulations-in-paris-f510aebc3408 (accessed 6/7/20).

10 Marcie Geffner. "FHA loans: Everything you need to know in 2020," Bankrate.com, undated, http://www.bankrate.com/finance/mortgages/7-crucial-facts-about-fha-loans-2.aspx (accessed 6/13/20)

11 Airbnb Automated, "How I AM NOT PAYING My Rent Right Now Airbnb Business Strategy 2020," 3/27/20, https://www.youtube.com/watch?v=Ojws-Vn_kXg (accessed 6/5/20).

12 Ibid.

13 TheRealDeal.com, "Hospitality startup Sonder slashes workforce," 3/24/20, https://therealdeal.com/2020/03/24/hospitality-startup-sonder-slashes-workforce/ (accessed

6/5/20).
[14] Airbnb.com, "Download the Airbnb cleaning handbook," https://www.airbnb.com/cleaning/handbook (accessed 6/13/20).
[15] Airbnb.com, "It's time to check your understanding," https://www.airbnb.com/hosting/cleaning/quiz (accessed 6/13/20).
[16] Airbnb.com, "Congrats! You're committed to clean." https://www.airbnb.com/hosting/cleaning/success (accessed 6/13/20).
[17] United States Environmental Protection Agency (EPA), Ozone Generators that are Sold as Air Cleaners, https://www.epa.gov/indoor-air-quality-iaq/ozone-generators-are-sold-air-cleaners#ozone-health (accessed 5/31/20).
[18] Ibid.
[19] US Food & Drug Administration, CFR – Code of Federal Regulations Title 21, Sec. 801.415(b), 1 April 2019, https://www.accessdata.fda.gov/scripts/cdrh/cfdocs/cfcfr/CFRsearch.cfm?fr=801.415 (accessed 5/29/20).
[20] Dain Evans, "Airbnb's future is uncertain as it continues to struggle through its Covid-19 response," May 6, 2020, https://www.cnbc.com/2020/05/06/can-airbnb-survive-the-coronavirus-pandemic.html (accessed 6/7/20).
[21] Airbnb.com, How is my refund calculated if I cancel my reservation? https://www.airbnb.com/help/article/1338/how-is-my-refund-calculated-if-i-cancel-my-reservation (accessed 5/31/20).
[22] Vrbo.com, "What is the Expanded Distribution Network?", https://help.Vrbo.com/articles/What-is-the-Expanded-Distribution-Network (accessed 6/2/20).
[23] Guesty.com, "FAQs," https://www.guesty.com/pricing/ (accessed 6/16/20).
[24] Guesty.com, "Features," https://www.guesty.com/features/ (accessed 6/16/20).
[25] Guesty.com, "Payment Processing," https://www.guesty.com/features/payment-processing/ (accessed 6/16/20).
[26] Guesty.com, "Frequently Asked Questions," https://www.guesty.com/features/api/ (accessed 6/16/20).
[27] Guesty.com, "Guesty Booking Website," https://support.guesty.com/en/article/guesty-booking-website-7019139 (accessed 6/16/20).
[28] Lodgify.com, "Easily Build a Bookable Vacation Rental Website," https://www.lodgify.com/vacation-rental-website-builder/ (accessed 6/16/20).
[29] Lodgify.com, "Multiply your bookings with our secure vacation rental booking software," https://www.lodgify.com/vacation-rental-booking-system/ (accessed 6/20/20).
[30] Lodgify.com, Vacation rental software pricing that scales as you grow, https://www.lodgify.com/pricing/ (accessed 6/2/20).
[31] Ashworth, Jess, "Vacation Rental Agreement Template for Your Total Peace of Mind," https://www.lodgify.com/blog/vacation-rental-agreement-template/ (accessed 6/15/20).
[32] Guesty.com, "Owner's Rental Agreement Template," https://support.guesty.com/en/article/owners-rental-agreement-template (accessed 6/15/20).
[33] Guesty.com, "What is a Rental Payment Agreement?" https://www.guesty.com/vacation-rental-guide/rental-payment-agreement/ (accessed 6/15/20).
[34] Airbnb.com, "Airbnb Highlights New Accessibility Filters and Features for Guests with Disabilities Worldwide," 15 March 2018, https://news.airbnb.com/airbnb-highlights-new-

accessibility-filters-and-features-for-guests-with-disabilities-worldwide/ (accessed 6/16/20).

[35] Ramit Sethi, "People don't value the things they get for free." Business Insider, 20 Jan 2017, https://www.businessinsider.com/people-dont-value-free-stuff-2017-6 (accessed 6/1/20).

[36] Hawkins, Andrew J. "Nearly two-thirds of Uber customers don't tip their drivers, study says." TheVerge.com, 21 October, 2021, https://www.theverge.com/2019/10/21/20925109/uber-tipping-riders-drivers-percentage-gender-nber-study (accessed 5/30/20).

[37] Such things are generally called *capital improvements*, and are not subtracted from revenues when calculating net income. Again, this is a simplification.

[38] This is the $1700 to $2300 we calculated earlier, minus $780 per month expenses.

[39] This is the $1230 to $1590 we calculated earlier, minus $630 per month expenses.

[40] Gothaus, Michael. "How to Make a Killing on Airbnb." FastCompany.com, 26 Mar. 2015, https://www.fastcompany.com/3043468/the-secrets-of-airbnb-superhosts (accessed 6/13/20).

[41] Here are the numbers, in case you're curious: Copenhagen 12.6%, Antwerp 32.8%, Chicago 45.6%, Athens (Greece) 43.8%, Brussels 36%, Berlin 21.8%, Asheville, NC 39.9%, Barcelona 57.5%, Amsterdam 24.6%, Austin, TX 32.2%, Dublin 43.8%. These data are from InsideAirbnb.com (accessed 9/6/17).

[42] Avakian, Talia. "16 Odd Things That Are Illegal in Singapore." BusinessInsider.Com, 4 Aug. 2015, http://www.businessinsider.com/things-that-are-illegal-in-singapore-2015-7 (accessed 6/13/20).

[43] Insurance Information Institute, "Peer-to-peer home rental," https://www.iii.org/article/peer-peer-home-rental (accessed 6/13/20).

[44] Airbnb.com. "Host Guarantee Terms and Conditions." Airbnb.com, undated, https://www.airbnb.com/terms/host_guarantee (accessed 6/13/20).

[45] Ibid.

[46] Vrbo, "$1M Liability Coverage." https://vrbo.com/l/liability-insurance/ (accessed 6/13/20).

[47] Ibid.

[48] Ibid.

[49] HomeAway, "Do I need a special vacation rental insurance policy for my property?" https://help.homeaway.com/articles/Do-I-need-a-special-vacation-rental-insurance-policy-for-my-property (accessed 6/13/20).

[50] Airbnb.com. "Terms of Service," https://www.airbnb.com/terms (accessed 6/14/20).

[51] *Ibid*. Section 8.1.2 (accessed 6/14/20).

[52] Airbnb.com. "What if a host asks me to sign a contract?" https://www.airbnb.com/help/article/465/can-hosts-ask-guests-to-sign-a-contract (accessed 6/13/20).

[53] Ibid.

[54] DocuSign.com, "US electronic signature laws and history," https://www.docusign.com/learn/us-electronic-signature-laws-and-history/ (accessed 6/16/20).

[55] Vrbo.com. "Why should I have a Rental Agreement?" https://help.Vrbo.com/articles/Why-should-I-have-a-Rental-Agreement (accessed 8/16/17). This page now (6/14/20) redirects to https://help.vrbo.com/articles/Why-should-I-have-a-Rental-Agreement.

[56] Vrbo.com, "What is a rental agreement?" https://help.vrbo.com/articles/Why-should-I-have-a-Rental-Agreement (accessed 6/14/20).

⁵⁷ *See* https://community.homeaway.com/docs/DOC-4094 (accessed 8/16/17), but the document was gone when checked 6/14/20.
⁵⁸ Vrbo.com. "How do I upload my rental agreement?" https://help.Vrbo.com/articles/How-to-upload-my-rental-agreement (accessed 6/13/20).
⁵⁹ Vrbo.com, "What Stay Taxes/Lodging Taxes do you collect and remit?" https://help.vrbo.com/articles/What-Stay-Taxes-Lodging-Taxes-does-HomeAway-collect-and-remit (visited 6/14/20).
⁶⁰ Airbnb.com. "What is the Airbnb Service Fee?" https://www.airbnb.com/help/article/1857/what-are-airbnb-service-fees (accessed 6/14/20).
⁶¹ Airbnb.com. "How does occupancy tax collection and remittance by Airbnb work?" https://www.airbnb.com/help/article/1036/how-does-occupancy-tax-collection-and-remittance-by-airbnb-work (accessed 6/14/20).
⁶² Ibid.
⁶³ Airbnb.com, "Listing photos & photography," https://www.airbnb.com/help/topic/1040/listing-photos-photography (accessed 6/9/20)
⁶⁴ Vrbo.com, "How do I add photos to my listing?", https://help.vrbo.com/articles/upload-photos-to-my-listing (accessed 6/9/20).
⁶⁵ Leshnower, Ron. "Does the Federal Fair Housing Act Apply to Your Rental Property?" Nolo.com, http://www.nolo.com/legal-encyclopedia/does-the-federal-fair-housing-act-apply-your-rental-property.html (accessed 6/14/20).
⁶⁶ 42 U.S.C. 3604 – Discrimination in the Sale or Rental of Housing and Other Prohibited Practices. https://www.gpo.gov/fdsys/pkg/USCODE-2010-title42/pdf/USCODE-2010-title42-chap45-subchapI-sec3604.pdf (bolding added) (accessed 6/14/20). *See also* 42 U.S.C. 3603.
⁶⁷ JDSUPRA, "Short-Term Rental Law Stumbles, But Survives Federal Court Challenge," 16 September 2019, https://www.jdsupra.com/legalnews/short-term-rental-law-stumbles-but-98938/ (accessed 6/9/20).
⁶⁸ PetMD.com. "Snail, Slug Bait Poisoning in Dogs." http://www.petmd.com/dog/conditions/neurological/c_dg_metaldehyde_poisoning?page=show (accessed 6/14/20).
⁶⁹ U.S. Department of Housing and Urban Development, "Assessing a Person's Request to Have an Animal as a Reasonable Accommodation Under the Fair Housing Act," 28 January 2020, https://www.hud.gov/sites/dfiles/PA/documents/HUDAsstAnimalNC1-28-2020.pdf (accessed 6/15/20).
⁷⁰ U.S. Department of Justice, Civil Rights Division, Disability Rights Section. "ADA Requirements, Service Animals," updated 24 February 2020, http://www.ada.gov/service_animals_2010.htm (bolding added) (accessed 6/15/20).
⁷¹ Ibid.
⁷² Ibid. (bolding added).
⁷³ Ibid. (line separations added for clarity)
⁷⁴ Ibid.
⁷⁵ FHEO-2013-01, p. 1 (accessed 9/11/17).
⁷⁶ HUD, "Assessing a Person's Request to Have an Animal as a Reasonable Accomodation Under the Fair Housing Act," 28 January 2020, p. 3, https://www.hud.gov/sites/dfiles/PA/documents/HUDAsstAnimalNC1-28-2020.pdf (accessed 6/14/20).
⁷⁷ Ibid., footnote 4.

78 Ibid., 2.
79 HUD, "Assessing a Person's Request to Have an Animal as a Reasonable Accommodation Under the Fair Housing Act," 28 January 2020, https://www.hud.gov/sites/dfiles/PA/documents/HUDAsstAnimalNC1-28-2020.pdf (accessed 6/14/20).
80 Ibid.
81 Ibid.
82 Ibid.
83 U.S. Department of Justice, Civil Rights Division, Disability Rights Section. "ADA Requirements, Service Animals." 12 July 2011, http://www.ada.gov/service_animals_2010.htm (accessed 9/9/17).
84 Ibid.
85 Airbnb.com. "What is an assistance animal?" https://www.airbnb.com/help/article/1869/what-is-an-assistance-animal (accessed 9/9/17).
86 New Orleans Code of Ordinances, Sec. 18-202. - Cats or dogs brought from other places, https://library.municode.com/la/new_orleans/codes/code_of_ordinances?nodeId=PTIICO_CH18AN_ARTVDOCA_DIV1GE_S18-202CADOBROTPL (bolding added) (accessed 9/11/17).
87 World Health Organization. "10 facts on rabies." Sept. 2016, http://www.who.int/features/factfiles/rabies/en/ (accessed 9/10/17).
88 World Health Organization. "Rabies Fact Sheet." March 2017, http://www.who.int/mediacentre/factsheets/fs099/en/ (accessed 9/10/17).
89 Airbnb.com, "How cancellations work for stays," https://www.airbnb.com/home/cancellation_policies (accessed 6/10/20).
90 Ibid.
91 Vrbo.com, "What are the cancellation policy options for my listing?" https://help.vrbo.com/articles/What-are-the-cancellation-policy-options (accessed 6/10/20).
92 Ibid
93 Elliott, Christopher, "This Is How To Buy Travel Insurance After The Pandemic," Forbes.com, 23 April 2020, https://www.forbes.com/sites/christopherelliott/2020/04/23/this-is-how-to-buy-travel-insurance-after-the-pandemic (accessed 6/10/20).
94 Vrbo.com, "How do I cancel a traveler's reservation?", https://help.vrbo.com/articles/How-do-I-cancel-a-reservation (accessed 6/10/20)
95 Airbnb.com, "What factors determine how my listing appears in search results?", https://www.airbnb.com/help/article/39/what-factors-determine-how-my-listing-appears-in-search-results (accessed 6/10/20).
96 Airbnb.com, "What factors determine how my listing appears in search results?", https://www.airbnb.com/help/article/39/what-factors-determine-how-my-listing-appears-in-search-results (accessed 6/10/20).
97 Ibid.
98 Homeaway.com, "How Best Match Works," https://www.homeaway.com/info/search-results/ (accessed 6/13/20).
99 Vrbo.com, "Understanding Search Results, https://www.vrbo.com/discoveryhub/tips-and-resources/improve-performance/market-rank-and-search-position (accessed 6/10/20).
100 Ibid.
101 *See* http://www.asecurelife.com/security-infographic/

102 Airbnb.com. "Hospitality Standards." http://airbnb.com/hospitality (accessed 8/14/17).
103 Airbnb.com, "Hosting on Airbnb," https://www.airbnb.com/hospitality (accessed 6/10/20).
104 Ibid.
105 Airbnb.com. "Responsible hosting in the United States." https://www.airbnb.com/help/article/1376/responsible-hosting-in-the-united-states (accessed 8/11/17)
106 Ibid.
107 Airbnb.com, "What regulations apply to my city?," https://www.airbnb.com/help/article/961 (accessed 6/10/20).
108 Airbnb.com, "What are Airbnb's standards for hotels and other hospitality businesses?" https://www.airbnb.com/help/article/1526/what-are-airbnbs-standards-for-hotels-and-other-hospitality-businesses?topic=206 (accessed 6/10/20).
109 Ibid.
110 Ibid.
111 HomeAway.Com. "What are the HomeAway Marketplace standards?" https://help.homeaway.com/articles/What-are-the-HomeAway-listing-policies (accessed 8/11/17).
112 Ibid.
113 Airbnb.com. "how do star ratings work?" https://www.airbnb.com/help/article/1257/how-do-star-ratings-work (accessed 8/26/17).
114 Airbnb.com. "how do reviews work?" https://www.airbnb.com/help/article/13/how-do-reviews-work (accessed 8/17/17).
115 Vrbo.com, "How does the review system work?", https://help.vrbo.com/articles/What-is-the-two-way-review-system (accessed 6/12/20).
116 Vrbo.com. "what is a traveler review?" https://help.Vrbo.com/articles/What-is-a-traveler-review (accessed 8/17/17).
117 Vrbo.com. "what is the property review process?" https://help.Vrbo.com/articles/What-is-the-review-process-for-a-traveler (accessed 8/17/17)

www.ingramcontent.com/pod-product-compliance
Lightning Source LLC
Chambersburg PA
CBHW080450220526
45465CB00006B/2224